I WILL POUR OUT MY SPIRIT

I WILL POUR OUT MY SPIRIT:

A HISTORY AND THEOLOGY OF REVIVALS AND EVANGELICAL AWAKENINGS

R. E. Davies

MONARCH
Tunbridge Wells

Unless otherwise indicated, biblical quotations are from the
New International Version.

ISBN 1 85424 160 5

British Library Cataloguing-in-Publication Data.
A catalogue record for this book is available
from the British Library.

Production and Printing in England for
MONARCH PUBLICATIONS
Owl Lodge, Langton Road, Speldhurst, Tunbridge Wells,
Kent TN3 0NP by
Nuprint Ltd, Station Road, Harpenden, Herts AL5 4SE

CONTENTS

PREFACE

T HIS WORK IS DEDICATED to the memory of two spiritual and theological giants, Jonathan Edwards (1703-1758) and Dr D. Martyn Lloyd-Jones (1899-1981), to both of whom the present author owes a tremendous debt for help and stimulus in Christian life and work. He first heard the latter preach soon after his conversion, in Bristol, and as a student in London from 1957 to 1961, he was privileged to attend Westminster Chapel and hear 'the Doctor' preach on Sundays and Friday evenings. He counts this as an invaluable part of the preparation for his life and future ministry, supplementing the formal course of theological education in which he was then engaged.

In 1957 he was also introduced to the writings of Jonathan Edwards, which have been an object of study, on and off, ever since. The opportunity to study Edwards' writings in depth as part of his Ph.D. work has immeasurably enriched him.

The interest in Revivals shown by both men, and their deep insights on the subject, are hopefully reflected in what follows.[1]

Notes

[1] Dr Lloyd-Jones was himself profoundly influenced by Edwards' works from very early on in his ministry, which, like that of Edwards nearly 200 years before, was blessed with revival (see Murray 1982:253-254; for the experience of revival see pp 203-227). In one address, given in 1976, he compared 'the Puritans to the Alps, Luther and Calvin to the Himalayas, and Jonathan Edwards to Mount Everest!' (Lloyd Jones 1989:355).

INTRODUCTION

E VERY SURVEY OF CHURCH HISTORY from the sixteenth century Reformation up to the present makes reference to a number of movements in the Protestant Churches which are usually described as 'revivals' or 'awakenings'[1]: spiritual movements of a dramatic kind when a great ferment seems to have occurred over a considerable area of the Church, which have resulted in growth and expansion in an accelerated fashion, and which have left marked changes, some of a beneficial nature, but others less so.[2]

The late Dr J. Edwin Orr, a leading authority on the history of revivals, gave considerable attention to the periodisation and classification of those revivals which had occurred in Protestantism since the eighteenth century. He grouped them under five major awakenings, two 'resurgences', and a number of smaller or more localised awakenings. The five major awakenings, according to Orr, occurred or began in 1725, 1792, 1857, 1904, and 1948,[3] with significant resurgences being observed in 1830 and 1882 (see Orr 1981a: 1-64).[4] All of these major awakenings (with the exception of the first), together with the 'resurgences' and more localised revivals, are dealt with in more detail and with documentation in his many writings (see Bibliography). The evidence amassed by Orr in his various books, together with that of Cairns and others (eg Gillies 1754, rev 1845, repr 1981) shows that even when more general revivals have not been

9

experienced, local awakenings have regularly occurred over the last two-and-a-half centuries.[5]

We shall follow Orr's classification for the awakenings of the last three centuries, and in our historical section will give a major amount of space to these events, but we will also give a survey of revivals and awakenings before that time, including those recorded in the Bible.[6]

However, while describing the historical events, this work also attempts to provide a *theology* of revivals, that is, to give a theological interpretation of those events in the life of the church, past and present, which are usually described as 'revival'. Particular use will be made of the analyses of revivals attempted by Jonathan Edwards. This is something which most previous studies of the subject have not undertaken. Orr's writings, while they are ostensibly historical, often contain normative judgments about the nature of historical events which are not really the concern of the historian *as* historian. Many other writers on the subject mix a few references to certain key awakenings in the past with some elements of theological interpretation and large amounts of spiritual exhortation! While the present writer hopes that his work will have practical results, his major purpose is to provide a theological framework for the understanding and assessment of revivals.

The theology of revivals also needs to be distinguished from a sociological approach to revivals, such as that of William G. McLoughlin. Again, while we need to note the various factors which (from a human point of view) prepared the way for different awakenings, from the biblical and theological perspective these do not provide an adequate explanation for the events. (See chapter 1).

The present work will include the following:

1. *A description and definition of Revival;* what it is, described biblically and theologically, together with other explanations which have been given of the phenomenon.

2. *A look at the classic theologian of revival, Jonathan Edwards,* noting, among other things, his descriptions of

Revival, his analyses of the essence of revival, his cautions against excesses, his analysis of the place of revivals in Salvation-history, past, present and future, together with his urgent call for united prayer for revival. (We shall also briefly note his doctrines of the Trinity, the Holy Spirit, conversion etc, seeing the implications of these for a full-orbed understanding of revival.)

3. *A survey of the major revivals of the past,* including those in Scripture and in the history of the Church, with concentration on those of the past 300 years in the Protestant Churches, together with a review of present-day revivals. This will occupy a major part of the work.[7]

4. *A study of the constants and variables of revival,* those aspects which seem to be always present at such times, together with other elements which are present in some revivals, but not in others.

5. *A look at what may be called 'aberrant accompaniments of revival',* excesses and other problems resulting from the presence in revival of influences from 'the world, the flesh and the devil'.

6. *A consideration of whether or not it is possible for Christians, by 'the proper use of means' to 'produce a revival'.* This was the view of the nineteenth-century American Charles G. Finney, and his influence has been very extensive for the past 150 years.

7. *A look at a related question: whether it is possible for human beings by their action to bring a revival to a premature end.* Many who have been involved in revival, while disagreeing with Charles Finney that we can start such an awakening, would believe that it is sadly possible for men to abort a revival and terminate its full effectiveness.

8. *A consideration of the connection between revival and holiness.*

9. *An enquiry into the connection between revival and evangelism.* Does one produce the other, and, if so, which precedes and which follows?

10. *A study of the relationship of revival to world wide*

mission. Can we establish a link between the two? Is a revival in the Church followed by new missionary thrusts?

11. *A look at the link between revival and social action.*

12. *A survey of the place that lay people have had in revival* and the way in which revival has often brought lay leadership to the fore.

13. *A consideration of the place of young people in revival.* Our historical survey will show that a number of revivals in the past have either begun with children, students or other young people, or have affected these groups in a special way. In a similar way, a number of revivals in our own century, particularly in North America, have involved young people in a particularly strong way.

14. *A study of the connection between revival, history, and the Parousia.* Is Jonathan Edwards right in saying that in history revivals are God's main method for advancing his purposes in salvation-history? And is he also right in his Post-Millennial hope for a great revival to bring in the end of history? (The modern 'Restorationist' expectation, although linked to a Pre- Millennial view, comes very close to Edwards in this respect.)

We shall attempt to deal with each of these topics in the chapters that follow.

Notes

[1] The two ways of describing this phenomenon will be defined later. Often we shall use them virtually interchangeably.

[2] According to some writers, eg Dolan 1978; Gilley in Robbins ed, 1990:99-108, there is evidence of similar movements in the Roman Catholic Church. For example, the movement of Quietism in the late seventeenth century is often cited as a contemporary parallel to Pietism, Methodism, and the Great Awakening. This is true in a broad sense, although the extent to which this can be described as a revival is debatable. Similarly, many church historians see the whole series of movements for the reform of the Western Church in the sixteenth century, including the Catholic Reformation as well as the Protestant Reformation, as part of a new impetus of spiritual life (eg

Latourette 1953:698). We will mention some of these various movements in Chapters 4 and 5.

[3] Although that of 1948 hardly deserves comparison with the previous ones mentioned.

[4] This was his final classification. In previous works he classified them differently. Earle E Cairns (1986:20,21) differs from Orr in the way he groups together the various awakenings, but there are no significant disagreements.

[5] As will become clear from our use of Orr's works, especially in Chapters 7-10, all students of the subject owe a tremendous debt to his exhaustive research. However, it has to be admitted that, particularly in his later writings, Orr is often doing no more than chronicling a long series of facts without much attempt at assessing their significance. The criticism has also been made, even by those who are in agreement with him on the nature of revivals, that sometimes he sees revivals where there are none! This highlights the difficulty involved in interpreting the evidence and the constant danger of broadening our definition until it embraces any kind of active spiritual work in which Christians engage.

According to Dr R H Lescellius, when Dr Orr died he left a further 800 papers on the subject which require editing for publication (Lescellius 1990:3)!

[6] Among writers who have also done this, we note Gillies (1754; revised and enlarged by H Bonar 1845; repr 1981), Cairns (1986).

[7] In the historical section, which takes up a sizeable part of the book, every effort has been made to include at least some reference to every movement of spiritual awakening that the author has been able to discover. However, there are probably a number of such movements that his reading and research have not turned up, and he would be extremely grateful to anyone who is able to fill the gaps for him. A certain unevenness of treatment is also present, partly due to the fact that in the case of some movements large amounts of research have been done, whereas in other cases, this is not yet so. The writer has tried to avoid a mere catalogue of revivals with a monotonous repetition of 'in...a revival broke out...', but at times the amount of evidence available makes it difficult to say much more. In some sections, the writer has had to rely excessively on the work of J. Edwin Orr, as he is the only researcher who has done any work at all on revivals in certain periods and places. Orr's pioneering work needs to be supplemented, and at times, possibly corrected, by further study, but, for the present, his is the only work which has been done in bringing together the host of evidence present in newspaper and magazine reports, and other contemporary writings.

CHAPTER 1

WHAT IS REVIVAL?

B EFORE WE GO ANY FURTHER, it is very important to
define in more detail what we mean by 'revival', as this
will determine which events we include in the category
and how we assess various movements in the history of the
Church.

DEFINING 'REVIVAL'
The working definition which we propose is as follows:

> A revival is a sovereign outpouring of the Holy Spirit
> upon a group of Christians resulting in their spiritual
> reviving and quickening, and issuing in the awakening of
> spiritual concern in outsiders or formal church mem-
> bers; an immediate, or, at other times, a more longterm,
> effect will be efforts to extend the influence of the King-
> dom of God both intensively in the society in which the
> Church is placed, and extensively in the spread of the
> gospel to more remote parts of the world.[1]

The word 'awakening' is often used as virtually syn-
onymous with 'revival'. On the use of the two words J. Edwin
Orr says:

> As the sense of the word 'revival' suggests a renewal of
> life among those already possessing it, and the sense of

the word 'awakening' suggests a coming alive to spirituality, the Oxford Association for Research in Revival [formed under the inspiration of Dr Orr in 1974] has adopted 'revival' for believers and 'awakening' for community (1981a:iv).

Elsewhere he comments: 'A revival may be described as the reviving of believers, an awakening as the winning of the related community' (1975:127).

We may compare other definitions of revival. For example, an older writer, James Buchanan, gives the following:

A revival of religion... consists in these two things: a general impartation of new life, and vigour, and power, to those who are already of the number of God's people; and a remarkable awakening and conversion of souls who have hitherto been careless and unbelieving: in other words, it consists in new spiritual life imparted to the dead, and in new spiritual health imparted to the living (Buchanan 1843, repr 1966:227).

J. I. Packer offers the following:

Revival...means God's quickening visitation of his people, touching their hearts and deepening his work of grace in their lives. It is essentially a corporate occurrence, an enlivening of individuals not in isolation but together (Ferguson & Wright eds 1988:588).[2]

Dr D. Martyn Lloyd-Jones, who, throughout his long ministry, was a tireless advocate of the need of the Church to pray for revival, used the centenary of the 1859 Revival to call special attention to the need of the modern Church for this. In 1959, he gave a lecture on the subject and also preached a series of twenty-four sermons.[3] In his lecture on 'Revival: An Historical and Theological Survey', given at the Puritan and Reformed Studies Conference,[4] he says,

It is an experience in the life of the Church when the Holy Spirit does an unusual work. He does that work, primarily, amongst the members of the Church; it is a reviving of the believers. You cannot revive something that has never had life, so revival, by definition, is first of all an enlivening and quickening and awakening of lethargic, sleeping, almost moribund Church members. Suddenly the power of the Spirit comes upon them and they are brought into a new and more profound awareness of the truths that they had previously held intellectually, and perhaps at a deeper level too. They are humbled, they are convicted of sin, they are terrified at themselves. Many of them feel they had never been Christians. And then they come to see the great salvation of God in all its glory and to feel its power. Then, as the result of their quickening and enlivening, they begin to pray. New power comes into the preaching of the ministers, and the result of this is that large numbers who were previously outside the Church are converted and brought in' (1960:38).

In the second of his sermons preached on the topic (on Genesis 26:17–18), he notes that every period of revival is 'a returning to something that had obtained before...a returning to what you can read in the book of the Acts of the Apostles' (1986:27-28).

This suggestion that revival is in reality a repetition of Pentecost in the life of the Church is quite common. The nineteenth century American evangelist D L Moody, in one of his last sermons in Boston before his death, said:

See how He [the Holy Spirit] came on the day of Pentecost! It is not carnal to pray that He may come again and that the place may be shaken. I believe that Pentecost was but a specimen day. I think the Church has made this woeful mistake that Pentecost was a miracle never to be repeated. I have thought too that Pentecost was a miracle that is not to be repeated. I believe now if we looked on Pentecost as a specimen day and began to pray, we should have the old Pentecostal fire here in Boston (cited in Greenfield 1929:13-14).

Edwin Orr comments similarly:

The Apostle Peter insisted that the events of Pentecost, the general outpouring of the Spirit on believers, fulfilled in part the prediction of Joel. History has shown that such happenings have been repeated in the Great Awakenings, not always in every detail but always in the major manifestations of prayer, conviction, repentance and the like (Orr 1984:4).[5]

While the Day of Pentecost itself marked the beginning of the unusual events which marked the new era of the Spirit, it is also true that the first few decades of the Church's life following Pentecost witnessed an intensity of the Spirit's work and a degree of growth that may properly be described as spiritual awakening and revival. It seems better, therefore, not to restrict ourselves to the Day of Pentecost alone for our paradigm of revival, but to use other New Testament material to fill out our understanding.

On the other hand we need to recognise that by the end of the first century, some churches were in need of revival. See, for example, what is said about some of the churches mentioned in Revelation 2—3 (eg Rev 2:4; 3:1–2, 15–16).

WHAT HAPPENS IN REVIVAL?

No two revivals are exactly alike. Their specific character is determined by the local situation and the period in which they occur. Nevertheless, there are a number of distinguishing features which seem to characterise all such events.

A revival usually begins with an unusual sense of spiritual interest or concern, often but not always over a wide geographical area and affecting a considerable number of people.

It may begin in a small way, affecting only a few, but it soon spreads, almost like a contagion, either by direct contact or at other times merely by report. In some cases (as in the Eighteenth-Century Awakening) while there is some contact, a number of similar awakenings occur independently of each other, with the participants completely unaware of what is taking place elsewhere.

It first manifests itself as a deep concern on the part of professing Christians regarding the shallowness and superficiality of their spiritual lives. They become profoundly conscious of the poverty of their relationship with God, the standard of their moral lives and their service for Christ. An awareness of the holiness of God, who is experienced as near but at the same time as angry or displeased with them, produces a deep sense of conviction of sin, which is often felt to be intolerable. It may cause weeping and other signs of grief, and may also have physical effects such as prostration or similar unusual actions.

Many Christians affected in this way eventually come to a new assurance of God's gracious forgiveness or restoration; they become enthusiastic witnesses to others, both Christian and non-Christian. They may be public preachers, or private Christians who testify joyfully to what God has done for them. In this way, the effect of the reviving experience spreads through a large section of the Church, bringing many to a new depth of Christian life and devotion, affecting many who had claimed or thought themselves to be believers with a realisation that hitherto they had been mere hypocrites, and bringing an increasing number of outsiders to initial faith.

The intensity of the experiences often results in excesses (including spiritual claims to direct 'revelations' from God) and in aberrant behaviour of different kinds. Great wisdom is needed, particularly from the leaders of the Church, both in assessing the validity of what is happening and in guiding the new life into right channels.

Where there is wise leadership and where other factors are favourable, the movement can have profound effects on the mission and activity of the Church in society and in outreach. As we shall see, great movements of social change and of missionary work have often resulted from revivals in the past.

The intensity of experience and the new conviction of truth in the minds of those affected often means that splits and divisions result from revivals. Sometimes these occur when groups of professing Christians are bypassed by the effects of the awakening, or are repelled by the events or by the excesses of some associated with the events. When leaders in the Church oppose the revival, the 'revived' group secedes or is forced out. At other times, two or more groups of those who have been revived differ from each other, often over their theological understanding, and the result is the formation of a number of new groups.[6]

One feature of a revival which is apparent to those who witness or who are involved in the events is the unexpectedness of the movement, its suddenness, and often its apparent violence as it erupts on to the religious scene. The explanations of historians who concentrate on social and other factors which in their understanding precipitate a period of awakening often appear inadequate to account for the 'violence' of the events.[7]

A number of other features which characterise some revivals but not others will be noted as we study past and present revivals. We shall take up some of these and examine them in later sections.

OTHER EXPLANATIONS OF REVIVAL

When we turn to non-Christian writers, and also to non-Evangelical Christian authors, we find different explanations than the ones we have quoted from various Evangelical sources.

Many secular writers dismiss revivals summarily as 'brief outbursts of mass emotionalism' or 'periods of social neurosis'. F M Davenport considers all aspects of awakenings that smack of emotional excess as 'retrogression and primitivism' (1917, cited in Smyllie 1979:40).

The Roman Catholic writer Ronald Knox, in his monumental study *Enthusiasm* (1950) is completely pessimistic about, and ultimately dismissive of, all revival movements, especially those in Protestantism.

Perry Miller, the twentieth-century American historian whose studies on Jonathan Edwards and the whole of early New England Puritanism have been largely responsible for the current scholarly interest in Edwards, tries to give a satisfactory explanation of the Great Awakening from his own philosophical viewpoint. He rejects such explanations as 'agrarian protest...an uprising of debtors against creditors, of the common man against the gentry, or even...the sheer panic resulting from a sore-throat epidemic', which some have suggested. He says:

> We are confronted with the problem of whether the Great Awakening is properly to be viewed as a peculiarly American phenomenon at all. It would be possible to write about it—as has been done—as merely one variant of a universal occurrence in Western culture. Between about 1730 and 1760 practically all of Western Europe was swept by some kind of religious emotionalism...Once this international viewpoint is assumed, the American outburst becomes merely one among many— a colonial one at that...What was at work throughout the Western world is fairly obvious: the upper or the educated classes were tired of the religious squabbling of the seventeenth century, and turned to the more pleasing and not at all contentious generalities of eighteenth century rationalism; the spiritual hungers of the lower classes...were not satisfied by Newtonian demonstrations that design in the universe proved the existence of God. Their aspirations finally found vent in the revivals...In this phraseology, the Great Awakening was an uprising of the common people who declared that what Harvard and Yale graduates were teaching was too academic...(Miller 1952, repr 1956:156-157).

Miller would add the distinctively American features of the Great Awakening, which he describes as 'the point at which the wilderness [ie the specifically American context, with the tasks of establishing a new society in a new and different setting] took over the task of defining the objectives of the Puritan errand' (*ibid* 151). In his view, Jonathan Edwards was the key thinker and catalyst in this.

Patricia Tracy, also writing of the Great Awakening, says, 'the Awakening can be seen as a manifestation of and a release from the tensions that accompanied social change' (Tracy 1979:4). She draws attention to the changing role of teenagers and young people in eighteenth-century New England, especially in the frontier areas, and notes that the ministers who experienced revival in their churches, such as Jonathan Edwards, concentrated particularly on this group.[8]

The most thorough modern attempt to explain the whole series of revivals in the life of North America over the last 400 years is that of William McLoughlin in his *Revivals, Awakenings and Reform* (1978). He says:

> Great awakenings (and the revivals that are part of them) are the results...of critical disjunctions in our self-understanding...Awakenings begin in periods of cultural distortion and grave personal stress, when we lose faith in the legitimacy of our norms, the viability of our institutions, and the authority of our leaders in church and state...They are times of revitalization. They are therapeutic and cathartic, not pathological. They restore our natural verve and our self-confidence, helping us to maintain faith in ourselves, our ideals, and our 'covenant with God' even while they compel us to reinterpret that covenant in the light of new experience (McLoughlin 1978:2).

Using the formulation of cultural change described by anthropologist Anthony F C Wallace in his essay 'Revitalization Movements' (*American Anthropology* 1956; see Wallace

1966), McLoughlin describes each of the various revivals in American history in terms of the five stages of a revitalisation movement as given by Wallace. He concludes

> In short, great awakenings are periods when the culture system has had to be revitalized in order to overcome jarring disjunctions between norms and experience, old beliefs and new realities, dying patterns and emerging patterns of behavior (*ibid* 10).

However, he later states that 'America's revitalistic movements...fall outside Wallace's model', and he uses another work, that of Peter Worsley, *The Trumpet Shall Sound* (1968), to supplement it.[9]

McLoughlin's explanation, while rather tortuous and laboured, is interesting, but, writing as a historian, he necessarily leaves out the whole dimension of divine activity in revival.[10] The theologian will prefer to say that while it is possible to discern certain factors in society which have prepared the way for religious awakenings, these are to be understood as aspects of God's providential preparation for a work he intends shortly to bring to pass. He would not see these factors as *alternative explanations* for the occurrence of religious awakenings. A view of God as the Lord of history will lead us to look for such preparations, while still seeing the element of unexpectedness and surprise when the revival actually occurs.[11]

Notes

[1] The *Oxford English Dictionary* suggests the following: 'A general reawakening of or in religion in a community or some part thereof'. According to the OED, the New England Puritan preacher and writer Cotton Mather was the first to use it in this way. In his *Magnalia Christi Americana* (1702) 3.71, he speaks of 'a notable revival of religion among them...', referring to the ministry of the seventeenth-century Puritan preacher Francis Higginson in Leicester.

Our definition seeks to exclude the modern, mainly American, use of the term to refer to evangelistic campaigns. J. Edwin Orr speaks of 'the American misuse of "revivalism" for "mass evangelism" ' as 'unscriptural and unhistorical, ambiguous, inadequate, pejorative and illogical, [and] therefore unscholarly' (1981a:viii)!

² This is his definition to the *New Dictionary of Theology* (1988). For other, earlier, discussions by Packer on different aspects of revival, see Packer 1961:13-28; 1971:97-100; 1980:2-16; 1984:255-258. Articles in other theological dictionaries focus on 'Revivalism' and are in danger of confusing the classical and modern uses of the word 'revival' which we have mentioned above (see eg Elwell ed 1984:948-952; Richardson ed 2nd ed 1983:506-507). It is interesting, and possibly significant, that the *Dictionary of Pentecostal and Charismatic Movements* (Burgess & McGee eds 1988) has an article on the 'Azusa Street Revival' but no general article on either 'Revival' or 'Awakening'.

³ Published under the title *Revival; can we make it happen?* (1986)

⁴ Reprinted in *How Shall they Hear?* (1960), also in *The Puritans: their Origins and Successors* (Edinburgh: Banner of Truth Trust) 1989. He returned to the subject in the last lecture he gave to the conference in 1974 before his death in 'Jonathan Edwards and the Crucial Importance of Revival', also included in the latter volume.

⁵ John Stott says in his exposition of Acts 2:

> Pentecost has been called—and rightly—the first 'revival', using this word to denote one of those altogether unusual visitations of God, in which a whole community becomes vividly aware of his immediate, overpowering presence. It may be, therefore, that not only the physical phenomena (vv 2ff), but the deep conviction of sin (v 37), the 3,000 conversions (v 41) and the widespread sense of awe (v 43) were signs of 'revival' (1990:61).

The fact that, on the Day of Pentecost, Peter cited the prophecy of Joel: 'I will pour out my Spirit...' leads many to speak of revival as 'an (or, the) outpouring of the Spirit'. This has much to commend it, and was, in fact, the way in which many older writers referred to such events.

⁶ Cf in general the section on 'Characteristics of Revivals' in Riss 1988:3-7. More briefly, Tony Lambert in his recent study of *The Resurrection of the Chinese Church*, in which he describes among other things the revival going on at present in many parts of China, says:

> 'A genuine spiritual revival may be defined as occurring when:
> 1. The people of God are stirred to pray fervently for the low state

of the church, and for the unconverted world.

2. Powerful preachers of the gospel are raised up by God to proclaim the gospel with unusual spiritual force.

3. The church is convicted of a deep sense of sin before a holy God.

4. Individuals and churches repent of specific sins.

5. A new sense of joy permeates the church, making the gospel and the things of God become real.

6. The Christian church has a marked impact upon the surrounding community.

7. God works visibly in supernatural ways' (Lambert 1991: 159-160).

[7] See, for example, the explanations of Perry Miller, Patricia Tracy and William McLoughlin cited below.

[8] It is an observable fact that a significant number of revivals in both past and present have begun with young people. See further below, Chapter 17.

[9] In an unpublished dissertation, William Howland Kenney argues that the revitalization theory applies to the Great Awakening in the Middle Colonies. He uses both Wallace's ideas and also Max Weber's theory of charisma, with George Whitefield in the role of charismatic leader. See a summary in Westerkamp 1988:11. She disagrees with Kenney's thesis.

[10] He says at one point: 'What I have to say will not necessarily contradict the faith system of...the Judeo-Christian theologian', but two paragraphs earlier he has stated: 'If we can rid ourselves of the old Protestant definition of revivalism and awakenings and think more sociologically and anthropologically about religion, we will better understand our past' (*ibid* 7-8). In making this kind of statement he is moving outside the realm of the historian's task. Divine causation does not submit itself to historical verification and hence is not the proper subject of the historian or sociologist. However, McLoughlin seems to want to *replace* the theological explanation by the sociological, rather than allow them to stand side by side as different explanations of the same events.

[11] The attempt has been made in two recent articles to suggest that the Great Awakening of the eighteenth century in the American Colonies was largely the result of skilful, and not always honest, use of newspapers and the printed page in general by George Whitefield and his 'press agent' William Seward! In the words of the author Frank Lambert, 'The network of colonial newspapers represents a necessary if not sufficient explanation for the Great Awakening' (Lambert 1991:224). The titles of the articles indicate their general approach: ' "Pedlar in Divinity": George Whitefield and the Great Awakening, 1737-1745', and 'The Great Awakening as Artifact: George Whitefield and the Construction of Intercolonial Revival, 1739-1745' (see Bibliography for full details).

CHAPTER 2

JONATHAN EDWARDS: THE CLASSIC THEOLOGIAN OF REVIVAL

N<small>O ONE WHO STUDIES</small> the topic of revival will dispute the statement that Jonathan Edwards, the eighteenth-century American preacher and writer, is the classic theologian on the subject.[1]

In the same way that any study of the doctrine of human sin and corruption should deal with the ideas of Augustine and John Calvin, and any investigation of the doctrine of justification by faith needs to include Martin Luther's views, so before we embark on a detailed study of revivals we shall be well advised to see what Edwards has to say on the subject.

EDWARDS' LIFE

A brief account of his life will help to see him as a real person, and not just as a theologian from the remote past. Jonathan Edwards was born on October 5 1703, the fifth child and only son, of the Rev. Timothy Edwards and his wife, who had a total of eleven children. He grew up in East Windsor, Connecticut, where his father was the minister, entered Yale College in 1716, graduated in 1720, and remained for another two years for advanced studies in theology. During that time he experienced what he described as 'a new sense of things', a new conviction of divine glory and excellence, which had a profound effect on his life and on his views.

After a short ministry in New York, in a Presbyterian church, and a summer of study in East Windsor, he returned to Yale in 1723 to receive his MA degree. He was appointed a tutor in 1724, but severe illness prevented him fulfilling his duties for several months.

In 1726 he accepted the invitation to join his ageing maternal grandfather Solomon Stoddard (1643-1729) of Northampton, Massachusetts as assistant pastor. In July 1727 he married Sarah Pierrepont, who bore him eleven children, eight daughters and three sons.

During Edwards' ministry at Northampton, a local revival broke out in 1734 and 1735, and a more extensive awakening covering the whole of New England and beyond, in 1740-1742. Edwards wrote a number of his key works describing, analysing and defending the revival as a genuine work of God.

Controversy with his congregation over a number of points in the late 1740s caused him to resign in 1750, and in 1751 he moved to Stockbridge, Massachusetts, a remote frontier settlement where he served as pastor of the church and missionary to the Indians. Controversy continued with some members of the church there, but was eventually resolved in Edwards' favour. He served as pastor and missionary administrator and continued to write.

In 1757 he was invited to the College of New Jersey as President; he reluctantly agreed, but when on reaching Princeton he was vaccinated against smallpox, he contracted the disease and died on March 22, 1758.

INFLUENCES ON HIS UNDERSTANDING OF REVIVAL

Before considering Edwards' published writings on revival, it may be interesting to look at some of the influences on him which helped him in his mature statements and assessments of the phenomenon.

The earliest known letter from his pen, written to his sister Mary in 1716 when he was only twelve years old, includes a reference to a revival taking place in the church at East Windsor, where his father was the minister. He begins:

Dear Sister,

Through the wonderfull mercy and goodness of God there hath in ths place been a verry remarkable stirring and pouring out of the Spirit of God, and likewise now is but I think I have reason to think it is in some mesure diminished but I hope not much. About thirteen have been joyned to the church in an estate of full communion...

I think there comes commonly a Mondays above thirty persons to speak with Father about the condition of their souls...(cited in *Christian History* vol IV no 4 1985:34).

While it was to be a few more years before he experienced fully[2] for himself the work of the Spirit in his own life, he was obviously no stranger to the observed phenomena of such 'stirring and pouring out of the Spirit of God' in his father's ministry. In a similar way, he knew by repute of the five spiritual awakenings, or 'harvests', which attended the long ministry of his maternal grandfather Solomon Stoddard (1643-1729) at Northampton in 1679, 1683, 1696, 1712 and 1718, to which he refers in his *Faithful Narrative*. In all probability, Edwards read, either on publication or at a later date, the series of sermons preached by Stoddard in 1712 during the fourth period of spiritual awakening which took place under his ministry. One of the sermons entitled 'On the Outpouring of the Spirit of God', and printed as part of a collection of sermons entitled *The Efficacy of the Fear of Hell* (Boston: B. Green 1713), has as its Doctrine: 'There are some special Seasons wherein God doth in a remarkable Manner revive Religion among his People'. To the question 'How is it with a People when Religion is revived?' Stoddard answers 'Saints are quickened...Sinners are converted...[and] many that are not Converted do become more Religious'. He further observes 'This reviving is sometimes of longer, and sometimes of shorter Continuance...God is very Arbitrary in this Matter. The People of God are praying, and waiting for this

Mercy...But God will take his own time for this Mercy' (cited in *Christian History* vol VIII no 3 1989:10).

Cotton Mather (1663-1728), the Boston minister who was Stoddard's contemporary, began in 1690 to urge the need of prayer for spiritual awakening (his father Increase Mather [1639-1723] had voiced hopes of such an awakening as early as 1678). Cotton linked this with the prophecy of Joel 2:28-32, which, he felt, was to be fulfilled in the final days before the pre-millennial return of Christ.[3] However, Edwards rarely refers to Mather in his writings, and Mather's pre-millennialism may have alienated him from Mather's presentation.

Edwards was influenced far more by the sermons of the English Puritan John Howe (1630-1705) which were published in 1725 under the title, *The Outpouring of the Holy Spirit; or, The Prosperous State of the Christian Interest before the End of Time, by a Plentiful Effusion of the Holy Spirit,*[4] and which articulated a post-millennial hope similar to his own.

Edwards was also aware of the work of Robert Fleming Sr (1630-1694), *The Fulfilling of the Scripture* (5th edn London 1726) and makes use of it in *Some Thoughts*. Fleming, in arguing for the reliability of Scripture, records instances of its fulfilment in history and including his own time. In describing the spread of Reformed Christianity since the Reformation, he gives instances from the ministries of a number of Scottish and English preachers where spiritual blessing was evident. His work was therefore to some extent a history of spiritual awakenings in a broad theological framework, which may also have influenced Edwards as he sought to integrate revivals into his own scheme of salvation-history in works such as his *History of the Work of Redemption*.

EDWARDS' MAJOR WRITINGS ON REVIVAL

Edwards' first work on Revival, *A Faithful Narrative of the Surprizing Work of God, in the Conversion of Many Hundred Souls in Northampton, and the Neighbouring Towns and Villages of Hampshire, in New England* (1737) describes and documents the revival which occurred in the Connecticut valley in 1734 and 1735. It had broken out in connection with his own preaching, and he was of the opinion that it was a genuine work of the Holy Spirit. In spite of a variety of experiences in those affected, Edwards draws out a number of significant similarities.[5] He is already developing at this point a morphology of conversion and of revival which he further hones and perfects in his later works.

In his *The Distinguishing Marks of a Work of the Spirit of God* (1741), based on a sermon he preached in Boston at the time when the 'great and general awakening' was spreading throughout New England and beyond, he first of all gives nine elements which some had fastened on to prove that the awakening was not genuine. He deals with each of these in turn, showing that, although a number of them are not to be approved, they do not of themselves prove that the revival was spurious. He then selects five characteristics of the revival, which in his view marked it as genuine, in spite of various excesses, namely: the fact that it exalted Jesus Christ,[6] it attacked the kingdom of darkness, it honoured the Scriptures, promoted sound doctrine, and resulted in an outpouring of love to God and man expressed in practical ways. These criteria, and their development by Edwards, remain permanently valid in helping us to assess various movements in the Church past and present.

In the application, he gives his reasons for not expecting a restoration of miraculous spiritual gifts in the Church (Edwards, ed Goen 1972:278-282). He had already made the same point in a series of sermons he preached in 1738 on 1 Corinthians 13[7], and returned to it at least once more in a sermon on 1 Corinthians 13:8–13 preached in 1748 (see refs in Edwards, ed Ramsay 1989:83 n 5; 169 n 7 etc). We shall return to this important subject at a later point (see below under 'Constants and Variables in Revival').

In *Some Thoughts Concerning the Present Revival of Religion in New England* (1742), and even more in *A Treatise Concerning Religious Affections* (1746), he tries to separate true experiences of revival and conversion—even if they are accompanied by errors and irregularities—from those which, while evidenced by high emotional states, extravagant spiritual talk and praise of God, are basically manifestations of self-love. True experiences of the renewing work of the Holy Spirit are God- and Christ-centred, focusing on an adoring appreciation of the divine glory and grace, divorced from self-interest and self-glory, leading to humility, meekness, a spirit of forgiveness towards others, and a hungering and thirsting for righteousness which is the antithesis of self-congratulation and a sense of 'having arrived'. True experience of the grace of God will lead on to works of mercy and justice towards others, and will show itself in personal concern for individuals and in social concern.

In the *Religious Affections*, which is based on the text from 1 Peter 1:8 'Whom having not seen, ye love: in whom, though now ye see him not, yet believing, ye rejoice with joy unspeakable, and full of glory', Edwards may occasionally be thought guilty of 'overkill' as he deals exhaustively with twelve things which 'are no certain signs that religious affections are truly gracious, or that they are not', and then even more exhaustively with the twelve which 'are distinguishing signs of truly gracious and holy affections'. However, his masterly justification of the statement that 'true religion, in great part, consists in holy affections' such as 'fear, hope, love, hatred, desire, joy, sorrow, gratitude, compassion and zeal', and especially love, and issues in Christian practice and a holy life, is a warning both to those who frown on all expressions of emotion in Christian experience, as well as those who feel that experience and high emotion are the only expressions of true spirituality.

In *Some Thoughts* Edwards is basically concerned to defend the revival which had become widespread throughout New England in the years 1740-1742 from the attacks of its critics.[8] He repeats what he has said in his previous publication about abuses not invalidating the whole work of revival, and adds further points in its defence. In Part I,

Section V, he gives an account of one person in Northampton whose experiences were highly ecstatic and quite remarkable. It is generally agreed that, although Edwards does not say so, he is giving an account of his own wife's experience.[9] In his view, hers is a good example of a number of the unusual phenomena manifest in the revival, but with a Christ-centred-ness and with practical outworkings which evidenced it as genuine (Edwards, ed Goen 1972:331-341). His concluding comment is:

> Now if such things are enthusiasm [a technical term for excessive concentration by an individual on their own spiritual experience, often with claims to divine revela-tions and a special divine authority], and the fruits of a distempered brain, let my brain be evermore possessed of that happy distemper! If this be distraction, I pray God that the world of mankind may be all seized with this benign, meek, beneficent, beatifical, glorious dis-traction!

In the same work he indulges in a little speculation regard-ing the place of the Great Awakening of the 1740s in the whole scheme of salvation-history. He says at one point,

> 'Tis not unlikely that this work of God's Spirit, that is so extraordinary and wonderful, is the dawning, or at least a prelude, of that glorious work of God, so often fore-told in Scripture, which in the progress and issue of it, shall renew the world of mankind (*ibid* 353).

His hope is that the millennium will shortly dawn in Amer-ica, and spread from there to the rest of the world. This expectation, usually characterised as Post-Millennialism, was developed by Edwards from earlier Puritan ideas of 'a hope of better times' before the end of the present age, which would come not from the Return of Christ but from a succession of ever greater revivals accompanied by the successful preaching of the gospel to all nations. While the hoped-for millennium did not dawn, it is interesting to note that the 250 years that have elapsed since Edwards wrote these words have seen a succession of revivals and the world-wide preaching of the gospel through the work of Christian missions. As we shall see later, Edwards' kind of Post-Millennial hope, which has been out of fashion for most of the twentieth century, is now making a come-back in some quarters. The expectation of a world-wide revival which is held by many of the leaders of the 'Restoration' Church movement in Britain has some similarities with the views of Edwards (see Wright 1991:7).

The fourth major section of *Some Thoughts* (the longest section in the work) is taken up with a vigorous exposé of errors which are to be corrected in revival. He deals powerfully and at some length with 'undiscerned spiritual pride', and mentions it as one way in which the Devil can trap those who are involved in revival (*ibid* 414-432). He also condemns a number of 'wrong principles' which those involved in revival can hold to, as well as a number of wrong and dangerous practices, among which he includes 'the mutual embraces and kisses of persons of different sexes, under the notion of Christian love and holy kisses', which, he says, can easily degenerate into 'unclean and brutish lust'!

He also expresses his unhappiness about 'lay-exhorting', which had become a feature of the revival. He expresses his views about this elsewhere, and shows that he holds very firmly to a clergy-centred view of Christian ministry and activity. While New England Congregationalism held the same views, the Separate Baptists who emerged from the Congregationalists had a much broader (and, we would judge, a more biblical) view of the ministry of the laity and, as a result, benefited considerably at the expense of their more traditional counterparts.

In Part V, 'Shewing Positively What Ought to be Done to Promote This Work', he mentions, among other things, the desirability of a day of united prayer and fasting to God:

...that he would continue and still carry on this work, and more abundantly and extensively pour out his Spirit...and that he would bow the heavens and come down...and erect his glorious kingdom through the earth (*ibid* 520),

a point to which he returns in the next work we shall mention.

In that work, entitled *An Humble Attempt to Promote Explicit Agreement and Visible Union of God's People in Extraordinary Prayer for the Revival of Religion and the Advancement of Christ's Kingdom on Earth* (1747) he again articulates his vision of a great revival, or succession of revivals, which will usher in the Millennium, and urges regular, united prayer for God to begin this work. He indulges in rather tortuous exegesis of the book of Revelation to try to prove that the slaying of the two witnesses spoken of in Revelation 11 has already happened, and that, therefore, the great victory of God over his enemies will soon take place. This he interprets as the triumph of the preaching of the gospel in a succession of ever-wider revivals (Edwards, ed Stein 1977:378-431).

However Edwards' eschatological speculations are interpreted (and even some of his best friends were dubious [see the preface to the work by five Boston ministers who were sympathetic to the call to prayer, but less certain about the eschatology, *ibid* 310]), the call to united prayer for revival, based on an expostion of Zechariah 8:20–22, was taken up by a number of his friends and associates in America. In Scotland, where the original 'concert of prayer' which provoked Edwards to write his *Humble Attempt* had been operating from around the time when he had first mentioned the usefulness of a united day of prayer and fasting, his prayer call was welcomed, although here too there was probably considerable hesitation about his detailed eschatological speculations.[10]

Edwards' *Account of the Life of the late Reverend Mr. David Brainerd...Missionary to the Indians* (1748), which he edited at Brainerd's request from the missionary's Diary after his death, tells of the awakenings which eventually, after much laborious toil and prayer, took place under his ministry to the Indians.[11] It is interesting in giving examples of the work of the Spirit among an 'unchurched' group of people.

In Edwards' 'Appendix' to Brainerd's Diary, he seeks to use the young missionary's life to reinforce a number of valuable lessons. Among other things Brainerd, according to Edwards, set an excellent example, to be followed by missionaries in particular but also by all God's people, of 'earnest prayers and endeavors for the advancement and enlargement of the Kingdom of Christ in the world' (*ibid* 531, 532). He was also able to cite the fact that, during his last illness at Northampton, Brainerd had 'expressed his wonder that there appeared no more forwardness to comply' with the proposal of the Scottish ministers, and had 'sent it as his dying advice to his own congregation, that they should practice agreeably to that proposal' (*ibid* 459, 460; cf 532). This provided, in Edwards' view, a powerful incentive to those who would be impressed by the account of Brainerd's life to join in the prayer concert which Edwards himself was now advocating.

One of the works on which Edwards was planning to concentrate when he was invited to Princeton was his *History of the Work of Redemption*, based on a series of sermons he had preached a number of years earlier in 1739. These were published posthumously, and show that his plan was to write a complete systematic theology in historical form. However, the published work only contains the outline of such a work, and we can only speculate on the detailed exposition that would have resulted had Edwards not died prematurely.

In spite of this, the published sermons show us how Edwards viewed awakenings and revivals in the whole of God's plan for man's salvation. He observes that:

> From the fall of man to this day wherein we live the Work of Redemption in its effect has mainly been carried on by remarkable pourings out of the Spirit of God. Though there be a more constant influence of God's

Spirit always in some degree attending his ordinances, yet the way in which the greatest things have been done towards carrying on this work always has been by remarkable pourings out of the Spirit at special seasons of mercy (Edwards, ed Wilson 1989:143).

As he proceeds through the story of God's saving acts, both in scriptural history and subsequent church history, he draws attention to a number of such outpourings, and when he looks at biblical prophecy to guide him on the course of events yet to take place before the End, he continues to see such activities of the Spirit as an important part in the progress of history towards its God-intended climax. The views he set forth in later works concerning the coming great revival which will inaugurate the Millennium are already here in embryo (*ibid* 460-462).

OTHER RELEVANT WORKS

A number of Edwards' other works, all published posthumously, are also relevant to the topic of revival. They include *A Dissertation on the End for which God Created the World* (prepared for publication by Edwards before his death and published together with *A Dissertation on the Nature of True Virtue* in 1765), *Charity and its Fruits*, a series of sermons on 1 Corinthians 13, preached in 1738, and published in 1852 by one of his relatives Tryon Edwards, and, finally, three small treatises which were excerpts from his unpublished *Miscellanies*. These were published at various points from 1854 to 1903, but have been reprinted most recently in 1971, namely *Treatise on Grace, Observations Concerning the Trinity and the Covenant of Redemption* and *An Essay on the Trinity*. These all give valuable background to his discussions on revival by expounding the essential nature of the Person of the Holy Spirit who is 'poured out' in revival and the nature of the work he does in human lives.

Edwards' restatement of the doctrine of the Trinity remained within the limits of orthodox Trinitarianism, while being at the same time a profound and reverent searching into the being and the ways of God. He states in *An Essay on the Trinity*,

> The Father is the deity subsisting in the prime, unoriginated and most absolute manner, or the deity in its direct existence. The Son is the deity generated by God's understanding, or having an idea of himself and subsisting in that idea. The Holy Ghost is the deity subsisting in act, or the divine essence flowing out and breathed forth in God's infinite love to and delight in himself. And I believe the whole Divine essence does truly and distinctly subsist both in the Divine idea and Divine love, and that each of them are properly distinct persons (Edwards ed Helm 1971:118).[12]

Again, concerning the relation of the Spirit to the other Persons in the Godhead, he says in the *Treatise on Grace*:

> The Holy Spirit does in some ineffable and inconceivable manner proceed, and is breathed forth both from the Father and the Son, by the divine essence being wholly poured and flowing out in that infinitely intense, holy, and pure love and delight that continually and unchangeably breathes forth from the Father and the Son, primarily towards each other, and secondarily towards the creature, and so flowing forth in a different subsistence or person in a manner to us utterly inexplicable and inconceivable...The Holy Spirit is the divine love itself, the love of the Father and the Son (Edwards, ed Helm 1971:63).

Thus the 'inner glory', the 'fullness' of God, the 'excellency' of the divine being, consists in the mutual happiness, delight and love of the persons of the Godhead.

But the essence of love is to communicate, 'God is a communicating being' (Edwards, ed Townsend 1972: 130).

> The great and universal end of God's creating the world was to communicate Himself...to intelligent beings....God created this world for the shining forth of His excellency and for the flowing forth of His happiness (*ibid*).

> God glorifies Himself towards the creatures...[in] two ways: 1. By appearing to them, being manifested to their understanding. 2. In communicating Himself to their hearts, and in their rejoicing, and delighting in, and enjoying, the manifestations which He makes of Himself (*ibid* 133).

This 'glorious and abundant emanation of his infinite fullness of good *ad extra*', 'consisting in the knowledge of God, love to God, and joy in God', is 'God's last end' and 'what moved him to create the world'; and the 'remanation',[13] the 'refulgence [being] reflected back to the luminary' means that 'the whole is *of* God, and *in* God, and *to* God; and God is the beginning, middle and end' (Edwards, ed Ramsay 1989:433, 531).

So the glory of God, defined in this way, is the chief end of all of God's works. But this includes

> the work of redemption, which is the chief work of providence towards the moral world....All God's works of providence in the moral government of the world...are...subordinate to the great purposes and end of this great work... The work of redemption is that work by which men...are restored to holiness and happiness. The work of redemption is a new creation...whereby men are brought into a new existence, or are made new creatures (*ibid* 489).

The work of redemption is thus the chief way in which 'God's chief end' is accomplished.

But Edwards has already established in his *History of the Work of Redemption*, (cited above) that 'from the fall of man to this day wherein we live the Work of Redemption in its effect has mainly been carried on by remarkable pourings out of the Spirit of God', thus contributing to the fulfilment of 'God's chief end' in creation. This analysis thus places revivals and awakenings in the broadest context possible, giving them an integral place in the fulfilment and outworking of God's eternal purposes for the manifestation of his own glory.

Edwards thus describes the Holy Spirit as the personal love of the Father for his Son, as well as the personal holiness and happiness of the Father in his communion with the Son. He further states that the Spirit, in his work in the saints, dwells within them and unites himself to them and works within them as a new, supernatural principle of life, holiness and action, communicating his own nature to them (Edwards ed Hickman 1834:II.13; Edwards ed Helm 1971:72-74). This means that love for Christ, holiness, and joy in Christ, which are the very nature of the Spirit, are the heart of true Christian experience, especially as evidenced in revival.

Edwards' sustained theological argument has thus succeeded in establishing revival as an important means in the accomplishment of God's grand design in creation, and also in showing that the essence of the revival experience arises from the inner trinitarian life of God. This is surely a considerable achievement, which confirms his position as undisputed theologian of revival!

Notes

[1] See, for example, J.I. Packer's lecture, 'Jonathan Edwards and the Theology of Revival' given at the Puritan and Reformed Studies Conference in London in 1960 (Packer 1961:13-28 [now reprinted in Packer 1991:408-432]); also Dr D. M. Lloyd-Jones' lecture at a later meeting of the same conference in 1976, 'Jonathan Edwards and the Crucial Importance of Revival' (Lloyd-Jones 1977: 348-371). Also, more recently, a paper by Peter Beale on 'Jonathan Edwards and the Phenomena of Revival' (unpublished EFCC Study Conference Paper 1986), and a lecture by Dr R. H. Lescelius on 'Revival and the History of the Church' at a 'Maranatha' Conference in

Worthington, PA (Lescelius 1990:3-10) make the same point.

Richard Lovelace, in his *Dynamics of Spiritual Life* (1979) uses Edwards' writings on the subject as 'the foundational theology of spiritual renewal in English, and perhaps in any language', and John White in his *When the Spirit Comes with Power* (1988) uses Edwards' criteria to assess the 'Signs and Wonders' phenomena associated with John Wimber. Edwards' call to united prayer for Revival and worldwide mission, which had a profound influence in the beginning of the modern Protestant missionary movement at the end of the eighteenth century, is looked to by many today as worthy of emulation: see eg David Bryant, *With Concerts of Prayer* (1985).

Even Charles Finney, whose approach was so radically different from that of Edwards, refers to Edwards a number of times in his own *Lectures on Revivals of Religion*. A later editor of the lectures, W.H. Harding, says, 'Finney was much influenced by the writings of Edwards. He first read them in the house of Dr Aiken (of Utica), who said that Finney "often spoke of them with rapture" ' (Finney ed Harding 1913:138).

[2] It is probably to this time of revival that he refers in his 'Personal Narrative', when he speaks of a period when he was 'very much affected for many months, and concerned about the things of religion, and my soul's salvation; and was abundant in duties'. However, he says, 'in process of time, my convictions and affections wore off' (Edwards ed Faust and Johnson 1935-57).

[3] For an expansion of this brief paragraph see R. Lovelace *The American Pietism of Cotton Mather* Wm.B. Eerdmans 1979:240-250. See also the final section of this present work on Revival and the Parousia.

[4] The volume of Howe's sermons is referred to by William Cooper in his preface to Edwards' *Distinguishing Marks* (1741), and by Edwards himself in his *Treatise on Grace* and his *Essay on the Trinity*, both of which were left unpublished at his death (see Edwards ed Helm 1971:59,112).

[5] After giving a broad description of the variety of people who were converted or revived, Edwards then describes in some detail the experiences of two notable converts, one of whom was a four-year old girl, Phebe Bartlet (Edwards ed Goen 1972:199-205).

[6] His words are worth quoting at length, but the reader can easily read the work for him/herself in the reprint of Edwards' complete works which is currently available. However, we give a sample to whet the reader's appetite!

> When that spirit that is at work amongst a people is observed to operate after such a manner, as to raise their esteem of that Jesus that was born of the Virgin, and was crucified without the gates of Jerusalem; and seems more to confirm and establish their minds in what the Gospel declares to us of his being the Son of God and the

Saviour of men; 'tis a sure sign that that spirit is the Spirit of God (Edwards, ed Goen 1972:249).

7 These were published postumously by one of his relatives Tryon Edwards under the title *Charity and Its Fruits* (1852, repr 1969)

8 One of the Awakening's strongest critics, Charles Chauncy (1705-1787) published his own critique about six months after Edwards' work appeared. Entitled *Seasonable Thoughts on the State of Religion in New-England*, and consciously modelled on Edwards' *Some Thoughts*, of which he had obviously seen an advance copy, Chauncy's book sought to discredit the revival by all kinds of horror stories about excesses and 'irregularities', as well as by linking it with some of the heresies of the previous century in the life of the New England churches.

9 See Tracy 1842:226-230; Miller 1949:201-206: Goen ed 1972:68-70; Murray 1987:193-197.

10 The full fruits came nearly forty years later in 1784, when a copy of the *Humble Attempt* was sent by John Erskine, one of Edwards' Scottish correspondents, to the Northamptonshire Baptist John Ryland Jr, who passed it on to John Sutcliff. At the latter's suggestion, the North-amptonshire Baptist Association resolved to devote the first Monday of each month to prayer for revival and the spread of God's kingdom. In 1786, the Midlands Association followed suit, and in 1789 a new edition of the *Humble Attempt* was published with a preface by Sutcliff. Sermons and tracts by Sutcliff, Ryland, Andrew Fuller (who was profoundly helped by others of Edwards' writings) and William Carey loosened the stranglehold which Hyper-Calvinism had on the thinking and activity of the Baptists, and also injected a missionary dimension. Carey's *Enquiry*, and the subsequent formation of the Baptist Missionary Society, were the result of this train of events. See further below Chapter 7.

11 Brainerd had himself published in 1746 two selections from his Diary giving an account of the awakenings among the Indians. Part 1 was published under the title *Mirabilia Dei inter Indicos, or the Rise and Progress of a Remarkable Work of Grace Amongst a Number of the Indians in the Provinces of New Jersey and Pennsylvania*, and part 2 as *Divine Grace Displayed, or the Continuance and Progress of a Remarkable Work of Grace among Some of the Indians Belonging in the Provinces of New Jersey and Pennsylvania* (Hickman ed *ibid* II.313-435).
In addition to the journal narrative detailing the work of exactly a year (June 19, 1745—June 19, 1746), the volumes contain three appendices, the first 'containing his [ie Brainerd's] general remarks on the doctrines preached, their extraordinary effects etc', the second 'containing an account of his method of learning the Indian language, and of instructing the Indians; together with the difficulties which lie in the way of their conversion', the

third being a letter to Ebenezer Pemberton, republished with an introduction describing the efforts of the Scottish society and its missionaries, notably Azariah Horton on Long Island.

[12] There are echoes of Augustine's trinitarian statements in what Edwards says here, particularly in his understanding of the Holy Spirit as the mutual love of the Father and Son. However, it is hard to prove any precise dependence. Indeed, according to one writer, 'Edwards does not refer to Augustine. The view which he develops implies a rejection of Augustine's' (Sairsingh 1986:144).

[13] Edwards seems at this point to have coined a new word to express his idea!

CHAPTER 3

REVIVALS AND AWAKENINGS IN THE BIBLE

I F REVIVALS ARE AMONG THE CHOICEST BLESSINGS which God gives to his Church, we should expect to find examples of such blessings in the Bible. Many writers, in addition to Jonathan Edwards, seek to trace through the pages of scripture, both Old and New Testaments, various instances of revival.[1]

REVIVALS IN THE OLD TESTAMENT

However, there is considerable disagreement among writers concerning which Old Testament events may be described as revivals. Bonar enumerates fourteen, Baker twelve, Smith sixteen and Kaiser ten. There is some overlap among them, as well as among the other writers mentioned, but also some individual writers include events not included by others.

As we have already noted, Jonathan Edwards integrates 'outpourings of the Spirit' into his whole scheme of the history of the work of Redemption. He notes at least five such outpourings. Apart from the first of these, which has a dubious exegetical basis, he appears to have focused on the major examples, although it is possible that at least some of the additional instances mentioned by other writers may be valid cases.

However, the evidence is uncertain. The problem in general is of reading back into the Old Testament period examples of the outpouring of the Spirit, who was certainly present and active among God's people before Pentecost, but whose coming in abundance on the whole people of God was only promised in the Old Testament itself for the messianic era (see, for example, Joel 2:28–32; Is 44:3; Ezek 36:27; 39:29).

Times of reformation and covenant renewal were not necessarily times of spiritual revival. The impetus for such action may come only from a godly leadership, and may be complied with by the people solely in outward form. This would certainly appear to be the case with the making of the Covenant at Sinai (Ex 19—24), as evidenced by the behaviour of the people subsequently, which was punished by the forty years of wandering in the desert until the whole of the adult generation who came out of Egypt had died, cf also Moses' statement in Deut 29:4: 'But to this day the LORD has not given you a mind [lit. heart] that understands or eyes that see or ears that hear'. The supposed repentance of Israel at Mount Carmel, following Elijah's triumph over the prophets of Baal (1 Kings 19) is another example of a temporary, outward change. It is also agreed among students of the book of Jeremiah that the prophet does not believe that Josiah's reformation achieved any lasting inward change in the people. The promise of the New Covenant (Jer 31:31–34) is a clear statement of the fact that only in the future Messianic Age will the whole people of God 'know' him and obey him.

Revival, therefore, in the sense of the outpouring of the Spirit in a general way, does not appear to be an expectation for the Old Testament period itself.

With these cautions, we will make a brief survey of those instances which different writers have mentioned as, in their view, examples of revival.

Both Edwards and Bonar draw attention to the statement in Genesis 4:26, 'Then men began to call on the name of the Lord'. While Edwards acknowledges that writers differ on the meaning of this verse, he feels that the first statement of men performing such a spiritual act must refer to an unusual 'addition to the performance of this duty [of corporate prayer, as he understands it]...carried far beyond what it had been

before, which must be the consequence of a remarkable pouring out of the Spirit of God' (Edwards, ed Wilson 1989:142). It
seems that Edwards and Bonar are alone among both ancient
and modern writers in understanding the verse in this way.[2]

Bonar feels that there was probably 'some special work of
the Spirit' in the days of Noah before the Flood, when 'there
were, in all likelihood, some with whom the Spirit not merely
strove, but strove effectually, and who were safely lodged in
the better ark before the deluge came, being taken away from
the evil to come'. Also, he thinks it likely that in the time of
Abraham 'the Spirit wrought mightily... when men such as
those we have named [Abraham, Lot, Melchisedek, Job] stand
forth as the representatives of the Church and monuments of
the divine grace and power' (in Gillies 1845:i-ii). At best, this
is arguing from silence. Indeed, the way in which the generation before the Flood is described (Gen 6:5) makes it unlikely.
Cf also Gen 8:21.

The events of Jacob's return to Bethel (Gen 35:1–15) are
seen by Kaiser as an example of personal revival which
affected his whole house (*op cit* 27-38).[3] Again, the evidence is
unclear.

According to Baker, Exodus 4:29–31 describes a revival
situation as Moses and Aaron return from meeting with God
and convince the Israelites by words and deeds that the Lord
is going to deliver them (*op cit* 9-17). Bonar says that 'during
the wilderness sojournings of Israel there were several indica-
tions of a work of God'; Kaiser (*op cit* 39-52) and Cairns (*op
cit* 22) are more specific, as they point to the renewal of the
covenant in Exodus 32ff as an example of revival. However, as
we have commented above, the conduct of Israel in the wilderness, as well as the explicit statement of Deut 29:4, would
seem to indicate that there was no genuine spiritual work
taking place in the hearts of the adult generation who left
Egypt.

Edwards is probably on sounder exegetical ground than he
was in his first example when he draws attention to what he
sees as 'a remarkable outpouring of his spirit on the younger

generation in the wilderness'. He notes the divine verdict and judgment on the generation who came out of Egypt, 'tainted with the idolatry and wickedness of Egypt and never weaned from it', but goes on to say that 'the younger generation were not so... This generation God was pleased to make a generation to his praise, and they were eminent for piety'. They saw the divine judgments of their fathers,

> and God poured out his spirit with those awakening providences towards their fathers, and their own wilderness travail together with his word preached to 'em by Moses, whereby they were greatly awakened and made to see the badness of their own hearts, and be humbled, and at length multitudes of 'em savingly converted.

He cites various passages in Deuteronomy (8:2–3, 15–16), Joshua (32:8; 24:31), Jeremiah (2:2–3) and Hosea (2:14; 13:5), including the renewal of the covenant in Deut 29ff, and comments that 'we find that such solemn renovations of the covenant commonly accompanied any remarkable pouring out of the Spirit'. The generation thus revived entered the Promised Land, served God, and continued to enjoy his blessings up to the death of Joshua and beyond (Joshua 24:31; Judges 2:7). Edwards sees a parallel between this 'good and orderly establishment of the church of Israel at its beginnings' and the similar establishment of the New Testament church through the events of Pentecost. 'Thus God at this time did gloriously advance the Work of Redemption both by his word and by his Spirit' (*op cit* 189-192).

Bonar, who also believes that the days of Joshua were 'days of blessing', mentions as 'the next great awakening' the incident in Judges 2, where the angel of the Lord confronts the people with their sins and they repent with tears. He also notes the several 'seasons of revival and decay' recorded in the book (*op cit* ii). Baker is another writer who believes that the Book of Judges records five 'seasons of Revival' as the people 'cried to the Lord' for deliverance from their enemies and repented of the sins which had brought them into bondage, and were answered by the Lord raising up judges to free them (*op cit* 18-25). However, in the light of the picture of religious syncretism and moral degradation presented to us in the book, especially in the appendices (chapters 17-21), it does not seem that either the repentance or the experience of revival—if that is what it was—was very deep or thorough.

Bonar, Baker, Kaiser, and Cairns all call attention to what they see as the revival that took place under the ministry of Samuel, who called the people to repentance and covenant renewal after the disasters of the previous years (1 Sam 7:1-13; see the various works cited for details). The incident was certainly significant as a time when Israel 'put away their Baals and Ashtoreths, and served the LORD only', and seemed to have an effect at least until the death of Samuel.

Bonar sees 'a most extensive revival of the work of God in Israel' under David, and also thinks that 'Solomon's days seem to have been days of refreshing'; in particular 'the Holy Spirit was manifestly present at the dedication of the temple, making the people's hearts to overflow with gladness when coming together to worship God' (*op cit*). At the risk of appearing negative, we must again comment that explicit statements are lacking in the Scriptures to justify such a conclusion.

After the division of the kingdom under Rehoboam, the northern kingdom of Israel experienced revival through the influence of Elijah on Mount Carmel, according to Kaiser and Cairns, although we have already expressed doubt regarding the depth of repentance and renewal evidenced in the incident (see above).

The southern kingdom of Judah experienced at least four revivals during the reigns of Asa, Jehoshaphat, Hezekiah and Josiah, according to Gillies, Baker, Kaiser and Cairns.[4] Kaiser draws attention to the central significance of 2 Chronicles 7:14 in what many commentators refer to as the writer's doctrine of immediate retribution, but which he prefers to speak of as the pattern of revival in the book. He notes (cf also Williamson 1982: 32, 225-226), that the four conditions 'If my people...will humble themselves and pray and seek my face and turn from their wicked ways' provide the key to the accounts of the four kings mentioned above, in whose reigns revival was experienced (*op cit* 14-15). If this is true, then the use of this verse, so beloved of popular preachers and writers on revival, is justified exegetically.

Once more, however, we should note that the revivals mentioned may not have affected the ordinary people to any great extent, either in their attitudes or their behaviour. As already noted, Jeremiah, who initially supported the reforms of the godly young king Josiah, later realised that they had not really changed the attitudes of the people. Only a new covenant which would be written by God on the people's hearts would cause them to truly obey him (Thompson 1980:61-62; Kidner 1987:17).

A number of writers mention revivals in the period after the return from the Babylonian Exile. Baker sees four (under Zerubbabel, under Haggai and Zechariah, under Ezra, and under Nehemiah), Kaiser two (under Zerubbabel and under Nehemiah), and Edwards one (that under the combined ministries of Ezra and Nehemiah).[5] Certainly, the scenes that occurred in the ceremony of covenant renewal described in Nehemiah 8—10 bear the marks of spiritual revival and awakening, which we shall encounter very frequently as we proceed through the pages of church history. Perhaps we may argue that, just as the 'New Exodus' prophesied by Isaiah (cf Isaiah 43:14ff) began with the Return from Babylon, so also the outpouring of the Spirit prophesied in such passages as Isaiah 44:3–4 began to take place after the Return.

REVIVALS IN THE NEW TESTAMENT
Moving on to the New Testament, Baker draws attention to the fact that 'the preaching of John the Baptist produced the first revival recorded in the New Testament'. He notes the vast numbers who flocked to hear John, the great majority of whom were baptised as evidence of their repentance (*op cit*

127-136). Certainly, there seems to have been a great awakening of religious interest. As Mark describes it, 'The whole Judean countryside and all the people of Jerusalem went out to him' (Mk 1:5a), showing the intense interest created by the appearance of such a prophet after centuries of prophetic silence. Matthew and Luke make clear that John did not automatically accept the sincerity of those who flocked to hear him. He addressed them (and particularly many of the Pharisees and Sadducees among them) as 'you brood of vipers', comparing them to snakes fleeing from a forest fire (Mt 3:7; Lk 3:7), and called for confession of sins before baptising them, as well as changed lives following their baptism. Whatever the possibilities of many being merely swept along by eschatological enthusiasm and the emotional response of the crowds, it is probably right to see this as a genuine movement of spiritual awakening produced by the prophetic preaching of a man of God.

While most writers ignore the fact, it may also be said that the ministry of Jesus himself manifested many revival features, as vast crowds also followed him, and as he preached and performed many remarkable miracles. Luke's description of him is of coming 'in the power of the Spirit' to Galilee, where news about him soon spread throughout the area and where his teaching was received with enthusiasm (Lk 4:14–15). In his home town of Nazareth, he received an ambivalent welcome (Lk 4:16–30), but elsewhere great crowds flocked to hear him and to bring the sick and demon-possessed to him to be healed (Lk 4:31–44; 5:12–16). Even as the opposition of the religious leaders grew, he continued to preach to large crowds wherever he went, and continued to heal and to cast out demons (Lk 5:17–26; 8:1–4). Luke presents a very high view of Jesus as the 'Saviour...Christ the Lord', but he also portrays him as the Spirit-endowed preacher of the Word (Lk 3:22; 4:1,14,16), with whom the power of the Lord is present (Lk 5:17), and in whose ministry the kingdom of God is clearly evident (Lk 11:20).

Similarly, the ministries of the Twelve and the Seventy

were accompanied by revival phenomena, according to the witness of the Gospel writers (Mt 10:1–8; Mk 6:7–13; Lk 9:1–6; 10:1–20).

It may be argued that the effects of the preaching of John and Jesus were as short-lived as some of the national reformations in the Old Testament period which we have considered, and that if we reject those as true awakenings, we should do the same with these. However, while it is true that the large crowds did not continue to accompany Jesus, this was due in part at least to a change of strategy which he adopted, as he increasingly concentrated on the Twelve in preparation for his physical departure from them. It is true that the Fourth Gospel records that 'from that time many of his disciples turned back and no longer followed him' (Jn 6:66), but after the Resurrection 'he appeared to more than five hundred of the brothers at the same time' (1 Cor 15:6), which argues for a large number of disciples who did remain faithful, possibly the fruit of his earlier 'revival preaching'.

As we have already noted, the events of Pentecost are often appealed to as providing the pattern by which all subsequent revivals may be judged. Baker says that 'the revival at Jerusalem on the day of Pentecost was the greatest of all time' (p 136). Edwards refers to the pouring out of the Spirit which began at Pentecost as 'Christ's coming ... in a spiritual manner for the glorious setting up his kingdom in the world' (p 377).[6]

The infant Church in Jerusalem in the first months of its existence, as portrayed for us in the early chapters of the Acts of the Apostles, was characterised by vigorous life, sustained growth, new accessions of spiritual power through new infillings of the Holy Spirit, and the presence of God experienced in an unusual way in miracles of both blessing and judgment. Problems arose, mainly caused by the large numbers of new converts from varying backgrounds; opposition and persecution occurred, but it failed to dampen the enthusiasm of the Christians.

The first really serious threat to the awakening in Jerusalem came through the martyrdom of Stephen and the more systematic persecution which followed. However, the effect was not to extinguish it, but rather to extend its influence, as 'those who had been scattered preached the word wherever they went' (Acts 8:4). By this means the awakening extended to places such as Samaria, through Philip (Acts 8:4–13, where many miracles occurred and great numbers of people were converted), the coastal towns from Azotus in the south to Caesarea about fifty miles further north, also through Philip, the city of Damascus,[7] the region of Phoenicia, the island of Cyprus and the Syrian city of Antioch (Acts 11:19).

In Antioch, as the gospel was first preached to Gentiles in large numbers,[8] there were unmistakable marks of a widespread spiritual awakening. Luke reports that 'the Lord's hand was with them, and a great number of people believed and turned to the Lord (Acts 11:21). The work continued to grow through the arrival of Barnabas from Jerusalem, as 'a great number of people were brought to the Lord' through his ministry (Acts 11:24); and continued to develop when Barnabas obtained Paul's help: '[he] met with the church and taught great numbers of people' (Acts 11:26). Out of the situation of such spiritual awakening the first planned missionary thrust began (Acts 13:1–3).

The mission in Paphos on the island of Cyprus (where Christians from Jerusalem had already preached the gospel to Jews [Acts 11:19], and from where preachers had gone to Antioch and spoken the Word to Gentiles [Acts 11:20]) was not the occasion of a large-scale awakening such as the one in Antioch, but it did produce a 'power encounter' between the Christian missionaries and the Jewish sorcerer Bar-Jesus, which resulted in the conversion of the Roman proconsul Sergius Paulus (Acts 13:6–12).

Back on the mainland, Paul and Barnabas preached in Antioch in Pisidia, where another spiritual awakening took place, as 'almost the whole city gathered to hear the word of the Lord' (Acts 13:44). Opposition from unbelieving Jews caused the missionaries to leave the city and region, but not before 'the word of the Lord spread through the whole region... and the disciples were filled with joy and with the Holy Spirit' (Acts 13:49–52). In Iconium 'they spoke so effectively that a great number of Jews and Gentiles believed' (Acts 14:1); in Lystra, unrestrained and uninformed religious frenzy soon changed from enthusiasm to an attempt to kill the messengers (Acts 14:8–19); in Derbe 'they preached the good news...and won a large number of disciples' (Acts 14:21). When they returned to Syrian Antioch they had quite a story to tell as they 'reported all that God had done through them' (Acts 14:27)!

On Paul's later journeys, the work in Philippi got off to a quieter start than that in many places, but grew more dramatically through the exorcism of the 'python' spirit of divination from the slave girl and the conversion of the jailer and his household (Acts 16:11–40). In Thessalonica, persecution cut short Paul's stay there, but not before he had preached to them 'not simply with words, but also with power, with the Holy Spirit and with deep conviction', as a result of which a vigorous church was established which 'became a model to all the believers in Macedonia and Achaia' and from which 'the Lord's message rang out... in Macedonia and Achaia [and their] faith in God has become known everywhere' (1 Thess 1:4–8).

In Corinth (Acts 18:1–17) and in Ephesus (Acts 19:1–41), in both of which places Paul spent an unusual amount of time in spite of opposition and persecution, awakenings took place which resulted in great numbers coming to faith in the cities themselves and in the surrounding areas (Acts 18:10–11; 19:10,20). In Ephesus, which was a centre of pagan worship and occult practices, during the awakening many miracles and exorcisms occurred (Acts 19:11–20). Presumably, similar awakenings took place in other places as 'by the power of signs and miracles, through the power of the Spirit...from Jerusalem all the way round to Illyricum [Paul] fully proclaimed the gospel of Christ' (Rom 15:19).

The New Testament therefore gives evidence of widespread spiritual awakening, although, as already noted, by the end of the century, some churches, including that at Ephesus, were in need of revival (Rev 2:4; 3:1–2, 15–16).

Notes

[1] Among these we note Bonar in Gillies 1845:i-iii; Baker 1906; Autrey 1960; Olford 1962; Kaiser 1986; Cairns 1986:22-24; Christian History 1989:6; Lescellius 1989:5-6. On individual revivals or awakenings in the Old Testament, see also Smith 1937; White 1986:99-109.

[2] Modern commentators on this verse usually discuss whether or not it contradicts the statement in Exodus 6:3 where God says to Moses: 'By my name the LORD I did not make myself known to them [the patriarchs]'. Whatever their conclusions on this point, they agree in general that the verse is noting the beginnings of public worship, possibly in the line of Seth (see eg Westermann 1974: I, 338-341; Wenham 1987:115-116; Hamilton 1990:242-244).

[3] His book is entitled *Quest for Renewal: Personal Revival in the Old Testament*, but in his Introduction (*ibid* 11-25) he discusses revival in general, his other chapters deal with general revivals, and each chapter is headed 'Revival under…'.

[4] Edwards also refers to the reigns of the last two kings, Hezekiah and Josiah (*op cit* 192,233). Wilbur Smith treats the reforms of Hezekiah in a work with the title *The Glorious Revival Under King Hezekiah* (1937).

[5] On this see also White 1986:99-109; 1988:26-27.

[6] He includes in this description the whole period of the New Testament terminating in the destruction of Jerusalem, taking note of stages within the period such as the 'glorious pouring out of the Spirit of God in the city of Samaria', the conversion of Cornelius and his family, and the work of the Spirit which began the Church at Antioch (pp 378-379 cf Baker pp 146-173). 'And after this,' says Edwards,

> vast multitudes were converted in many different parts of the world, chiefly by the ministry of the apostle Paul, a glorious pouring out of the Spirit accompanying his preaching in one place and another. Multitudes flocked into the church of Christ in a great number of cities where the apostle came (*ibid*).

He notes particularly 'the most remarkable pouring out of the Spirit…in the city of Ephesus', and 'a very extraordinary ingathering of souls at Corinth' (p 380), and concludes

> Thus the gospel sun...now rose and began to enlighten the heathen world...This was a great thing, and a new thing such as never had been seen before...And in almost all countries throughout the known world were assemblies of the people of God, and joyful praises were sung to the true God, and Jesus Christ the glorious Redeemer (*ibid*).

[7] Presumably, many of the Hellenistic Jewish Christians had fled here, and Saul went there to bring them back to Jerusalem (Acts 9:1–2; see Longenecker in Gaebelein ed 1981:370).

[8] Peter had already opened the door of faith to Cornelius and his household, who were 'God-fearers', which event had been preceded by visions granted to both Peter and Cornelius, and accompanied by unusual activity of the Holy Spirit (Acts 10:1–48).

CHAPTER 4

REVIVALS IN THE HISTORY OF THE CHURCH UP TO THE SEVENTEENTH CENTURY

B EFORE WE COME TO LOOK IN DETAIL at the revivals which have taken place in the past three hundred years, we will first give a brief survey of those revivals which occurred up to the seventeenth century.

THE EARLY AND MEDIEVAL PERIODS
When we come to study the subject of revivals in the early Church, we encounter a number of difficulties. The first arises from the fragmentary nature of the evidence for what happened in the first few centuries of the Church's existence. Up until the time of Constantine when official persecution ceased, the Church had no opportunity to keep full accounts of its life and activity. In fact, a complete record with details of such matters as leadership and activities could itself have caused problems if it had fallen into the hands of the authorities.

A second difficulty arises from the fact that writers who did keep some record of what happened may have had concerns other than those in which we are interested. We, therefore, need to read between the lines in their accounts in order to see whether they provide us with evidence for revivals or spiritual awakenings.

A third problem, which will also recur in the Medieval period (and which is, in fact, a perennial danger), is that movements of spiritual awakening or revival may be rejected by the leadership of the mainline Church and be dismissed as a heretical or fringe movement. This often means that we are only able to read about the movement through the writings of its opponents, because the mainline Church in the past usually destroyed any writings of the group even if they had the time and leisure to produce any writings of their own.

In the period up to the accession of Constantine,[1] the Church grew and spread in a remarkable way, especially considering the periods of persecution which it suffered from time to time. The church grew rapidly in many areas, including the great city of Alexandria in Egypt, and along the coast of North Africa among the Latin-speaking population. The city of Carthage had a very strong church at an early date.

A considerable spiritual awakening seems to have taken place in Lyons, in southern Gaul, under the ministry of Irenaeus (fl c 175-c 195) who in addition to his literary activity and other episcopal duties learned the local dialect and preached to the local non-Hellenistic population; exorcisms occurred, gifts of the Spirit were evidenced, and some people were reportedly raised from the dead (see Irenaeus *Against Heresies* 2.32.4; 2.31.2; Riss 1988:8[2]).

The same was probably true in the next century at Neo-Caesarea in Pontus under the ministry of Gregory the Wonderworker (c 213-270) who was converted through contact with Origen (c 185-c 254). He returned to his native Pontus, where he was elected bishop somewhat against his will. He gave himself to the task of the complete conversion of the population of his diocese. Such was his success that it was said that when Gregory became bishop (c 240) he found only seventeen Christians in his diocese; when he died only seventeen remained pagan (Latourette 1953:76).

The first half of the third century, up until the persecution of Decius who became emperor in AD 249, saw thousands flocking into the churches all over the Roman Empire. The persecutions of Decius and his successor Valerian continued until AD 260, and were followed by what was the most severe, and, mercifully, the last outburst of such persecution under Diocletian before Constantine's espousal of Christianity in AD 312 dramatically reversed the situation. In the forty years of peace from AD 260 to 303, great gains were made. By the beginning of the fourth century, some estimate that up to half of the population of the empire had professed faith. Other estimates are more sober, and speak of around twenty per cent of the population, but even this figure is amazing (Latourette 1953:90).[3] The persecutions often caused many to renounce their faith, and probably served to purify the church; but the growth of the Christian movement over the previous two-and-a-half centuries must surely be attributed, in part at least, to a succession of spiritual movements which deserve to be included in our survey.

Outside the Roman Empire, the mass conversion of the kingdom of Armenia took place in the latter part of the third century through the work of Gregory the Illuminator (c 240-332). He succeeded in bringing the king, Tiridates, to faith, and the rest of the population soon followed. Whatever may be thought of the depth of such mass conversions,[4] it is probably right to see the movement as the result in part at least of a spiritual awakening.

Montanism or 'the New Prophecy', a movement which flourished in Phrygia from the middle of the second century, is an early example of what was probably a genuine spiritual impetus, but which through some of the excesses of its leaders and adherents was rejected by the main-line Church and for centuries was viewed as a heresy. Recent study, however, has vindicated the movement's orthodoxy[5] and it is probably true to say that it was the result of a genuine movement of spiritual renewal protesting against the institutionalising of the Church and calling, among other things, for a renewed emphasis on spiritual gifts such as prophecy. Tertullian of Carthage (c 160/170-c 215/220) was attracted to the movement, particularly because of its protest against the moral laxity which was invading the Church at the time, and in later life joined the group.

Another movement which also began as a protest against

the laxity which came into the life of the Church, this time through the large numbers who were flocking into the Church in the third century, was the phenomenon of monasticism. Some of the motivation towards the withdrawal from the life of the Church itself, as well as from ordinary life in the family and the community, came from false ideas such as the belief in the evil of material things. However, there was also present the desire to live wholeheartedly and completely for God without any encumbrance and distraction such as ordinary life in society inevitably brought.

According to Athanasius, who wrote the biography of Antony (251-356), one of the pioneers of the monastic movement, the latter was responsible for a strong spiritual movement as large numbers followed him in taking up the monastic life and as he performed many miracles, healings, exorcisms. Martin of Tours (335-400) who was a bishop and a missionary, as well as being a pioneer of monasticism, was also involved in a spiritual impetus which brought multitudes to living faith. He too had many miracles attributed to him.[6] His influence on his own generation may be measured by the fact that even during his lifetime churches were dedicated to him, and soon after his death the numbers of such dedications greatly increased. Theodoret (c 393-c 458) gives a vivid contemporary account of the thousands who flocked to Simeon the pillar ascetic (c 390-459), renouncing their former religion, destroying their idols, and being baptised (cited in MacMullan 1984:2).

The success of the missionary work of Patrick (389-c 461) in Ireland—where thousands were baptised, the power of heathenism was broken and the church firmly established— was quite clearly the result of a spiritual awakening.[7] Similarly, the vigour of Irish monasticism, which in the next century produced missionaries such as Columba (521-597) and his fellow monks, who evangelised much of Scotland, together with Columban (c 543-615) and others who evangelised and re-evangelised in France, Switzerland and northern Italy, bears witness to the continuation and renewal of the original spiritual movement. Furthermore, the works of Aidan (d 651), Cuthbert (c 634-687), Chad (d 672), and others from Lindisfarne in Northumbria who evangelised England from the North, shows that the spiritual impulse continued into the next century. When English missionaries such as Willibrord (658-739) and Boniface (680-754) took up the torch, their success in evangelising and in overcoming the power of heathenism among the Frisians and the various Germanic tribes shows evidence once more of spiritual awakening.[8]

The legends which grew up around the lives of many missionary leaders, such as Patrick, Columba, Aidan, Boniface and others need to be treated with caution, particularly when they multiply the miracles which were claimed for such men, but they bear witness to the powerful influence which was made by their work. Possibly, they also show that a number of healings and other miracles were performed by them, even if the numbers were nowhere near as great as those claimed. Riss notes that Augustine of Canterbury (d 604) was told by Gregory, bishop of Rome, not to be puffed up with pride that great miracles were taking place in his missionary work in England (Riss 1988:8, citing Bede *Ecclesiastical History* Book I ch 31). Riss comments, 'This is a good indication that revival had taken place during the course of his ministry'. However, miracles are not in themselves proof of revival, and we shall return to the question of revival and miracles at a later point.

By the end of the fifth century monasticism was firmly established in the life of the Church in both East and West. It was in the various monastic orders and movements, as well as in the many protest movements which like Montanism were often marginalised and rejected by the main-line Church, that new impulses of spiritual life were to be seen for the next 1,000 years. Concerning monasticism, Latourette wrote:

> In its numerous ramifications it was to be the main channel through which bursts of new life were to find

expression in the various churches...One of the best gauges of the vitality of these churches, and especially of the Roman Catholic Church, is to be found in the number and strength of the reforms of existing monastic houses and of the new monastic or near-monastic movements which emerge in any one era. When vigour has been at a low ebb, the monastic life has languished and become sluggish or corrupt. In times of revival, the monastic life has attracted ardent souls who wish to give themselves unreservedly to the faith and has taken on fresh variety and new forms (Latourette 1953:233).

Within Western Catholicism the movements for monastic reform associated with Cluny in the tenth century and with the Cistercians and other new orders in the twelfth century should possibly be included in the account of revivals and awakenings (Latourette 1953:416-427). Even more, the advent of the mendicant orders of Franciscans and Dominicans in the thirteenth century shows evidence of new spiritual life in the Medieval Church (Latourette *ibid* 427-444 [note the summary on pp 443-444]). The preaching of Francis of Assisi (1182-1226) was the occasion of spiritual awakening for great numbers (Burns 1909: 57-96). The preaching of one of his early followers Antony of Padua (1195- 1231) was accompanied by all the signs of revival. When he preached a series of Lenten sermons in Padua in 1231, 30,000 gathered to hear one sermon in an open field. A massive number of reconciliations and restitutions took place, and there were not enough clergy to cope with those who wished to confess their sins (Rogers in Douglas ed 1978:51).

Among the various protest movements which arose, but which were rejected and suppressed by the main-line Church, it is very difficult, if not impossible, for us to determine whether or not they were genuine movements of revival and spiritual awakening. A number of them seem to have contained elements of error or heresy, although this perception may have been created in part by the official Church as it

sought reasons to suppress the particular group. The Pauli-
cians in the seventh century (see Norman in Douglas ed,
1978:755), the Bogomiles in the eleventh (Giacumakis in
Douglas *ibid* 139), and the Albigenses or Cathari in the same
century (Latourette *ibid* 453-455) may have been originally
the result of genuine spiritual impulses, which were possibly
corrupted.[9]

The Waldensian movement which began in the eleventh
century with the activity of Peter Waldo and the Poor Men of
Lyons, and which spread rapidly through much of Catholic
Europe, is another example of spiritual awakening and revival
in the Medieval period. Due to the determined efforts of the
Catholic Church to stamp it out, it is not possible to discover
the full extent and depth of its impact, but it is likely that it
had a profound influence on the lives of large numbers over a
considerable area of Central and Southern Europe (see *Christian History* 1989).

In fourteenth-century Prague, a reform movement was
begun through the preaching of an Augustinian canon from
Vienna, Conrad of Waldhausen, who was succeeded by a
Moravian Jan Milic of Kromeriz (d 1374) and then by a
Bohemian preacher Matthew of Janov (c 1355-1393). These, in
turn, were followed by Jan Hus (1373-1415), Jerome of Prague
(c 1371-1416), and others. Through the activities of these men,
a movement of reform was begun which had many revival
characteristics. As a result of Milic's ministry, the 'red light'
district in Prague was transformed into a hostel for converted
prostitutes, and renamed 'Jerusalem'. A school for preachers
was established, named 'Nazareth', and a special chapel was
built, capable of holding 3,000 people for the large crowds to
gather to hear the preaching of the Word, named 'Bethlehem'.
When Hus preached in the Bethlehem Chapel, the Queen and
her ladies attended, together with thousands of the ordinary
people. A number of the preachers were silenced through the
activity of the monks and clergy, and both Hus and Jerome
were eventually burned at the stake (Spinka
1968:3-21,288-299). After their deaths, a popular revolution

took place which resulted in Hussite armies proving invincible against the might of Catholic opposition. The movement splintered, and one branch established a theocracy in the south of Bohemia on a hill-top fortress renamed Tabor (Heymann 1955). A more pacific stream from the Hussite Revolution eventually produced the Unity of Brethren in 1457, a 'Protestant' Church sixty years before Luther nailed his theses to the door of the church in Wittenburg (Brock 1957: Wagner 1983).

Other reform movements, such as the Brethren of the Common Life in Germany and the Netherlands in the fourteenth and fifteenth centuries, and John Wycliffe (c 1329-1384) and the Lollard preachers in England, should probably also be included as examples of revival in the late medieval Church (see Clouse in Douglas ed 1978:153-154, 601-602, 1064-1065).

Within the Catholic Church a number of mystics, several of whom were women, such as Catherine of Sienna (1347-1380), Catherine of Bologna (1413-1463), and Catherine of Genoa (1447-1510), exercised considerable spiritual influence. The Dominican preacher Vincent Ferrer (1350-1419) travelled widely in Spain, Northern Italy, Switzerland and France, preaching to enormous crowds. In Spain he is said to have won thousands of Jews and Muslims to faith in Christ. He also involved himself in politics, acting to protect Jews from persecution; he gave himself to tending sick children and adults, especially in the plague in Genoa; marvels accompanied his prayers, and many miracles were attributed to him (Latourette *ibid* 652-653; Thorne in Douglas ed *ibid* 1019).

In Florence, Italy, there was a significant revival between 1494 and 1498 under the ministry of Girolamo Savonarola (1452-1498). In his fiery sermons he called for repentance on the part of the people and their leaders, and championed the cause of the poor and the oppressed. He warned of judgment to come on the city, which occurred when Charles VIII of France invaded Italy. As the result of his preaching, the citizens made a bonfire of their cosmetics, false hair, pornographic books, and gambling equipment. However, when he denounced the corruption of the Papal court, he was tried and executed (Burns 1909: 97-141).

THE SIXTEENTH AND SEVENTEENTH CENTURIES

The Protestant Reformation of the sixteenth century is judged by most writers on the subject of revival to be, in Edwards' words, the result of 'a glorious outpouring of the Spirit of God...not only to convert multitudes in so short a time from popery to the true religion, but to turn many to God and true godliness' (Edwards [1774] in Wilson ed 1989:438; see also Gillies 1845:36-83; Burns 1909:142-262 [on Luther, Calvin and Knox]; Allen 1951:11-13; Lloyd-Jones 1960:48-49; Murray 1971:3-7; Riss 1988:9-10. See also Reid ed 1968; Jones 1985).[10] Revival phenomena were certainly evident in the ministries of men like Hugh Latimer (1485-1555) and many others. At times, Latimer preached in the open-air to 6,000 people at a time. Murray (1971:6) notes an entry in the records of St Margaret's Church, Westminster, where one shilling and sixpence was expended 'for mending diverse pews that were broken when Doctor Latimer did preach', presumably as a result of the great numbers crowding into the building to hear him!

In the Puritan era of the late sixteenth and the seventeenth centuries there were many significant local revivals, and, indeed, the whole Puritan movement should probably be considered as a revival movement (Packer 1980:2-16, reprinted in Packer 1991:41-63), although some would disagree (eg Cairns 1986:25).

In Scotland there were notable preaching ministries such as that of John Welch, the son-in-law of John Knox, under whose preaching there was revival in Ayr between 1590 and 1606; that of John Davidson in 1596 at a meeting of the General Assembly of the Church of Scotland;[11] that of David Dickson from 1625 to 1630 in Stewarton in the West of Scotland;[12] and that of Robert Bruce of Kinnäird in 1627 at Edinburgh and Inverness (see the references in Gillies cited by Riss 1988:10,169; Douglas 1964; Murray *ibid* 25-29; Packer

1991:56-57). The best-known of the early seventeenth-century revivals in Scotland took place on June 21, 1630 under the preaching of John Livingstone at Kirk of Shotts in Scotland, which Robert Fleming describes as 'so convincing an appearance of God and down-pouring of the Spirit' (cited in Gillies 1845;198; see also Murray 1971:28-29; Riss 1988:10-11). Following a weekend of communion services[13] at which a number of ministers had preached, many spent the Sunday night in prayer. On the Monday morning John Livingstone, a young minister, preached at a further service. Fleming says that, as a result of that sermon, 'it was known, which I can speak on sure ground, near five hundred had at that time a discernible change wrought on them, of whom most proved lively Christians afterward' (Murray *op cit*).

The plantation of Ulster in Northern Ireland, which in the 1620s became a haven for both English and Scots ministers of Puritan conviction, saw a number of revivals under the preaching of Robert Blair, Josias Welch (son of John Welch), John Livingstone, and others who moved from Scotland; and also that of John Ridge, an English minister. The first revival began around 1626 in Oldstone, near the town of Antrim, through the preaching of a rather eccentric minister, James Glendinning. According to a contemporary witness, Andrew Stewart:

> Behold the success! For the hearers finding themselves condemned by the mouth of God speaking in His Word, fell into such anxiety and terror of conscience that they looked on themselves as altogether lost and damned...I have seen them myself stricken into a swoon with the Word; yea a dozen in one day carried out of doors as dead, so marvellous was the power of God smiting their hearts for sin, condemning and killing. And of these were none of the weaker sex or spirit, but indeed some of the boldest spirits... The stubborn, who sinned and gloried in it...are now patterns of sobriety... and this spread through the country to admiration, so that, in a

manner, as many as came to hear the word of God, went away slain with the words of his mouth (cited in Murray *ibid* 30 and Westerkamp 1988:15).

The revival spread widely and continued into the 1630s, when a number of the ministers involved died and episcopal opposition, under the influence of Archbishop Laud, excluded the remainder from preaching (see Murray *ibid* 29-33).

In England, there were similar awakenings under the ministry of a number of the Puritan preachers, especially in East Anglia. Men such as Richard Greenham at Dry Drayton, seven miles from Cambridge, from 1570 to 1590; Samuel Fairclough vicar of Kedington, seventeen miles from Cambridge from 1627 to 1662; his son, Richard Fairclough rector of Mells in Somerset from 1647 to 1662; and John Rogers of Dedham in Suffolk saw revival phenomena as a result of their preaching (See Murray *op cit* 11-13 and Packer 1980: 11-12 for contemporary descriptions). We have already noted the ministry of Francis Higginson in Leicester before his emigration to New England. Cotton Mather mentions the 'notable Revival of Religion' resulting from his preaching (Mather 1702, Book I:72). The ministry of Richard Baxter (1615- 1691) in Kidderminster, Worcestershire, saw a prolonged awakening over a period of several years, which resulted in the vast majority of the town coming to a profession of faith (Murray *op cit* 13-14; Packer *op cit* 12). Baxter affirms that there were scores of godly ministers in the Commonwealth period whose preaching was remarkably blessed by God, so much so that Packer comments,

> Further study of the Puritan ministry in seventeenth-century England...would, I think, warrant the conclusion that in the middle of that century a work of grace was in progress in England that was every whit as potent and deep as its better-known counterpart a hundred years later (*ibid* 13).

All of this came to a tragic and premature end through the Great Ejection of Puritan ministers in 1662, following the Restoration of Charles II in 1660. However, at the time of the Great Plague in London in 1665 there was an awakening in the city, particularly through the preaching of a number of the ministers who had been ejected from their pulpits in 1662. Many of the ministers who had replaced them after the Great Ejection fled from the capital when the plague broke out, and their places were taken by those they had displaced (Gillies *op cit* 124-128).

In mainland Europe a century earlier, the rise of the Anabaptists is surely to be seen as a revival movement, even though many of their radical ideas, reinforced by the excesses of its militant arm, brought the whole phenomenon into disfavour with the leaders of the magisterial Reformation (see Littell 1964; Verduin 1964; Durnbaugh 1968). The doctrinal errors of some of the groups, particularly in the direction of Unitarianism, brought the movement into further disrepute (see Williams 1964), but, as we see constantly in the history of revival, this does not of itself prevent us from judging it in general to be a true revival, at least in its beginning.

The same is probably true of the Society of Friends, or 'Quakers', at the beginning, especially as seen in the life and ministry of George Fox (1624-1691), their founder. His powerful preaching in England, Ireland, Wales, in Continental Europe and in America, accompanied by many reported miracles of healing,[14] brought large numbers to join his societies. In spite of persecution, imprisonment and opposition from nearly all other groups of Christians (from whose ranks many of his converts came), their numbers multiplied throughout the century (Braithwaite 1912 rev ed 1955).

Notes

[1] The works of Harnack ET 1908; Latourette I. 1937; Bruce 1959; Green 1970; Hinson 1981; and MacMullen 1984; provide us with the basic facts,

together with their own assessments of the reasons for the amazing growth of the first few centuries. Latourette lists ten factors which contributed to the success of the faith, but gives as the underlying cause of the 'vast release of creative energy' the influence of Jesus, his crucifixion, resurrection and 'the continued living presence with his disciples of his spirit' (*ibid* 162-170).

[2] For an excellent discussion of miracles in the early Church see Bradley nd 1-28. See also Harnack 1962: I. 199-218; Kydd 1984. Bradley claims that prophecy and other spiritual gifts were present in the Church after the first century. He notes both the enthusiasm and the sobriety of the Church in the second and third centuries on the subject, but sees a degeneration in attitude after AD 325 when the church became legalised. Miracles became trivialised as healings supposedly performed by the relics of the martyrs became indistinguishable from popular magic.

[3] Latourette himself speaks of 'the probable tenth of the population of the Roman Empire who called themselves Christian at the accession of Constantine' (Latourette 1937: I. 169; cf Harnack [1908: II. 327-331]). According to Hinson (1981:25n.), recent evidence which has come to light 'would raise the percentage considerably'.

[4] A deepening and purification of the nation's Christianity was effected a century later through Nerses, a descendant of Gregory (Latourette 1953:102).

[5] See Wright 1976:15-22; also Snyder 1989:15-28. Leading historians of Christian doctrine such as von Campenhausen (1964) and Pelikan (1971) have vindicated the orthodoxy of the movement, and modern church historians, almost without exception, have argued that it was not heretical, although it was schismatic (see eg Johnson 1976:50). According to Wright, 'They were fanatics but not heretics.'

[6] Septimius Severus, Martin's biographer, mentions his powers of exorcism, prophecy and healing as decisive factors in his success in winning large numbers of pagans (Hinson 1981:276-177).

[7] In his 'Confessions' he claimed a special dispensation of the Spirit which enabled him to convert the heathen, escape perils, and do 'signs and wonders' (Hinson 1981:277).

[8] This is not to say that all missionary activity is evidence of revival and spiritual awakening, although, as we shall see later, revival has often produced a new missionary impulse. In the Medieval period, it is interesting to see the missionary work which was often undertaken at great cost, and in many cases with great results, which show the power of God active in and through the lives of a small number of his servants, even when the Church at large was moribund. The Nestorian missionary A-lo-pen reached China

with the gospel in AD 635. Irish monks continued to undertake missionary work in areas remote from the safety of the confines of the Holy Roman Empire; evidence of their work is found in the Orkneys, the Faroes, Bohemia, Moravia and Russia. The two brothers Constantine and Methodius from Byzantium established the Church in Moravia in the ninth century.

The whole question of the relation between revival and the expansion of the Church, particularly with reference to the Medieval period, requires further work.

[9] See Broadbent (1930 and often reprinted) for a sympathetic treatment of a number of these, and similar groups, all of which the author, a leader in the Plymouth Brethren, sees as representatives of the 'True Church' which has always existed, even at times of general corruption in the official Church.

[10] Some Church historians also see the Catholic Reformation as a movement of genuine spiritual awakening. They would include in that description the formation of the Society of Jesus (the Jesuits) through Ignatius Loyola (1491-1556) together with the early missionary activity of the Society, as well as the influence of the great Spanish mystics such as Teresa of Avila (1515-1582), John of the Cross (1542-1605) and others, and other new religious orders such as the Capuchins (see Latourette *ibid* 840-883).

[11] 'In this he was so assisted by the Spirit working upon their hearts, that within an hour after they had convened, they began to look with another countenance than at first, and while he was exhorting them to their duties, the whole meeting was in tears, whereby that place might justly be called Bochim', according to a contemporary witness (cited in Murray 1971:23-24).

[12] This was described by outsiders as 'the Stewarton sickness' as they observed the deep conviction of sin experienced by many. Robert Fleming (cited in Murray 1971:27-28) spoke of 'a very solemn and extraordinary outletting of the Spirit' when 'many were so choaked and taken by the heart, that through terror the Spirit in such a measure convincing them of sin, in hearing of the Word they have been made to fall over, and thus carried out of the church...'.

[13] On the sixteenth-century revivals in Scotland and Northern Ireland and the relation of religious fervour to the large communion services, see Westerkamp 1988:28-34.

[14] Over 150 in all, see Cadbury 1948:ix; Fox, ed Penney 1911, *passim*; Fox ed Nickalls 1952.

CHAPTER 5

THE GREAT AWAKENING OF THE EIGHTEENTH CENTURY

THE MOVEMENT OF REVIVAL known as the Great Awakening, or the Evangelical Revival[1], began in the early part of the eighteenth century. It profoundly influenced Protestantism in Continental Europe, the United Kingdom and the Colonies on the Atlantic seaboard of America.[2]

PRECURSORS OF THE GREAT AWAKENING
Before we look at the revival as it manifested itself in the different areas, we shall first of all notice a number of precursors to the Great Awakening. These preliminary manifestations of a new surge of spiritual life are also found in the three geographical areas where the revival later took hold.

Precursors: Europe
In Germany the Pietist movement in Lutheranism, begun by Johannes Arndt (1555-1621), and given further impetus by Philip Jacob Spener (1635-1705), came to its full flowering in the work of August Hermann Francke (1663-1727) at Halle, as well as in Wurttemberg, Swabia, with men like the biblical commentator Johann Albert Bengel (1687-1752), and in many other places.[3]

Under Francke's vigorous leadership, Halle became a centre for Bible translation and distribution, with orphanages and schools, a seminary for the training of evangelical preachers and missionaries, and many other Christian and phil-anthropic enterprises. Jonathan Edwards comments on the 'remarkable revival of the power and practice of religion in Saxony in Germany' connected with Francke, involving the schools and orphanages, all of which 'was accompanied with a wonderful reformation and revival of religion, and a spirit of piety in the city and university of Halle' (Wilson ed 1989:436). Gillies, in his 'Historical Collections' of revivals, has extracts from Francke's own account of the rise and growth of Pietism and of his own work at Halle, together with a letter from Francke to Cotton Mather in Boston which gives details of the missionary work in India which was begun by two men from Halle, Bartholomew Ziegenbalg and Henry Plutschau (Gillies 1845:234-252). Pietism was certainly a precursor of, as well as a preparation for, the Evangelical Revival of the eight-eenth century in Europe, Britain, and North America.

A number of local revivals broke out in Central Europe in the first decades of the century, a number of them with influence from Halle. These also became part of the prepara-tion for the awakening among the Moravians at Herrnhut in 1727, which, as we shall see, through their missionary out-reach brought the gospel to many places in the world and eventually motivated other parts of the Protestant Church to engage in world mission. In Lower Silesia, a revival which began with children's prayer meetings (known as 'the uprising of children') soon spread to Breslau in 1708, and also to Teschen in Upper Silesia, where from 1717 to 1730 the power-ful preaching of Johann Adam Steinmetz, a Halle graduate, at the Jesus Church produced unusual psychological and phys-ical phenomena. In Upper Lusatia around Niederwiesa and Gorlitz, there was revival, particularly through the preaching of Johann Schwedler (who preached nine-hour sermons!) and Melchior Scheffer. In Salzburg there was a spiritual movement among the Protestant minority, which grew in influence and power from around 1710, and which by 1732, when there was a large-scale exodus to more favourable territory away from the harrassment of the Jesuits, numbered several thousands.

In Siberia there was an awakening among thousands of Swedish prisoners-of-war, through the influence of preachers from Halle. (For more information on all of these, see articles by W.R.Ward [1979, 1980, 1982, 1988, 1989]; also Gillies 1845:292-296 on the Protestants at Salzburg).

In villages such as Litomysl and Litice in northern Bohemia and also in Moravia, where secret members of the 'Hidden Seed', the remnants of the Unity of Brethren who had been persecuted by the Jesuits for the past century, still held to the faith of their fathers, there were revivals in 1720 (de Schweinitz 1885:640-641; Hamilton 1967:14). It was from these areas that the first refugees came to Herrnhut under the leadership of Christian David (1691-1751) in 1722. Christian David had himself been influenced by Scheffer in Gorlitz, and had contact with Steinmetz and Schwedler.

When, in 1727, the Moravians at Herrnhut experienced their own revival, these other awakenings—some of which were still in progress—provided the background out of which the new revival movement sprang. However, Church historians, both Moravian and others, have not usually referred to these contemporary awakenings which were taking place in the same general area (Gorlitz and Herrnhut are only about twenty miles from each other), and which made their contribution to the better-known movement which had such far-reaching effects.

Precursors: The British Isles

In England, the precursors of the Evangelical Awakening are to be found in the religious societies which had grown up in the Church of England[4] over the previous forty years or more, having been introduced from the Continent around 1678 by the Rev Dr Anthony Horneck (1641-1697) who had come to England from his native Germany in 1661.[5] Horneck had grown up in Reformed Pietist circles, and at Heidelberg University had studied under Friedrich Spannheim the Younger, who had been a follower of Jean de Labadie (1610-1674), one of the leaders of Reformed Pietism in the Netherlands

(Stoeffler 1965: 162-169). Horneck, when in Germany, had also known Philip Jakob Spener, who in 1675 published his *Pia Desideria* with its proposals for the formation of *collegia pietatis*, or small cell groups for the nourishing of spiritual life, which he had already begun in his church in Frankfurt-am-Main five years before. It seems certain, then, that the Religious Society movement derived a considerable amount of its inspiration from Pietism.[6]

In England the Anglican religious societies spread and had considerable influence on the spiritual life of members of the church. In the early 1700s there were at least forty such societies meeting in London alone (Overton 1885:210). According to the classic account of the societies, Josiah Woodward's *Account of the Rise and Progress of the Religious Societies in the City of London* (1689), the members, in addition to observing strict devotional rules,

> visited the poor at their houses and relieved them, fixed some in a way of trade, set prisoners at liberty, furthered poor scholars at the University and established scores of charity schools for the poor (cited in Overton *ibid* 211).

By the year 1700, this form of religious organisation had established itself in the structure of the Anglican Church as a viable expression of Christian piety and social concern. The church authorities permitted, and even encouraged, these societies, an interesting phenomenon at a time not generally noted for spiritual life (Heitzenrater 1972: 8,9; cited in Snyder *ibid* 15. See also Simon 1921; Snyder 1989:184-191).[7]

The Religious Societies, therefore, fostered a desire for deeper spirituality, which can be seen as a preparation for the Revival itself. They also provided a network through which the Revival could spread. In addition, they gave a model for the societies which John Wesley used so successfully to organise the many converts of the Revival. The 'Holy Club' which Charles and John, together with George Whitefield and others, organised in Oxford before any of them had experienced a true evangelical conversion, was modelled on the existing societies. Samuel Wesley, the father of John and Charles, was an advocate of the societies, and their mother Susannah organised one in the rectory at Epworth.[8]

In Wales, an Anglican vicar, Griffith Jones (1683-1761) is often referred to as 'the morning star of the Revival'. Beginning as a curate in 1710, he soon began itinerant preaching, which resulted in great numbers of converts but also provoked strong opposition. Later leaders in the revival in Wales, Daniel Rowland (1713-1790), Howell Harris (1714-1771) and Howell Davies (1716-1770), all looked to him as their spiritual father. He also developed the Charity School movement in Wales (see Wood 1960:40-45).

Rowland and Harris were both converted in 1735; the former was already a vicar, the latter was, and remained, a layman. Their preaching ministries were soon being wonderfully blessed by God, and also violently opposed by men (Bennett 1987). Davies was converted through Harris, and soon began to experience the same contrasting responses to his itinerant ministry. As we shall see, the year 1739 marked the point when the Welsh and the English revival movements came together, mainly through the friendship of George Whitefield and Howell Harris. As with the later Great Awakening in the Thirteen Colonies, Whitefield was the connecting link, at least on the human level.

In Scotland, the dead hand of Moderatism controlled the Church of Scotland at the start of the eighteenth century. Some Evangelicals seceded from the Church in 1733, and others in 1761. However, when the Revival came it was the Evangelicals who remained who were affected, and even in the dark years before that time, Evangelical parishes experienced foretastes of the later awakening. In 1724 the parish of Easter Ross in the Northern Highlands experienced the first stirrings, and similarly from 1730 onwards the parish of Nigg in the Southern Highlands witnessed a gradual quickening in the spiritual life of the people, 'with stops and intermissions', until 1739, when it reached a climax (MacInnes 1951:156 cited in Wood 1960:117).

Precursors: North America

In New England, the sixty-year ministry of Solomon Stoddard (1643-1729) in Northampton, Massachusetts, was punctuated by five periods of revival, described by Stoddard as 'harvests', in 1679, 1683, 1696, 1712 and 1718 (see Jonathan Edwards' account in his *Faithful Narrative* [Smith ed 1972:146]; *Christian History* Vol VIII no 3 1989:8-9). In 1705 there was an awakening in Taunton, Massachusetts, under the ministry of Samuel Danforth, and in 1721 at Windham, Connecticut, through the visit of Eliphalet Adams.

Further south, in the Middle Colonies, revival broke out in the 1720s and 1730s under the preaching of Theodore Jacob Frelinghuysen (1691-1747), a German-born minister who came from Holland in 1720, where he had been trained and had served as pastor of a small Dutch church. Influenced by both German and Dutch Pietism, his intense preaching to congregations of scattered Dutch settlers in the Raritan Valley in New Jersey provoked opposition, but also produced revival (Tanis 1967:42-78; *Christian History* 1989:10-11).

Frelinghuysen in turn influenced Gilbert Tennent (1703-1764), the son of William Tennent (1673-1746) an Irish immigrant, who in his 'Log College' was seeking to prepare ministers who were more than merely orthodox but were also spiritually alive. Gilbert Tennent arrived in New Brunswick, New Jersey, in 1726 and was immediately impressed by the powerful effects of Frelinghuysen's ministry. When he adopted his method, he soon saw similar results in his own ministry (Tanis 1967:67-71; Coalter 1986:12-25). His brother John experienced similar effects in his ministry further south in Freehold, New Jersey from 1730 to 1732,[9] and in 1735 the preaching of John Cross (died c 1750) was attended with the same kind of results in his itinerant ministry in the area of Newark, New Jersey.

In December 1734 a new period of revival began in Northampton, Massachusetts, this time under the ministry of Jonathan Edwards, the grandson of Solomon Stoddard who had died in 1729. Beginning in a village nearby about six months before, it soon swept through the town of North-ampton, and over the next year spread to at least thirty-two other communities in the Connecticut Valley, all mentioned by Edwards in his *Faithful Narrative* (Goen ed 1972:152-155).

Edwards describes the height of the revival as follows:

> The work of conversion was carried on in a most astonishing manner, and increased more and more; souls did as it were come by flocks to Jesus Christ...This work of God, as it was carried on, and the number of true saints multiplied, soon made a glorious alteration in the town; so that in the spring and summer following, *anno* 1735, the town seemed to be full of the presence of God...Our public assemblies were then beautiful; the congregation was alive in God's service...On whatever occasions persons met together, Christ was to be heard of, and seen in the midst of them. Our young people, when they met, were wont to spend the time in talking of the excellency and dying love of Jesus Christ...Those amongst us that had been formerly converted, were greatly enlivened and renewed with fresh and extraord-inary incomes of the Spirit of God (*ibid* 150-152).

It was brought to a premature halt, at least in North-ampton, by the suicide of Joseph Hawley, Edwards' uncle, in June 1735, but it continued in some of the other towns of the Connecticut Valley until the end of 1736. What was described as the 'Great and General Awakening' did not begin in New England until 1740, mainly in connection with the arrival of George Whitefield. For this reason, it seems best to see the awakening in the Connecticut Valley in the 1730s as one of the precursors of the Great Awakening, rather than part of the awakening itself.

In Continental Europe the Great Awakening in its full force began in 1727; in the British Isles it started about ten years later, around 1737; in North America, as we have just mentioned, it began in 1740.

THE MORAVIAN RENEWAL IN GERMANY

The Moravian Church, or the Renewed Unity of Brethren, commonly reckons its 'birthday' to be August 13, 1727, the 'day of the outpouring of the Holy Spirit upon the Congregation', 'its Pentecost', in the words of Zinzendorf (cited in Benham 1895: 103 ff). 'Then were we baptized by the Holy Spirit Himself to one love', according to August Gottlieb Spangenberg, Zinzendorf's successor (*ibid*); 'from that time on Herrnhut became a living Congregation of Christ', according to the testimony of David Nitschmann, another of the early leaders (*ibid*). Christian David, another key figure in the beginnings of the movement, wrote: 'It is truly a miracle of God that out of so many kinds and sects as Catholics, Lutheran, Reformed, Separatist, Gichtelian and the like, we could have been melted into one' (*ibid*).

The occasion was a special Confirmation and Communion service in the parish church at nearby Berthelsdorf, where Johann Rothe, a Pietist friend of Zinzendorf, was the minister. It had been preceded by prayer and mutual confession of hard words and thoughts by the members of the various groups who made up the community. Zinzendorf, in particular, had laboured night and day to reconcile the disparate groups and prevent the whole community from breaking up. Reconciliation had been achieved by the time of the special Communion service.

What took place at the service on that Wednesday morning none of the participants could fully describe. 'They left the house of God that noon "hardly knowing whether they belonged to earth or had already gone to Heaven" ', according to one Moravian writer, citing a contemporary witness (Greenfield 1929:15).

Verily the thirteenth of August, 1727, was a day of the outpouring of the Holy Spirit. We saw the hand of God and His wonders, and we were all under the cloud of our fathers baptized with their Spirit. The Holy Ghost came upon us and in those days great signs and wonders took place in our midst. From that time scarcely a day passed but what we beheld His almighty workings amongst us. A great hunger after the Word of God took possession of us so that we had to have three services every day, viz. 5.0 and 7.30 a.m. and 9.0 p.m. Every one desired above everything else that the Holy Spirit might have full control. Self-love and self-will, as well as all disobedience, disappeared and an overwhelming flood of grace swept us all out into the great ocean of Divine Love (*ibid* 14).

Another writer, also cited by Greenfield, says:

Zinzendorf, who gives us the deepest and most vivid account of this wonderful occurrence, says it was 'a sense of the nearness of Christ' bestowed, in a single moment, upon all the members that were present; and it was so unanimous that two members at work twenty miles away, unaware that the meeting was being held, became at the same time deeply conscious of the same blessing (*ibid* 16).

Five years before, Christian David (1691-1751), an itinerant Pietist preacher, had led a group of German-speaking refugees, who were remnants of the Unity of Brethren in Moravia which had been proscribed by the Catholic Church for over a hundred years, to the estate of a sympathetic nobleman, Nicholas von Zinzendorf (1700-1760), in Saxony. The group had grown over the years with the addition of more remnants from the ancient Unity in Moravia and Bohemia, together with other religious refugees. After a number of tensions and problems had been resolved, a period of great spiritual peace and blessing was experienced in the summer of 1727, culminating in the profound experience of August 13 referred to above. (For a description of the events of the 'Golden Summer of 1727' see Lewis 1962: 51-62). Subsequent events showed this to be of epochal significance.

Two weeks later, twenty-four brethren and twenty-four sisters covenanted together to spend one hour each, day and night, in prayer for the divine blessing on the Congregation and its witness. Thus began the 'Hourly Intercession', which spread as the Moravian witness spread, and which continued for over a hundred years (Lewis *ibid* 60).

The renewed community at Herrnhut soon became the sending centre of what became known as the *Diaspora*, the scattering of the witnesses of the renewal, messengers going out singly or in pairs to establish centres of fellowship and new life in Germany, Austria, and beyond (Weinlick 1956: 88, 89). These witnesses were laymen, and laywomen, whose qualifications were a living experience of 'heart religion', focused on 'the Lamb of God' (*Ibid* 187, 190-193).

In the same year, two of the Nitschmann brothers were sent by the community at Herrnhut to Copenhagen, to initiate enquiries concerning the group's possible participation in missionary work. Five years later, in 1732, the first two missionaries, both laymen, left for the island of St Thomas in the West Indies, to work among the slaves. The following year, the first Moravians, again laymen, set out for Greenland—the modern Protestant missionary movement had begun in earnest, a direct result of the revival of 1727 (Lewis *ibid* 79-89).

The Moravians did not meet with universal acceptance among Protestants of the time, either in Germany or elsewhere. The orthodox Lutheran theologians, including those of Wurttemberg who were generally of an eirenic disposition, felt uncomfortable in the presence of their religious enthusiasm. More surprisingly, other Pietists were critical of them and their theological novelties. At Halle, one of the most prominent leaders Joachim Lange (1670-1744), wrote against them, as did Johann Albrecht Bengel (1687-1752), the Pietist biblical scholar in the Duchy of Wurttemberg.

In Britain, John Wesley and his followers, after an initial period when they felt themselves at one with the Moravians, broke from them, feeling increasingly unhappy at a number of their emphases. In North America, Zinzendorf crossed swords with the Lutheran Pietist Henry Melchior Muhlenberg (1711-1787), and with Gilbert Tennent (Smith, Handy & Loetscher I. 1960:280-285; Coalter 1980:35-46). In general, in North America the Moravians were not welcomed, even by those who were sympathetic to revival.[10]

The years from 1743 to 1750, known as the 'Sifting Period' by Moravian historians, marked the time when for Zinzendorf and the Moravians, especially those in Herrnhag and Marienborn in Wetteravia, 'childlikeness' and 'simplicity of spirit' became childishness and puerility. Not only did they adopt a sickly sentimentality, especially in their hymns, in describing the relationship between Christ and his followers, as well as other excesses, but the Count formed the 'Order of Little Fools', and encouraged his followers to behave like little children. He and his wife were addressed as 'Little Papa' and 'Little Mama', and Christ was spoken of as 'Brother Lambkin' (Weinlick 1956:198-206). The naivity shown in the 'Sifting Period' also extended to financial matters. Although the Church was already under some financial strain, during this period further expansion and new obligations were undertaken, without sufficient guarantees to cover them. The Church was burdened for many years after this time with the problems of debt resulting from the irresponsibility of the period (Hamilton 1967:107-112).

Zinzendorf's dislike of the intricacies of theology led him to a radical restatement of his Christocentric faith which many felt to be less than fully orthodox (see his lectures given in Fetter Lane Chapel in 1746, [Zinzendorf, ed Forell 1973]; also Stoeffler 1973:145-155).

There is much that we can learn from the eighteenth-century history of Moravianism which can help us in our

assessment of present-day movements of the Spirit. The genuineness of the initial spiritual impulse is no guarantee of the
later direction of the movement, and does not allow us to
canonise all the behaviour of its adherents. Actions which at
the time may be characterised as bold steps of faith, may be
seen later as foolhardy and irresponsible. In addition, a faulty
understanding, especially in a strong leader, can lead the
whole movement into serious error.

THE EVANGELICAL REVIVAL IN THE BRITISH ISLES

1735 was the year that the revival in Northampton, Massachusetts, and other places in New England was coming to a
premature end. It was also the year that the Moravians established a settlement in Georgia several hundred miles further
south; the year, too, when the Wesley brothers set sail for
Georgia as missionaries to the Indians, and the year when
Howell Harris and Daniel Rowland were converted in Wales.

It was also the year when the young George Whitefield
(1714-1770) was converted in Oxford. Shortly after, he
returned to his home town of Gloucester and soon began to
speak of his new-found faith. When some young people
responded, he organised them into a small society, along the
lines of the Holy Club in Oxford, but with an evangelical
emphasis (Dallimore 1970: I. 83). On his return to Oxford to
complete his studies in preparation for ordination, he was able
to inject a more evangelical spirit into the Holy Club, which
was still in existence but struggling following the departure of
the Wesleys for Georgia.

In the months that followed his ordination in Gloucester
on Trinity Sunday, June 20 1736, his preaching became the
means of awakening increasing numbers of people to their
need of peace with God. He was also the instrument through
whom new life was injected into many of the existing religious
societies, and at whose instigation many new societies were
formed. For the next eighteen months he preached with
increasing frequency and with ever-increasing results

attending his ministry. For two months he held a temporary post at the Chapel of the Tower of London, during which time his preaching proved a steady attraction, especially for a number of young men who were probably members of the religious societies in the capital. He returned to Oxford for six weeks, and his room became the daily meeting place for a number of students who were concerned about spiritual matters. He then spent a short time in a village church in Dummer, Hampshire, officiating in the place of the rector who was away in Oxford, and while there decided to respond to the appeals of John Wesley to become a missionary to Georgia.[11]

He visited Gloucester to say farewell to his relatives and friends, and was invited to preach for two Sundays, which he did, to large congregations. Moving on to Bristol, where he stayed for four weeks, he preached daily to large crowds who filled the churches to overflowing. Growing numbers of people needing spiritual counsel sought his help. His preaching in Stonehouse, Gloucestershire, in Bath, and in Oxford met with similar response, reaching a climax in the capital itself, where for four months he engaged in a furious round of activities, seeking to respond to the many requests to preach and minister in churches and religious societies. The awakening in England had begun, around the same time that the preaching of Harris, Rowland and others in Wales was beginning to attract great throngs (Dallimore *ibid* 103-140; Whitefield 1960:86-92).

Among many exciting events recorded in his journal, Whitefield mentions a daily prayer meeting which he and his friends began in October 1737, and to which he attributes much of the blessing which followed in succeeding years. He says,

> We began to set apart an hour every evening, to intercede with the Great Head of the Church to carry on the work begun...Once we spent a whole night in prayer and praise: and many a time, at midnight and at one in

the morning, after I have been wearied almost to death in preaching, writing, and conversation, and going from place to place, God imparted new life to my soul, and enabled me to intercede with Him for an hour-and-a-half and two hours together...I cannot think it presumption to suppose that partly, at least, in answer to prayers then put up by His dear children, the Word, for some years past, has run and been glorified, not only in England, but in many other parts of the world (*ibid* 91).

For most of 1738 Whitefield was out of the country on the first of his many visits to America. John and Charles Wesley had both returned to England from Georgia, and in May of that year through Moravian influence both experienced their evangelical conversion. A society had already been formed by the Wesleys and certain Moravian brethren in Fetter Lane, and three weeks after his conversion John Wesley made a three-month visit to Germany to meet Zinzendorf and to spend time learning more at first hand of the Moravian communities. He also wished to clear up problems he had over 'the full assurance of faith'. Some of his doubts and uncertainties were removed, but others remained. On his return he preached in the existing religious societies as well as at Fetter Lane, increasingly preaching now on the basis of personal experience the doctrine of salvation by faith which he had gradually come to believe through conversations with the Moravians David Nitschmann, August Gottlieb Spangenberg, and Peter Bohler.

Bohler had advised him in March 1738 to preach saving faith until he experienced it himself, and this Wesley had proceeded to do. Even before this he began to experience opposition and exclusion from the churches in which he preached. His messages on the new birth and the radical nature of discipleship, and possibly his forthright manner, offended both clergy and patrons (Wesley nd:I.82; Wood 1967:84). This opposition, which increased following his conversation with Bohler, became even more marked after his evangelical conversion experience and came to a new height after his return from Germany in September. Following Charles' evangelical experience on May 21, three days before that of his brother, he too began to speak with a new assurance concerning faith in Christ alone for salvation, both in personal conversation, and, increasingly, in public. He also visited condemned prisoners in Newgate prison, and led at least one man to faith in Christ hours before he was hanged. As with John, he too found churches being closed to him, although in a few places he was still accepted. One of these was St Mary's Islington, where the rector was the Rev. George Stonehouse, who the following year resigned his position and joined the Moravians.

While the number of churches where they were still acceptable continued to shrink following their conversion experience in May, and even more when John returned from Germany in September, the evidence of blessing on their ministries where they were accepted, both in the churches and the societies, began to increase. In two letters, both written on October 14 four weeks after his return, John wrote (firstly, to the Moravians at Herrnhut),

> We are endeavouring...to be followers of you, as ye are of Christ. Fourteen were added to us [the Fetter Lane Society] since our return, so that we now have eight bands of men, consisting of fifty-six persons...As yet we have only two small bands of women—the one of three and the other of five persons...Though my brother and I are not permitted to preach in most of the churches in London, yet (thanks be to God) there are others left wherein we have liberty to speak the truth as it is in Jesus. Likewise every evening...we publish the word of reconciliation, sometimes to twenty or thirty, sometimes to fifty or sixty, sometimes to three or four hundred persons, met together to hear it (cited in Dallimore 1988:74).

And to a Dutch physician in Rotterdam, for whom he had promised to transcribe some papers he had brought from Germany,

> I find I cannot have time for this yet, it having pleased God to give me full employment of another nature. His blessed Spirit has wrought so powerfully, both in London and Oxford, that there is a general awakening, and multitudes are crying out, 'What must I do to be saved?' So that, till our gracious Master sendeth more labourers into His harvest, all my time is much too little for them (cited in Wood 1967:90).

When Whitefield returned from Georgia in December 1738, he resumed his preaching ministry alongside the Wesleys, and soon began to meet the same opposition from many of the London clergy. However, in the churches still available to them, their preaching was attended with amazing results. Whitefield speaks in his journal of 'a great pouring out of the Spirit' as he preached at Great St Helen's Church and at St Mary's Islington. He writes,

> I had an opportunity of preaching in the morning at St. Helen's, and at Islington in the afternoon, to large congregations indeed, with great demonstration of the Spirit, and with great power. Here seems to be a great pouring out of the Spirit, and many who were awakened by my preaching a year ago, are now grown strong men in Christ, by the ministrations of my dear friends and fellow-labourers, John and Charles Wesley (Whitefield *ibid* 193).

Three weeks later he writes,

> Preached nine times this week, and expounded near eighteen times ['preaching' refers to sermons in churches, 'expounding' to his ministrations in the reli-

gious societies], with great power and enlargement. I am every moment employed from morning till midnight. There is no end of people coming and sending to me...What a great work has been wrought in the hearts of many within this twelvemonth!...Glory be to God that He fills me continually, not only with peace, but also joy in the Holy Ghost. Before my arrival, I thought I should envy my brethren's success in the ministry, but, blessed be God, I rejoice in it, and am glad to see Christ's Kingdom come, whatsoever instruments God shall make use of to bring it about (*ibid* 195).

Whitefield became a regular attender of the Fetter Lane Society from the day he arrived back in London, and the fellowship of prayer which was enjoyed there may very possibly be seen as the vital background to the successful and arduous public preaching of Whitefield and the Wesleys. The love-feast held throughout the night of January 1 1739 was particularly memorable and has been referred to as a 'New Year Pentecost'. In John Wesley's words,

About three in the morning, as we were continuing instant in prayer, the power of God came mightily upon us, insomuch that many cried out for exceeding joy, and many fell to the ground. As soon as we were recovered a little from that awe and amazement at the presence of His majesty, we broke out with one voice, 'We praise Thee, O God; we acknowledge Thee to be the Lord!' (Wesley ed Curnock 1938 II:121-122).

A number of the former Holy Club members joined them in London for a week of prayer and consultation on Friday January 5, and the love feast at Fetter Lane on Sunday January 7 was again the occasion of 'a great pouring out of the Spirit amongst the brethren' according to Whitefield (1960:197). Of this, and of other meetings at Fetter Lane, Whitefield says:

Sometimes whole nights were spent in prayer. Often have we been filled as with new wine. And often have we seen them overwhelmed with the Divine presence and crying out, 'Will God indeed dwell with men upon earth! How dreadful is this place! This is none other than the house of God and the gate of heaven!'(cited from Gillies 1772:34, in Dallimore 1970 I:221).

1739 was a crucial year in the growth of the revival in the British Isles. Whitefield began open-air preaching in Bristol in February. John Wesley, very unwillingly and initially against the advice of brother Charles, eventually yielded to Whitefield's encouragement to follow his example in May. Whitefield met Howell Harris for the first time in March and preached with him in Wales in March and April, thus beginning a very fruitful connection which linked together the English and Welsh movements. In April Whitefield also began open air preaching in London. In June John Cennick (1718-1755) became involved in the revival preaching, even though he was not ordained. Throughout the year the effects of the revival were increasingly evident, both in the thousands who were now responding, as well as in the increasing number of physical phenomena being manifested in those under conviction of sin.[12] In the same year problems were experienced with the 'French Prophets'.[13] In April Wesley began to organise the societies and become increasingly prominent in their supervision (this also was initially at the suggestion of Whitefield, who was planning to return to America in June).[14] In June, problems began to appear in the Fetter Lane Society, which were exacerbated in October with the arrival from Germany of Philip Henry Molther (1714-1780), whose 'quietist' teaching eventually caused Wesley to separate from the Society in July 1740.

In 1739 Wesley also (after casting lots to determine God's will on the subject) preached and published a major sermon against Predestination, which seemed to be intended to drive a wedge between himself and Whitefield who had just sailed for

America. In fact it did so very effectively (Dallimore 1970 I:233-331, 379-392).

Finally, 1739 saw a revival in the Scottish Highlands; stirrings had been evident for a number of years, but they came to a climax in the parish of Nigg, on the Moray Firth north of Inverness, under the ministry of John Balfour in 1739 (Wood 1960:117). Five years later, the revival was still being experienced at Nigg (Gillies 1845:453-454, who cites contemporary accounts from the minister, John Balfour).

The subsequent history of the Revival in the British Isles is quite involved, having both positive and negative aspects. The break between the Wesleys and Whitefield came to a decisive point in 1741 on the latter's return from his second American trip. John Wesley's strong opposition to the doctrine of Predestination and his equally determined espousal of a doctrine of Perfectionism made the rift inevitable. When Whitefield returned, he showed that he also was firmly convinced on the two subjects, positively regarding the first and negatively regarding the second, partly through his contacts with New Jersey Presbyterians like the Tennents and New England Congregationalists like Jonathan Edwards. The societies were firmly under the influence of Wesley and his doctrines, and the subsequent Methodist movement grew under his direct control. Whitefield chose not to split the movement but rather to continue his itinerant ministry among those sympathetic to his views. This he did in England (eventually receiving the support of Selina Countess of Huntingdon), in Wales with Howell Harris, forming the Welsh Calvinistic Methodists, in Scotland where his preaching was used by God in many places[15] but especially at Cambuslang in 1742, and in America, which he visited a total of seven times, and where he eventually died in 1770.

In Scotland there were a number of remarkable awakenings in addition to the one at Nigg which began in 1739. Among the most notable were those at Cambuslang (five miles southeast of Glasgow), where William McCulloch was the minister, and at Kilsyth (about thirty miles northeast of Glasgow),

where James Robe was the parish minister (Gillies
1845:441-452; Robe 1840; Macfarlan 1847), but there were also
notable awakenings at Campsie, Calder, Cumbernauld and
Glasgow (Westerkamp 1988:129-130). The revival at Cambuslang had begun in February 1742 with around 500 of the
900 parishioners being awakened and 'savingly brought home
to God', but reached its climax later in the year with upwards
of 20,000 people attending open-air communion services
where Whitefield was preaching (Dallimore 1980 II:121-137;
Wood 1960:114-126, esp 120-123; Fawcett 1971; Westerkamp
ibid 130-131).[16] At Kilsyth, the first signs of revival appeared
in May 1742 with evidences of deep conviction of sin affecting
many in the parish. Within a short time around 300 were said
to be awakened, 200 being from within the parish and the
remainder from outside. At a communion service in October,
nearly 1,500 took part (Murray 1971:119, citing the account by
James Robe published in 1742).[17]

In Wales, as we have seen, the revival continued through
the labours of Howell Harris, Daniel Rowland, Howell
Davies, George Whitefield and many others.

In England the Methodist societies retained a loose connection with the Anglican Church, at least until John Wesley's
death in 1791, but in addition an Evangelical group developed
within the national Church, which included a number of
ministers who experienced revivals in their own parishes and
often beyond, as many of them engaged in itinerant preaching. Among these were William Romaine (1714-1795) in
London; Samuel Walker (1714-1761) in Truro, Cornwall;
James Hervey (1713-1758) in Bideford, Devon, and Weston
Favell, Northamptonshire; John Berridge (1716-1793) in Everton, Cambridgeshire;[18] and William Grimshaw (1708-1763) in
Haworth, Yorkshire. Later in the century the numbers grew,
and places like London, Bristol, Oxford and Cambridge had a
number of local parishes where evangelical doctrines were
strongly held and preached (Wood 1960:129-147, 205-220).
Henry Venn (1724-1797) in Huddersfield, John Newton
(1725-1807) in London and Charles Simeon (1759-1836) in

Cambridge are three well-known names among a host of lesser-known but no less faithful ministers who preached the Evangelical truths and experienced the blessing of God on their service.

NOTE ON THE 'FRENCH PROPHETS'

During the Evangelical Revival in England, a sect which had been formed in 1706 by French Protestant refugees fleeing from persecution in Catholic France made its influence felt with the leaders of the revival. The Camisards, as they were known in France, had for many years resisted the attempts of Louis XIV to make them conform. They suffered terribly, many of them being put to death. All Protestant pastors were prohibited and public assemblies were banned. Consequently, they resorted to secret meetings in private and to the ministrations of lay-preachers.

Under the worst of the persecution, the Camisards took comfort from the *Pastoral Letters* of Pierre Jurieu who, on the basis of his studies of the Book of Revelation, forecast a speedy deliverance, which sadly did not arrive. Many of the Protestants of Languedoc, who were subject to the worst kinds of persecution, began to experience all kinds of extraordinary manifestations of an apparently spiritual kind. They heard supernatural voices, spoke in tongues and saw visions. Young children in particular were the subjects of these manifestations. Also, uneducated people, 'seized by the Spirit' spoke prophecies in perfect French. A number of these spoken by Elias Marion were taken down and published in England in 1707 under the title *A Cry from the Desert*.

In England they gained a considerable following in the first few years, claiming the powers of prophecy and the working of miracles. They advocated the community of property and foretold the speedy coming of the messianic kingdom, which was to be accompanied by wonders and the infliction of severe judgments on the wicked. In London they made a deep impression and numbered some of the nobility among their followers, including Lady Jane Forbes and Sir Richard

Bulkeley. Sir Richard claimed to have been miraculously healed of continuous headache, stone, and rupture, and gave large amounts of money to support the sect. John Lacy, who was a member of the church pastored by Edmund Calamy, the well-known historian of Nonconformity, became a seer and a healer, and published several works containing his own prophecies and those of French prophets (including *A Cry from the Desert*).

In 1707, they were convicted of publishing false and scandalous pamphlets and holding tumultuous assemblies, and some of them were placed in the pillory. However, this made them more popular, and soon there were over 400 prophets spreading their increasingly fanatical ideas in different parts of the country. In 1708, when one of their number, Thomas Emes, died, a pamphlet entitled *The Mighty Miracle, or the Wonder of Wonders* issued by John Lacy foretold that he would rise from the dead on May 25, 1708, and invited everyone to come to Bunhill Fields to witness the event. When Emes failed to appear from the grave, the influence of the sect weakened, and from that time they fell into disgrace.

When the religious societies were touched by the Evangelical Revival under Whitefield's ministry, the French Prophets decided that they offered potential for proselytes. They influenced a number of the leaders of the Fetter Lane Society and also some from the Methodist Society in Bristol. Charles Wesley came to the conclusion early on that they were deluded and even demonically inspired. His brother John was initially more cautious, but eventually recognised that they were no allies of the revival (see Schaff-Herzog 1909: iv. 383; Scott in Hastings ed, 1910:iii.175-176; Dallimore 1970: I. 174-177, 326-327; Garret 1987).

Notes

[1] 'Great Awakening' is the title usually found in American literature. 'Evangelical Revival' is the normal British way of referring to the events.

[2] Because this is the first widespread revival in Protestantism, and because of its far-reaching results, we will devote considerable space to it. In many ways it serves as a paradigm for future awakenings, although these also manifest new features. A very good over-all survey of the eighteenth-century Awakening in its European, British and American phases is Wood 1960.

[3] Twentieth-century scholars, such as F E Stoeffler (see Stoeffler 1965; 1973), are only now discovering the full extent of the spread and influence of Pietism in its various forms within the Reformed Churches, as well as in Lutheranism, and its influence in Anglo-Saxon Christianity on both sides of the Atlantic (see also Stoeffler ed 1976; Manton 1969; Prozesky 1977; Lovelace 1979b; Christian History 1986; Snyder 1989:71-120). The roots of Pietism itself can be traced, in part at least, to English Puritanism (Spener acknowledged his debt to Lewis Bayly's *The Practice of Piety* [3rd edn 1613], one of the seminal books in English Puritan devotional writings), and probably also to German and Dutch Reformed Christianity. The subject is a large and complicated one, and there is disagreement among scholars, including those mentioned above.

[4] Among the Nonconformists, men such as Matthew Henry (1662-1714) the biblical commentator, Isaac Watts (1674-1748), John Guyse (1680-1761) and Philip Doddridge (1702-1751) had a widespread spiritual influence.

[5] After his emigration he identified himself closely with the Church of England. In 1670 he was preacher at the Savoy Chapel, in 1689 he became chaplain to William III, and in 1693 a prebendary of Westminster Abbey, where he was subsequently buried. He wrote a number of books (Stoeffler, in Stoeffler ed 1976:185,186).

[6] According to Snyder, the relationship between Pietism and the Religious Society movement has been largely ignored by writers in the past, as has also the relationship between Pietism and Methodism (Snyder 1980:169), although we should note Nagler (1918:147,148), and Stoeffler (in Stoeffler ed 1976:185-188).

[7] For a balanced account of the state of the Anglican Church in the early part of the eighteenth century see Wood 1960:15-25.

[8] As rector of Epworth Samuel had organised a society for promoting Christian knowledge in his parish in 1702, following the pattern of the SPCK in 1699. The purposes were for the development of the spiritual lives of his

parishioners, and for doing good to those in need (Snyder *ibid* 15,16). In a 'Letter Concerning the Religious Societies' he wrote

> I know few good Men but lament that after the Destruction of Monasteries, there were not some Societies founded in their stead, but reformed from their Errors, and reduced to the Primitive Standard. None who has but lookt into our own Church-History, can be ignorant how highly instrumental such Bodies of Men as these, were to the first planting and propagating Christianity amongst our Fore-fathers...A great part of the good Effects of that way of Life, may be attained without many of the Inconveniences of it, by such Societies as we are now discoursing of (quoted in Hietzenrater *ibid* 22, cited by Snyder *ibid* 16).

Samuel Wesley's enthusiasm for such institutions seems, however, to have been more theoretical than practical, as shown by subsequent events. Early in 1712, when he was away for a long period (Snyder says that he was in London on church business, but in fact he was serving a sentence in a debtors' prison in Chester!) his wife Susannah began a small meeting in the rectory. It developed out of the family devotional time which she held for her children, and which a number of neighbours asked to attend. Soon the group grew from about thirty to more than two hundred! Susannah would read a sermon, pray, and talk with those who attended. When Samuel heard about the practice, he voiced his objections, mainly because the meetings were led by a woman, and also because they might be seen as a separatist conventicle. Susannah defended herself in two masterly letters, noting that church attendances had jumped dramatically since the meetings began. However, although the meetings continued while Samuel was away, they seem to have stopped soon after his return (Snyder *ibid* 16-18)!

[9] He settled there in 1730 and died two years later.

[10] The references to the Moravians in David Brainerd's Diary, which Jonathan Edwards edited for publication, are unfavorable (Edwards ed Pettit 1985:30-32, 324).

[11] For a variety of reasons, he did not leave for America for another year.

[12] These first began to appear during Wesley's seven-months' ministry in Bristol in 1739 (see Dallimore 1960: I. 321-331). See further below under 'Constants and Variables of Revival: Physical Accompaniments'.

[13] Dallimore 1970:I. 174-177. See Note on the 'French Prophets' at the end of this chapter.

[14] For a detailed account of the way in which Wesley organised the societies, and eventually took control of them, see Snyder 1980:33-64.

[15] See MacFarlan 1847 reprint 1980.

[16] Dallimore (1980:II. 135-136) notes a number of the characteristics of the awakening at Cambuslang. Among other things, he points out:

> It began under the ministry of a man who did not possess outstanding pulpit gifts—William McCulloch—and who was simply doing his regular task, but with grave earnestness...
> The Revival was born in and produced much prayer. McCulloch and Robe were men of prayer and under their influence the Societies for Prayer in their areas came into a new strong life and Christians prayed with new intensity and power...
> There was no attempt at sensationalism, showmanship or entertainment. Rather, this work was of an opposite nature. As a report approved by McCulloch stated, '...this work was begun and carried on under the influence of the great and substantial doctrines of Christianity.'...
> The declaration of these great doctrines, under McCulloch, Whitefield and others, was used to effect a deep consciousness of the reality and character of God and a corresponding awareness of sin. It brought deep and lasting repentance...
> Bodily distresses were not encouraged, but when they occurred they were considered of value only inasmuch as they arose from a sorrow for sin so intense they could not be restrained.

[17] As noted earlier, the revivals took place in Church of Scotland parishes, not among the recently-formed Secession Church (see Westerkamp *ibid* 103-135 esp 129).

[18] John Berridge became vicar of Everton in Cambridgeshire in 1755. Two years later he was converted and his ministry took on an Evangelical hue. He soon began to itinerate around the county, and particularly in 1759 his ministry resulted in many conversions and was accompanied by physical and psychological phenomena, such as hysteria, convulsions and trances, as he preached in church buildings as well as in the open air (Pibworth 1987:49-70).

CHAPTER 6

THE GREAT AWAKENING OF THE EIGHTEENTH CENTURY (CONCLUDED)

THE GREAT AWAKENING IN THE AMERICAN COLONIES[1]

ALTHOUGH THE REVIVAL of 1734/1735 began to decline in Jonathan Edwards' church at Northampton in May 1735, it continued in some of the other towns of the Connecticut Valley until the end of 1736. In 1739 and 1740 there were new revivals in such places as Newark and New Brunswick in New Jersey, in Harvard, Massachussetts, and at New Londonderry, Pennsylvania (Tracy 1842:18-35). In Northampton also there were hopeful signs of a new work in the spring of 1740, before George Whitefield arrived in New England. However, the 'great and general awakening'[2] did not break out until the arrival of George Whitefield from England.

Whitefield arrived in America for his second visit in October 1739.[3] He preached in Philadelphia, New Brunswick, New York City[4] and Neshaminy, Pennsylvania during November, and then journeyed south to Georgia, where he remained until April. For four weeks from the middle of April until the middle of May he itinerated around Philadelphia and New York; he then spent another spell in Georgia, and in August sailed north to Newport, Rhode Island, where he arrived on Sunday September 14, 1740 (Dallimore 1960: I.431-525). Having preached there on the Monday and

Tuesday, he left for Boston, where he arrived on the Thursday evening.

Everywhere he preached in the Middle Colonies and in the South, great crowds flocked to hear him, many of whom were deeply affected by the preacher's powerful exposure of sin and proclamation of Christ. He also experienced opposition, especially in Charleston, where the rector, Alexander Garden, who was the Commissary of the Bishop of London, cited him before an ecclesiastical court and tried to secure his removal from the office of priest. However, this did not prevent a revival taking place in Charleston itself. Josiah Smith, the pastor of the Independent Congregational Church in Charleston, described something of the effects of Whitefield's preaching:

> He is certainly a finished preacher, and a great master of pulpit oratory and elocution,[5] while a noble negligence ran thro' his style. Yet his discourses were very extraordinary when we consider how little they were premeditated, and how many of them he gave to us, the little time he was with us. Many, I trust, have felt, and will long feel the impressions of his zeal and fire, the passion and flame of his expressions...He appeared to me, in all his discourses, very deeply affected and impressed in his own heart. How did that burn and boil within him, when he spake of the things he had made touching the King?...The awe, the silence, the attention, which sat upon the face of so great an audience, was an argument, how he could reign over all their powers...So charmed were people with his manner of address, that they shut up their shops, forgot their secular business, and laid aside their schemes for the world...(Heimert and Miller eds 1967:67-68).

On his arrival in Boston, he preached in various of the churches in the city, as well as to the students at Harvard College and to great crowds on Boston Common. In one of the churches the gallery collapsed under the numbers of people, killing five and injuring several others. He made a week's preaching tour up the coast as far as York, (now in Maine, but then in Massachusetts) and returned to Boston for a final open-air meeting, where around 20,000 heard him preach.

The great majority of the Boston ministers supported Whitefield, and many of them helped in counselling the great number of people who came under spiritual conviction through his preaching. The revival continued under their preaching for at least eighteen months after Whitefield left Boston, being further helped by a four-month visit made, at Whitefield's suggestion, by Gilbert Tennent.

Tennent's personality and style were very different from those of Whitefield, but the results were the same. According to the Rev. Thomas Prince,

> He seem'd to have no regard to please the Eyes of his Hearers with agreeable Gesture, nor their Ears with delivery, nor their Fancy with Language; but to aim directly at their *Hearts* and *Consciences*, to lay open their ruinous Delusions, shew their numerous, secret, hypocritical Shifts in Religion, and drive them out of every deceitful Refuge wherein they made themselves easy, with the Form of Godliness without the Power (Prince 1745:2,385, cited in Goen 1962:16).

Whitefield journeyed west to Northampton, where his preaching had the same effects as elsewhere, then southward to Yale, stopping off at East Windsor where Timothy Edwards, Jonathan Edwards' father was still ministering, and thence to New York, Philadelphia, and Savannah from where he sailed for England on January 24 1741. His itinerating had taken him over hundreds of miles to hundreds of places where he had been used by God to kindle, or rekindle, the fires of revival.[6] Such ministry had not been seen before in the Thirteen Colonies.

The revival continued to grow and spread among the churches in New England, partly through the preaching of ministers, some of whom had themselves been quickened and revived by Whitefield's preaching, and partly through the ministry of laymen, who first of all began to exhort their fellow men and women to repentance and conversion, and later, to preach in churches and in the open air.

In Boston, the revival continued under the preaching of such men as Benjamin Coleman and William Cooper at Brattle Street, Joseph Sewell and Thomas Prince at the Old South Church, Joshua Gee at the Second Church, John Webb at the New North Church, and Samuel Checkly of the New South Church. Colman wrote to Whitefield in June, 1741, three months after Tennent had left Boston, 'The Work of God with us goes on greatly...our crowded serious assemblies continue, and great Additions are made to our Churches' (cited in Gaustad 1957:51). Ten months later, in April, 1742, he closed a mid-week lecture by

> giving Glory to God for the Great and good Work of his Grace, which He has so visibly begun, spread and is carrying on, in every Part almost of our Provinces (Gaustad *ibid* 52).

Outside of Boston, in scores of other towns and rural communities, the revival was felt, not only in places visited by Whitefield, but throughout New England. Tracy (1842:120-229) gives contemporary accounts from Natick, Wrentham, Bridgewater, Lyme, Plymouth, Sutton, Taunton, Middleborough, Halifax, Portsmouth, Gloucester, Reading, Newcastle, Westerly, Northampton, and Enfield, together with extracts from the journals of ministers such as Eleazer Wheelock, who engaged in widespread itinerant preaching.[7]

Jonathan Edwards, whose own church continued to experience abundant revival blessing for the next twenty months or so following the visit of George Whitefield in October, 1740, and even after that enjoyed occasional 'extraordinary appearances', itinerated extensively through most of 1741 and also in the early part of the following year. His well-known sermon on 'Sinners in the Hands of an Angry God' from Deuteronomy 32:35 given at Enfield Connecticut on July 8, 1741 'was the cause of an immediate and general revival of religion throughout the place', according to Sereno Dwight, his great-grandson and biographer (in Hickman ed 1834: I.li).

While Edwards was away on a preaching tour in January-February, 1742, a young man who had recently been licensed to preach, Samuel Buell, began with Edwards' permission to preach every day in the church at Northampton. During this time there was a new movement of the Spirit which touched many, including Sarah Edwards, Jonathan's wife. Her experience is recorded in an account drawn up in her own words (cited in Hickman ed 1834: I.lxii-lxvii), and by her husband in *Some Thoughts...* (Hickman *ibid* I.376-378; Goen ed 1972:331-341).

A number of ministers, including Jonathan Edwards, were unhappy about the practice of lay-exhorting and lay-preaching, feeling it would introduce excesses into the revival and bring it into disrepute. This may have been the case in part, but it was nothing to the excesses introduced through the fanaticism of Rev. James Davenport (1716-1757), whose antics brought the revival in New England to a virtual end in 1742, and hardened many ministers against it.

During his studies at Yale, as well as in his first pastorate, Davenport, the grandson of the founder of New Haven, had come under the influence of men who emphasised 'inner light' doctrines and special 'impressions' and revelations of the Holy Spirit. While at Yale, he had suffered a breakdown which affected him mentally and physically; he continued to suffer physical weakness and illness throughout his life. His background and condition gave him 'an unusual earnestness [and] a kind of ascetic fervour' which was heightened by his claim that it had been revealed to him that the last days of Acts 2:17 had arrived, and that he had been divinely chosen to receive the visions and dreams (Dallimore 1980: II. 184). His contacts with Gilbert Tennent in Philadelphia in 1740, the year that the latter preached his scathing sermon on 'the danger of an unconverted ministry', and the time he spent with Whitefield in the autumn of the same year, accompanying him on a preaching tour from New York to Philadelphia, fired him up for an itinerating ministry among the churches of New England in the summer of 1741.

Arriving in New London, Connecticut in July, he preached in one of the churches, where

> Divers women were terrified and cried out exceedingly. When Mr. Davenport had dismissed the congregation some went out and others stayed; he then went into the broad alley [aisle], which was much crowded, and there he screamed out, 'Come to Christ! come to Christ! come away!' Then he went into the third pew on the women's side, and kept there, sometimes singing, sometimes praying; he and his companions all taking their turns, and the women fainting and in hysterics. This confusion continued till ten o'clock at night. And then he went off singing through the streets (*Diary of Joshua Hempstead of New London, Connecticut*, cited in Goen 1962:21).

The next day, he publicly announced his fear that one of the town's pastors was unconverted, and moved on to the next town, where similar scenes and activities occurred, and continued thus through several of the towns of southern Connecticut. He withdrew for the winter to his pastorate on Long Island, but resumed his itinerating the following spring, accompanied by a ministerial friend from his days at Yale, Benjamin Pomeroy, and some zealous laymen.

He continued his highly emotional and eccentric practices in churches where he was allowed, and in the open-air where he was not, and also his habit of pronouncing upon the spiritual state of the various ministers he encountered. He was twice arrested and tried, once for itinerant preaching, which was now outlawed in some places, and once for disturbance of public order—due to his practice, after an incredibly boisterous meeting, of leading 'a large mob through the streets, all singing at the top of their voices in such disorderly fashion that it shocked the sensibilities of the whole town' (Goen *ibid* 24). At his first trial he was pronounced guilty, and was deported back to Long Island, it being judged that

> the said Davenport is under the influences of enthusiastical impressions and impulses, and thereby disturbed in the rational faculties of his mind, and therefore to be pitied and compassionated, and not to be treated as otherwise he might be (*Public Records of the Colony of Connecticut*, cited in Goen *ibid* 23).

Similarly in Boston, he was judged '*non compos mentis*, and therefore *not guilty*' (Tracy 1842:248). As before, he was deported. He was also censured by the ecclesiastical council at Southold, Long Island, for neglecting his responsibility to his own people there, but he ignored this, as he did the other measures taken against him.

Finally, in March, 1743, he returned to New London,

> 'sent from God' to purify and perfect the organization of a group of his followers who had withdrawn from the church there. 'His mind was in a state of fervid exaltation, amounting to frenzy. Bodily ailments and overstrained faculties had so disordered his reason that he could no longer keep within the bounds of order and propriety.' He first ordered his devotees to burn all their wigs, fine clothes and jewelry, in order to cure them of 'idolatrous love of worldly things.' He then demanded that they bring all their 'unsafe' religious books, and on Sunday evening, March 6, he led the company down to the wharf, where they set fire to works by such authors as William Beveridge, John Flavel, Increase Mather, Benjamin Colman, Joseph Sewall, and Jonathan

> Parsons! They marched around the pyre shouting 'Hal-
> lelujah!' and 'Glory to God!' declaring that 'as the
> smoke of these books ascended up in their presence, so
> the smoke of the torment of such of their authors as died
> in the same belief, was now ascending in hell.' (Goen
> *ibid* 25, citing Tracy *op cit* and Caulkins, *History of New
> London*).

This event, 'the zenith of his fanaticism', was also 'the nadir
of his career' (Goen *ibid*). He returned to Long Island utterly
exhausted, physically, mentally, and spiritually. He wrote to
two well-known ministers, asking to be shown the error of his
ways, and shortly after published his *Confessions and Retrac-
tions* (reprinted in Hemert and Miller 1967:257-262), in which
he acknowledged the wrongness of his behaviour over the
three previous years, including the final episode at New
London. The detailed retraction mentioning most, if not all,
of the offending practices suggests that the accounts of the
opponents of the revival were not exaggerated when they
reported on his excesses (Garret 1987:119-126).

However, the damage had been done; the revival ceased
dramatically, those opposed to it had abundant ammunition
for their counterattacks,[8] and lay exhorting and lay preaching
were excluded, even by the friends of the revival.[9] The lessons
of such behaviour should not be lost on the evangelical church
today, where lay activity is more and more encouraged especially where 'renewal' is experienced, but where adequate
ways of training the laity have not always been fully
developed.

Whitefield returned to New England in October 1744 and
did his best to heal the wounds inflicted on the revival by
Davenport and by the wilder kinds of lay exhorters and
preachers. He preached to large numbers of people at nearly
every place he visited, but the general revival of the previous
years had definitely ceased, at least in New England.[10] He
encountered opposition, particularly from the faculties at
Harvard and Yale (for the 'Testimony' of the Harvard faculty,

see Heimert and Miller 1967:340-353; for selections from Whitefield's reply, see Dallimore 1980:II. 197-199; see also a letter from a senior New England minister, William Shutleff, in defence of Whitefield, in Heimert and Miller *ibid* 354-363).[11]

Whitefield made further trips to America in 1751-1752, 1754- 1755, 1763-1765, and 1769-1770, and continued to see great blessing from his ministry right up to the time of his death in 1770. His ministry in New York in 1764 was attended with greater results than any of his previous visits there (Beardsley 1904:66).

There were a number of awakenings among the Indians in the 1740s, notably those associated with the ministry of David Brainerd in 1745 and 1746 at Crossweeksung in New Jersey and the Forks of Delaware in Pennsylvania (Brainerd in Hickman ed 1834:II. 387-415). Extensive revivals also occurred among them at Stonington, Connecticut and at Westerly, Rhode Island (Beardsley *ibid.* 67).

In New England, the revival produced first the Congregational Separatists and then the Separate Baptists, of whom Isaac Backus became the leader and main spokesman (McLoughlin 1967). They continued to experience local revivals from time to time until well into the 1760s (Goen 1962:183-185). The establishment of Dartmouth College in New Hampshire, which grew out of Eleazar Wheelock's attempts to form a school for the Indians, resulted in a series of revivals, which extended to a number of communities in the area and continued for many years.

A series of more general awakenings occurred in New England in 1763 and 1764 (Hardman 1983:119), and a number of more local ones in Connecticut, such as that at Norfolk in 1767, at Lebanon in 1781, and at New Britain in 1784. Other local revivals were reported at Thetford, Vermont and at Brentford, New Hampshire in 1781, and at Boscawan, New Hampshire in 1782. Yale College Church saw a revival in 1783, and in the same year there were also awakenings in West

Simsbury, Massachusetts and several towns in Litchfield County, Connecticut.

In the Middle Colonies, the Presbyterians divided between the 'Old Side', who opposed the revival, and the 'New Side', who supported it. The latter, among whom the Tennents[12] and Jonathan Dickenson were prominent, were ejected from the Synod of Philadelphia in 1741, and later joined the New Brunswick Presbytery to form the Synod of New York. The College of New Jersey (later Princeton) was founded in 1746 by New Side Presbyterians in conjunction with the pro-revivalists of New England, being born out of the awakening, and further revivals were experienced there in 1757, 1762 and 1771/2. Similarly, King's College in New York (founded in 1754), and Queen's College in New Brunswick (founded in 1770), together with other educational institutions, were all begun as a direct result of the Awakening in the Middle Colonies.[13]

The work of the Moravian settlements in Pennsylvania (founded in 1740 with help from George Whitefield after they had moved north from their earlier settlement in Georgia) and later in 1753 in North Carolina did not seem to share in any large way in the revival impulses of the Great Awakening in America, even though it had grown directly out of the Moravian Revival in Germany, and the Moravians themselves were committed to an 'enthusiastic' form of Christianity. This was also the case with the German Lutherans in Pennsylvania, although the organising genius was Henry Melchior Muhlenberg (1711-1787) who had been sent by Halle Pietists.

In the Southern Colonies, a revival in Hanover county in central Virginia began as a spontaneous movement among a small group of laymen led by Samuel Morris. They met together to read the sermons of George Whitefield and some of Martin Luther's writings, and soon they had to meet in special houses constructed for the purpose, as thousands crowded into the meetings to hear what was being read. In 1742-1743 William Robinson, a graduate of the Log College, visited Hanover county as part of a larger preaching tour of

Virginia and North Carolina, and assisted in the revival already taking place. He was followed by other preachers; eventually in 1748 Samuel Davies (1723-1761) was sent as the first settled Presbyterian minister. Through his preaching a number of churches were formed and in 1755 the Hanover Presbytery came into existence, which in its turn became the 'Mother' Presbytery of the South and Southwest. Davies continued his itinerant ministry over seven counties with great success until 1759, when he accepted the presidency of the College of New Jersey. The Presbyterian revival in Virginia was 'the first mass movement that was to bring about a social and political upheaval in Virginia—the first breach in the ranks of privelege' (Sweet 1973:149; see also Davies' account of 'The State of Religion among the Protestant Dissenters in Virginia' [1751] in Heimert and Miller 1967:376-393).

Separate Baptists from New England were also used to bring revival to Virginia and North Carolina. Shubal Stearns (1706- 1771), a convert of the Great Awakening in New England who first became a Separate and then a Baptist, began to preach and was ordained in 1751. In 1754 he and his brother-in-law Daniel Marshall moved to Virginia, where they began to engage in itinerant evangelism. Because of opposition from Baptists who were there already and others, they moved to Sandy Creek in Guilford County, North Carolina. A church was organised of which Stearns became pastor. The membership soon grew from 16 to 606, and very soon other churches were planted as the result of the itinerant preaching of Stearns, Marshall and others. In 1760 the Sandy Creek Association was formed, and from the original church a total of 42 churches were formed. The next ten years saw unparalled growth as whole communities were affected and strong Baptist churches formed.

The revival spread back into Virginia and some of the rash attacks on the established Anglican Church by the Baptist evangelists led to imprisonment and persecution. From 1768 to 1770 more than thirty Baptist ministers were imprisoned.

The Baptist preachers at times also encouraged extravagant behaviour in their meetings. One eyewitness saw

> multitudes, some roaring on the ground, some wringing their hands, some in extacies(sic), some praying, some weeping; and others so outrageously cursing and swearing that it was thought they were really possessed of the devil (Sweet 1973:150-152; see also Smith, Handy & Loetscher 1960: I.360-366).

What has been described as the 'Methodist phase' of the Great Awakening in Virginia was associated with the preaching of Devereux Jarratt (1733-1801), an Anglican minister from England who was ordained in 1763 and became rector of Bath parish in Dinwiddie County, Virginia. His fervent evangelical preaching in his own parish resulted in great crowds flocking to hear him, and he was soon itinerating in Virginia and North Carolina. He organised prayer meetings at which laymen spoke, and from 1764 to 1772 revival attended his ministry. In 1773 he met the English Methodist Robert Williams, and from then until 1784, when Methodism was organised as an independent body, Jarratt and the Methodist laypreachers cooperated in evangelism.

The revival reached its climax in 1775-1776, accompanied by some emotionalism which Jarratt was unhappy about, but which he faithfully describes in 'A Brief Narrative of the Revival of Religion in Virginia'. Jarratt reported on May 7, 1776:

> The work of God still increases among us: I believe, within these eight days, more than forty here have been filled with joy and peace in believing. Of these I have had an account; but there may be many more...I have no doubt but that the work now carrying on is genuine: yet there were some circumstances attending it which I disliked—such as loud outcries, tremblings, fallings, convulsions. But I am better reconciled, since I read

President Edwards on that head, who observes, 'That wherever these most appear there is always the greatest and the deepest work.' (cited in Smith, Handy & Loetscher *ibid* 367-371; another contemporary description is cited in Sweet *ibid* 153-154; see also Gewehr 1930:149. For an up-to-date treatment of the various phases of the revival in Virginia see Isaac 1988).

Effects of the Great Awakening in the American Colonies
The Great Awakening in the American Colonies had many results. It brought great numbers to faith in Christ and into membership of the various churches;[14] it also quickened the spiritual life of large numbers of existing church members. It stimulated missionary work, particularly among the Indians, and also humanitarian and philanthropic efforts of different kinds. It produced controversies in the various denominations, particularly creating pro- and anti-revival parties, but it also united pro-revival groups across denominational lines. While the revival emphasis was very strongly critical of those who seemed to advocate merely theoretical or intellectual approaches to religion, it produced large numbers of colleges, some of which developed into universities and others into theological seminaries. The Awakening gave a new place of importance in the life of the churches, and by implication in society, to the common man. Lay activity in both realms dramatically increased. Finally, the Awakening hastened the separation of church and state, together with the American Revolution (on various aspects mentioned here see Heimert 1966; Bononi 1986; Westerkamp 1988).

NOTE ON ROMAN CATHOLIC REVIVAL MOVEMENTS IN THE EIGHTEENTH CENTURY
In the eighteenth century, a number of mission preachers in the Catholic lands of Italy, Spain and France sought to bring about the conversion of many estranged from the church as well as nominal Catholics and many of the parish clergy. The

success attending their efforts, in spite of official opposition at times, seems to indicate a genuine revival impulse.

In the sixteenth century the Theatines, the Jesuits and the Oratorians had sought to implement the Counter-Reformation on a popular level. St Philip Neri (1515-1595), the founder of the Oratorians, won the title 'Apostle of Rome', and should probably be credited with converting the pagan Renaissance city back to Christianity. Ronald Knox has drawn attention to the similarity between the itinerant ministry of John Wesley and that of the seventeenth-century Jesuit Paolo Segneri who walked barefoot 800 miles a year to preach in missions in northern Italy (Knox 1950:423).

Two new Italian missionary orders were established in the eighteenth century, the Redemptorists, founded by Alphonso Maria del Liguori (1696-1787; canonised as St Alphonsus Liguori) and the Passionists, founded by Paul Danei (1694-1775; canonised as St Paul of the Cross).

One of the most popular and successful preachers of the first half of the eighteenth century was Paolo Girolamo Casanova (canonised as St Leonard of Port-Maurice). St Leonard in northern Italy and St Alphonsus in the south preached powerfully to both urban and rural populations with great effect. The former had been a professor of theology, and the latter's output of over a hundred books on moral theology raised him to the rank of Doctor of the Church. He also produced many popular devotional and mystical works and composed a number of hymns.

St Leonard declared in one of his first missions that he 'only intended to preach Jesus Christ and Him crucified'. In a six-month mission to Corsica in 1744, he preached in churches packed with rival bands of banditti, many of whom were converted. At Sarno the taverns were closed for ten years following a mission there, and of the great international port of Leghorn it was said that 'it seemed another Nineveh was converted' (Maria 1852:53, cited in Gilley 1990:102). In 1750 he preached in the great penitential mission for the Roman Jubilee before the Pope and Cardinals and an audience of

100,000 people. Some of the methods he employed to produce reconciliation of former enemies might strike us as questionable; he savagely beat himself with a flail until he had secured the necessary repentance!

In Spain and France also, mission preachers were active. A historian of Spanish Catholicism has compared them to the Moravians (Noel 1985:888 cited in Gilley 1990:99). French scholars have maintained that levels of religious practice in modern France have tended to remain high where the mission preachers before 1789 were successful; contrariwise, popular religious practice has been eclipsed in areas not so affected (Gilley 1990:108).

Notes

[1] The Thirteen Colonies in the eighteenth century are normally thought of in three groups: the four New England colonies of Massachusetts (which included what is now the separate state of Maine), New Hampshire, Connecticut and Rhode Island, colonised mainly from England; the five Middle Colonies of New York, New Jersey, Pennsylvania, Maryland and Delaware, with a mixture of English, Scottish, Irish, Dutch, Swedish and German colonists; and the four Southern colonies of Virginia, North Carolina, South Carolina and Georgia, predominantly settled by the English, but with some ethnic minorities.

[2] This was the way in which the revival of 1740-1742 was referred to by contemporaries (Gaustad 1957:42).

[3] For the suggestion that the Great Awakening was largely the result of a skilfully-managed press campaign by Whitefield and his 'press agent' William Seward, see Lambert 1991:223-246.

[4] See a report on Whitefield in New York quoted from the *New York Weekly Journal* in Bushman 1969 (1989):22-23.

[5] It is often assumed that Whitefield had never consciously studied such subjects, but learnt 'on the job'. However, a new work by Harry Stout on Whitefield, *The Divine Dramatist* (1991) seeks to show that he had indeed studied elocution, or at least those forms of expression and gesture that produce effect, by imitating no less a person than the actor David Garrick!

However, the evidence he seeks is present for his thesis is mainly indirect and inferential.

6 For an eye-witness account of Whitefield's visit to Middletown, Connecticut on October 23, 1740, see the quotation from 'The Spiritual Travels of Nathan Cole' cited from *The William and Mary Quarterly* (1950) in Whitefield 1965:561-562.

7 See a number of letters written to and by Wheelock in Bushman *ibid* 39-45.

8 Charles Chauncy (1705-1787), who had preached a sermon at the Harvard Commencement in 1742 on 'Enthusiasm Decribed and Caution'd Against' (in Heimert and Miller 1967:228-256), spent part of the winter of 1742/1743 journeying around New England collecting materials which he included in his *Seasonable Thoughts on the State of Religion in New-England*, published in September 1743 (Reprint Edition 1975).

Also in September, Timothy Cutler, a previous rector of Yale College, who had left Congregationalism to become an Anglican in 1722, and was now the most eminent Anglican clergyman in Boston, wrote to a fellow clergyman in England, making wild charges against Whitefield, alleging that he was responsible for all kinds of excesses in the behaviour of those who heard him (Letter cited in Dallimore 1980: II. 189).

Four months previously, in May, 1743, thirty-eight ministers meeting in Boston had produced a *Testimony* critical of the Awakening, but this was answered two months later by another *Testimony* signed by sixty-eight, and with Attestations from a further forty-three who could not be present at the meeting. The second Testimony acknowledged a number of abuses, but declared that the Awakening was a mighty work of the Spirit of God. As Gausted says, 'In Boston the established ministers who resisted the Great Awakening were outnumbered three to one' (Gaustad 1957:55; see Tracy [1842:286-302] for the texts and signatories of the two Testimonies).

9 Jonathan Edwards' ideas on lay ministry were those of classical Puritanism. The clergy-centredness of such an approach required that the life of the church focused on the Sunday meetings for worship, the climax of which was the (lengthy) sermon delivered by the minister, with a week-night 'lecture' thrown in for good measure. The place of the laity was to listen, and then to put the teaching of the sermon into practice in their various 'callings'. The days when laymen were allowed to preach were long past; the only exceptions were those who had been duly licensed to do so by an official body (as was David Brainerd [Pettit ed 1985:174]), and who usually were later ordained to the ministry.

In *Some Thoughts Concerning the Revival*, written in 1742, when zealots were in danger of wrecking some of the good effects of the awakening, and when opposition was hardening, partly as the result of this, Edwards addressed himself to the question of the part that the laity have to play in the revival. Civil rulers are to encourage it (Goen ed 1972:370-373), as is 'every living soul' (*ibid* 379-383), but he contents himself with generalised exhortations to 'promote' it, 'take notice of' it, and 'rejoice' in it. The press is singled out as having a duty not to oppose it (*ibid* 380, 381), and in a later section he speaks of the duty of the rich and powerful to use their possessions and position to further the work (*ibid* 513-515). All Christians should seek to promote the work of God by prayer and fasting, by attending more diligently on the Lord's Supper, by abounding in moral duties, and by renewing their covenant with God (*ibid* 515-529).

Lay exhorting, however, is to be firmly discouraged (*ibid* 483-489), unless it is on a one-to-one basis, or confined to a very small, informal group. Some enthusiasts, with great zeal, and (sometimes) with little understanding or discretion, had brought the revival into disrepute (through their imitation of ordained enthusiasts like Rev. James Davenport!). Edwards expresses his disapproval on the basis of its supposed invasion of the special prerogatives of the clergy, rather than the excesses associated with it. In his view

> The common people in exhorting one another ought not to clothe themselves with the like authority with that which is proper to ministers... (*ibid* 484).
> No man but only a minister that is duly appointed to that sacred calling ought to follow teaching and exhorting as a calling, or so as to neglect...his proper calling (*ibid* 487).
> Speaking in the time of the solemn worship of God...should not be allowed (*ibid* 488).
> There ought to be a moderate restraint on the loudness of persons talking under high affections...There should also be some restraint on the abundance of persons' talk under strong affections... (*ibid* 488,489).

In a letter to a friend in Goshen, Connecticut, written on May 18, 1742 (published in Bibliotheca Sacra 1871: 95,96), he rebukes him because he had 'done that which did not belong to you, *in exhorting a public congregation*'. The argument that such activities 'do a great deal of good for the present, and within a narrow sphere' is not good enough; 'appearing events are not our rule, but the law and the testimony'.

> You ought to do what good you can, by private, brotherly, humble admonitions and counsels; but 'tis too much for you to *exhort public congregations*, or solemnly to set yourself, by a set speech, to counsel a room full of people, unless it be children, or those that are much your inferiors, or to speak to any in an authoritative way (*ibid*).

He concludes, 'I hope these lines will be taken in good part, from your assured friend, Jonathan Edwards'. We do not have any record of the response, or whether the friendship survived!

Edwards was not alone in these sentiments; he mentioned in his letter the opposition of Gilbert Tennent to the practice. Those who opposed the revival as a whole directed their invective and scorn at the lay exhorters (Gaustad 1957:72). The whole question of the role of the laity, especially among the Middle Colony Presbyterians, is handled by Westerkamp 1988.

10 Among other factors which diverted people's attention in this and in succeeding decades, and which, therefore, may have contributed to the decline and cessation of the awakening, we may note 'King George's War' against France (1743-1748), and the French and Indian War (1755-1763).

11 For many details of the various events of the Great Awakening in New England see Tracy 1840:114-301; Gaustad 1957:25-60; Whitefield 1965:457-483; Dallimore 1980:II.179-191, especially the summary on pp 181-182.

12 Gilbert Tennent's blistering attack on those who opposed the revival in his sermon *The Danger of an Unconverted Ministry* (1740) hastened the division (see Coalter 1986:55-89 esp 64-67; the full sermon is reprinted in Heimert & Miller 1967:72-99 and selections in Bushman 1969 [1989]:87-93).

13 On the Great Awakening in the Middle Colonies, see Maxson 1920; Coalter 1986. It is the thesis of Marilyn Westerkamp that the Great Awakening in the Middle Colonies was the continuation of the tradition of revivals which the Scots-Irish Presbyterians brought with them from the Old World. It was not 'innovative religious behaviour...[but] was actually part of the Scots-Irish religiosity, a tradition that flourished under the encouragement afforded by the colonial ministers' (Westerkamp 1988:14). On the British background to the New England Revival tradition see Crawford 1991.

14 The precise numbers are impossible to determine with accuracy. Estimates range from 25,000 to 50,000 (see Tracy 1842:389). It has often been suggested that Whitefield's estimates of those attending his meetings are exaggerated and need to be revised downwards.

This raises the problem of what has been described as 'evangelical exaggeration' where the number of legs are counted and then multipled by two! In the historical section of this book, while every effort has been made to avoid this fault (which is really the Evangelical counterpart of Roman Catholic hagiography with its multiplication of miracles performed by saints), in the last resort we often have to rely on the accounts of those who were present. However, we need to avoid on the one hand an excessive gullibility which believes everything that is claimed, and on the other a cynicism and scepticism which believes nothing!

CHAPTER 7

THE SECOND EVANGELICAL AWAKENING

I N NORTH AMERICA, the Revolutionary War and the need to establish the newly independent nation absorbed much energy in the 1770s and 1780s, but local revivals continued to occur sporadically, such as those mentioned above at Lebanon, Connecticut, at Thetford, Vermont, and at Brentford, New Hampshire in 1781, at Boscawan, New Hampshire, in 1782, at Yale College Church, in West Simsbury, Mass. and several towns in Litchfield County, Connecticut, in 1783, and at New Britain in 1784.

In Virginia a new revival began in 1785 which benefited the newly organised Methodist Church, and which, combined with the effective organisation, simplified theology, democratic appeal, and revivalistic fervour of Methodism, contributed greatly to the Methodist expansion (Smith, Handy & Loetscher *ibid* 367; see also Hardman 1983:106,119). The year 1787 saw revivals among both the Methodists (Smith, Handy and Loetscher *ibid* 520) and the Baptists.[1] In the same year a significant revival took place at Hampton-Sydney College, a small Presbyterian college in Virginia, from where it spread to a similar establishment, Washington College, and then radiated out into the whole of Virginia (Cairns 1986:98). Gewehr describes it as the centre of 'the great interdenominational Awakening which marked the final triumph of evangelical Christianity in Virginia' (1930:230).

In Canada, the work of Henry Alline (1748-1784), a 'New Light' Congregationalist, and one of his converts William

Black, who became a Methodist, was instrumental in bringing revival to a number of towns in the Maritime Provinces from 1779 onwards (Cairns *ibid* 86-88; see also Armstrong 1948).

The 1790s witnessed a number of local awakenings, for example in North Yarmouth, Maine, in 1791, in Lyme and East Haddam, Connecticut in 1792, in Lee, Massachusetts, in 1792-1793, and in Farmington, New Hartford and Milford, Connecticut, in 1795, as well as in other places (Griffin in Sprague 1832: Appendix 151-152). The Methodists were already seeing considerable response in a number of places.

However, in other parts of North America the spiritual and moral state of both Church and society following the War of Independence was at a low ebb, aggravated by the spread of rationalistic deism and outright atheism, partly through the influence of the French Revolution (Orr 1981:9).[2]

The same was true in continental Europe (Latourette 1953:1001-1013), and in Britain, where the revival had spent its force by 1776 (Orr *ibid* 8-10, who cites Trevelyan as saying that 1776 belonged to 'the period most marked by infidelity and lack of doctrine').[3]

In England, the tide began to turn in the 1780s with a number of local awakenings which soon began to gather in strength and spread, although the flood was not reached until the next decade (Orr 1975:13). Methodists, Congregationalists, Baptists and the newly-registered Countess of Huntington's Connexion all saw significant growth. In Wales and Ireland, although there were a number of local revivals in the 1780s (Orr 1975:28-29,40), by and large the churches were at a low spiritual ebb.

THE PRAYER CALL

In 1784, a significant chain of events began, which directly contributed to the next major spiritual awakening. John Erskine (1720-1803) of Edinburgh, who had been one of Jonathan Edwards' Scottish correspondents,[4] re-published Edwards' *Humble Attempt to Promote Explicit Agreement...in Extraordinary Prayer for the Revival of Reli-*

gion...[5] He sent a copy to an English Baptist, John Ryland Jr., who passed it on to another pastor, John Sutcliff. At the latter's suggestion, the Northamptonshire Baptist Association resolved to devote the first Monday of each month to 'prayer for the general revival and spread of religion'. In 1786, the Midlands Baptist Association followed suit, and in 1789 a new edition of the *Humble Attempt* was published with a preface by Sutcliff.

The prayer call was taken up by evangelical groups in other denominations, both in England and Scotland, and soon spread to other countries. In 1792 in the United States, Baptists in Boston adopted it, having been informed of what was happening in England, and in 1794 Isaac Backus and his friends enlisted support from all the major American denominations for the monthly concert of prayer (Orr 1975:52,194).

In 1795, the directors of the newly-formed London Missionary Society recommended that the prayer meeting on the first Monday of each month should be made a missionary prayer meeting. The idea met with immediate success, and prayer meetings in London began to proliferate. The practice then spread to 'all the principal cities and towns of the Kingdom', as well as to 'Holland, Switzerland, Germany, America, India, Africa, and wherever there are any missionaries from the Societies in England'.

> Thus an immense number of praying persons are engaged at the same hour in their supplications to the God of all grace, in behalf of a world lying in the Wicked One, and for the spread of that glorious gospel which is the power of God to human salvation; and thus the plan of union, which good Mr. Edwards so strongly recommended, is, in no inconsiderable degree, adopted in the Christian world (George Burder's preface to an abridged copy of Edwards' *Humble Attempt* published by the LMS in 1814, cited in Beaver 1957-8:426).

In 1798, the New York Missionary Society, a group comprising Baptists, Presbyterians, and other Reformed Christians, summoned its members and friends on 'the second Wednesday evening of every month, beginning at candlelight' to united prayer to

> the God of grace, that he would be pleased to pour his spirit on his Church, and send his gospel to all nations; and that he would succeed the endeavours of this Society, and all Societies instituted on the same principles, and for the same ends (*New York Missionary Magazine* [1800], cited in Beaver *ibid* 427, who gives other examples of societies making similar prayer calls).

These efforts were rewarded in the Second Evangelical Revival and all that followed from it in evangelism, church growth, missions, social concern etc (Payne 1941:4-11; *ibid* 1943:223-237; Foster 1948:375-381: Beaver 1957:420-427).

THE SECOND EVANGELICAL REVIVAL IN THE BRITISH ISLES

In England the revival began in the northern industrial cities of Yorkshire, but soon spread to rural areas as well, eventually affecting all parts of the land.

The Methodists probably benefited most, being less afraid than some other groups of the phenomena of mass awakening; their total membership grew from 72,000 in 1791 when John Wesley died to almost a quarter of a million within a generation. Cornwall, which had been a very fruitful field for Wesley himself, was again the scene of amazing growth for Methodism. 1799 and 1814 were especially remarkable years. In 1799 the Society in Penzance received 100 new members; that at Zennor increased from seventeen to 100; the Society in St Ives grew from 160 to 550. In 1814 a revival began in Redruth, which soon spread throughout Cornwall; 500 were added to the Methodist Societies in a few weeks. At nearby Tuckingmill, 2,000 were converted in a meeting which lasted from Sunday 27 February to the following Friday, with people coming and going all the time (Edwards 1990:179)!

The adoption of 'camp meetings' by Hugh Bourne (1772-1852) and others, on the analogy of the American model and influenced by the American preacher Lorenzo Dow, caused the expulsion of Bourne and others from the Methodist Church in 1808. Bourne formed the Primitive Methodist Church and continued to use the camp meeting in evangelism with great results (Morrell 1987:10-48 which contains a wealth of detail).

The Baptists, both General and Particular, and the Congregationalists also continued the pattern of growth begun in the previous decade with further momentum, engaging in vigorous itinerant evangelism.[6] From these groups the first foreign missionary societies were formed, the Baptist Missionary Society in 1792, with William Carey (1761-1834) as its first missionary, and the London Missionary Society in 1795.[7] The modern Protestant missionary movement was a direct result of the Second Evangelical Revival (Payne 1943:223-236).

The revival also strengthened and accelerated the Evangelical influences in the Church of England, with such men as Thomas Haweis (1734-1820, a co-founder of the London Missionary Society), John Newton (1725-1807), the biblical commentator Thomas Scott (1747-1821), John Venn (1759-1813) and others. In Cambridge Isaac Milner (1750-1820), as Professor of Natural Philosophy in 1783, President of Queen's College, and finally as Vice-Chancellor of the University in 1792, had a profound influence on the spiritual life of the university, as did Charles Simeon (1759-1836), the vicar of Holy Trinity Church from 1782 (Hopkins 1977).

Simeon's influence extended far and wide, through his sermons (2,536 of which were published), his sponsoring of Evangelical candidates for the Anglican ministry, his support of charitable work of many kinds, and his advocacy and support for foreign missions. He obtained chaplaincies in India for men like David Brown and Henry Martin, and played an important role in the founding of the Church Missionary Society in 1799. On a preaching holiday in Scotland with James Haldane (1768-1851, see below) in 1796, he preached at Moulin in Perthshire, as a result of which a revival occurred.[8]

The 'Clapham Sect',[9] comprising Anglican Evangelicals who were concerned to implement social reforms as the outworking of their evangelical commitment, laboured for years to abolish slavery and other social evils from the national life. Men like William Wilberforce (1759-1833), Zachary Macaulay (1768-1838), Thomas Clarkson (1760-1846), James Stephen Jr, Thomas Fowell Buxton, and Henry Thornton used their time, talents, wealth and political influence in the abolition of slavery (on the Clapham Sect, see Howse 1971).

The Religious Tract Society (1799) and the British and Foreign Bible Society (1804) also grew out of the revival, as Christians sought to print and distribute Bibles and Christian literature both at home and abroad.

Other evangelical Christians who were involved in the revival and who sought to work out their Christian principles in redressing social injustices included Robert Raikes (1735-1811) and Hannah More (1745-1833), who founded the modern Sunday School movement in England, Elizabeth Fry (1780-1845) the prison reformer and, a little later, Anthony Ashley Cooper, the Earl of Shaftesbury (1801-1885) who successfully campaigned for improvement in the inhuman factory conditions, especially those of children.

In 1798 and 1800 there were remarkable revivals in Moulin, Scotland, under the ministry of Alexander Stewart[10]. The Haldane brothers, Robert (1764-1832) and James, were involved in a wide variety of spiritual activity. Along with Alexander Stewart, James had been spiritually renewed through his association with Charles Simeon on holiday in 1796, and subsequently became a travelling evangelist in northern Scotland, the Orkneys and Ireland, often preaching to enormous crowds. He eventually settled as a pastor in Edinburgh, where he remained for fifty years. His brother

Robert was frustrated in his plan to become a missionary, but used his wealth in the work of the gospel. Among other things he established a 'Society for the Propagation of the Gospel at Home' which sent out 114 catechists and missionaries, together with a Missionary Training Institute in Edinburgh where he personally financed the training of 300 students and paid for twenty-eight Africans to come to Scotland for training as missionaries to their own people. He also supported Bible distribution, and paid for the construction of many chapel buildings, including the one where his brother ministered. From 1816 to 1818 he was in Switzerland and France, where a number of those converted through his ministry later became leaders in the *Reveils* in those countries. The Haldanes were brought up in the Church of Scotland, but left it in 1799, and became first Congregationalists and later Baptists.

Among those who remained in the Kirk and maintained a strong stand against the deadening Moderatism, was Thomas Chalmers (1780-1847). His parish church ministry, especially in Glasgow, his teaching position in St Andrews University and later in Edinburgh, and his leadership of the Evangelical Party, were all remarkably successful and influential (Orr 1975:32-39).

On the island of Skye there was a revival in 1812, and in the north of Scotland the ministry of John MacDonald of Ferintosh, Ross-shire, the 'Apostle of the North', was attended by large crowds which often numbered up to 10,000. In the parish of Breadalbane, where Robert Finlater was the minister, there were the first stirrings of spiritual concern in 1812, which developed into a full-scale revival through MacDonald's preaching; the revival continued from 1816 to around 1820.

In Wales, the sporadic awakenings of the 1780s were followed by waves of revival from 1791 until 1814 through the ministries of men like Thomas Charles of Bala (1755-1814), John Elias (1774- 1841), Christmas Evans (1766-1838), William Williams (1781- 1840), and many others[11]. Amazing scenes of conviction of sin coming simultaneously on whole congregations over a large area were recorded. Thousands gathered in the open-air to hear the preaching, as well as packing the churches. Baptist, Congregational and Wesleyan Methodist Churches experienced accelerated growth; the Welsh Calvinistic Methodist Church grew out of the revival (Orr 1975:29-31).

Ireland, which was the scene of political unrest and economic hardship in the 1790s, also experienced revival, particularly among the Methodists whose travelling evangelists were extremely effective. Among these was the eccentric American Lorenzo Dow (1777-1824), who also preached in England among the Methodists from 1805 until the split of 1808 (see above). He returned to Britain in 1817 for a further round of itinerant preaching (Kent 1978:43,48-59).

SCANDINAVIA
In Norway, Denmark, Sweden and Finland there were revivals associated with Lutheran Pietism. In Norway, a nationwide revival developed through the itinerant preaching of Hans Nielsen Hauge (1774-1824), a lay preacher who for eight years travelled around on foot or on skis, covering over 10,000 miles in this way. He was often opposed by the Lutheran clergy, was arrested ten times, and was imprisoned for ten years from 1804 till 1814. Laymen were active in the societies he formed, but ordained pastors were involved in later revivals. The work of Hauge made a lasting impression on Norwegian Lutheranism, where his societies remained within the Church. His work also had an effect in Denmark. In Sweden there were similar movements, and these in turn affected Finland, where Paavo Ruotsalainen (1777-1852) exercised a ministry very similar to that of Hauge (Cairns *ibid* 114-116).

SOUTH AFRICA
Among the Dutch settlers in the Cape Colony, a young minister named Helperus van Lier exercised an evangelistic

ministry in the 1790s which resulted in many being converted from a nominal faith; a number of these became missionaries to the Hottentots. Among the English garrison in the Cape Colony, a number of Methodist soldiers sought to witness to their faith, but with little result until an earthquake in 1809, the aftershocks of which lasted for eight days, produced a solemnity previously lacking. This was followed by an outpouring of the Spirit which resulted in hundreds being converted (Orr *ibid* 83).

NORTH AMERICA

Henry Alline died in 1784, but the movement begun in Canada by his preaching continued. In 1791 a series of revivals began in the Canadian Maritime Provinces, affecting Methodists, Baptists and New Light Congregationalists. As Upper Canada (now Ontario) was opened up to immigrants, the churches sent evangelists; widespread revivals occurred, particularly among the Methodists. In 1797 there were 800 Methodists in the Canada Conference; by 1805 this had grown to 1,800. In 1810 a notable revival occurred in Western Ontario under the preaching of a Methodist evangelist William Case (Orr *ibid* 71-77).

In the United States, the sporadic instances of revival in some New England towns were followed by a general awakening at the turn of the century affecting towns all over the states of New England and extending also to the cities of New York and Philadelphia, as well as western parts of New York State and Pennsylvania. As a result of the spread of the Concert of Prayer, prayer meetings multiplied as the first Monday of each month became the occasion of fervent intercession. By 1795 support for the Concert was general among churches of all denominations, apart from those which, explicitly or implicitly, were Unitarian.[12]

By 1798 the awakening was general and widespread, covering churches in all the New England states,[13] Long Island, New Jersey, New York, Philadelphia and Maryland, and involved Congregationalists, Baptists, Presbyterians,

THE SECOND EVANGELICAL AWAKENING 121

Methodists, Dutch Reformed, a number of Episcopal churches and some German-speaking groups. In most places it continued until at least 1812, when the war interrupted the work, and resumed after the peace of 1815; in other places it continued on into the 1820s and even later (details in Orr 1975:53-58).

A series of notable awakenings occurred at Yale College during the presidency of Timothy Dwight (1752-1817), the grandson of Jonathan Edwards. When he became president in 1795, he began immediately to preach against the rationalism which at the time gripped Yale and many other centres of higher education. Revival came in 1802, when one-third of the entire student body professed conversion. In succeeding years there was a steady stream of professions of faith, and in 1808, 1813, and 1815, there were further notable movements of the Spirit. These were paralleled in many other colleges, including Dartmouth, Bennington, Princeton, Amhurst, Andover, and Williams (see the various letters in the Appendix of Sprague 1832; also Tyler 1846; Humphrey 1859; Keller 1942).

It was at Williams College, Williamstown, Massachusetts, during the revival there in 1805-1808,[14] that Samuel John Mills (1783-1818) and his friends formed their resolution in the famous 'haystack prayer meeting', to commit themselves to the work of foreign missions. As a result, the American Board of Commissioners for Foreign Missions was formed in 1810, and the first missionaries sailed for India in 1812. For the next several years, students from the various colleges and seminaries which experienced revival, were to provide the majority of recruits for the ministry in the already existing churches, for the task of evangelism on the expanding frontier, and for the work of foreign missions in the newly formed societies.

In the college revivals, as in those on the Eastern Seaboard in general, there was a complete absence of emotional extravagance among those affected,[15] but in western parts of New York State and Pennsylvania there were more startling scenes of excitement. The awakenings which began in 1798 in Kentucky and Tennessee and later spread to Virginia, North and South Carolina and Georgia, taking place among the rough, illiterate and lawless frontiersmen, were characterised by extremes of conviction and response, such as trembling, shaking, fainting, weeping for sorrow and shouting for joy.

The southern phase of the awakening was associated with the 'camp meeting' which developed out of open-air sacramental preparation weekends climaxing in communion services, which were borrowed from Scottish Presbyterian practice. In 1798 revival broke out at Red River, Kentucky, in a sacramental weekend meeting where Rev James McGready (c 1758-1817), a Presbyterian minister and evangelist, preached; similar revival was experienced in many places as McGready, William and John McGee and others preached at a number of such occasions over the next two years.

The first 'camp meeting' proper was held in July 1800 at Gasper River, Kentucky, when services were held in the open air and families lived in thirteen wagons over the weekend. Barton Stone (1772-1844), a Presbyterian minister, journeyed from the other side of Kentucky to observe what went on, and in August 1801 organised a similar meeting at Cane Ridge, Kentucky, which lasted for six days and to which around 12,500 came. There were at least 125 wagons from various parts of Kentucky and from as far afield as Ohio and Tennessee. A prayer meeting was held at 7.00 am and sermons delivered at 11.00 am, 3.00 pm, and 7.00 pm, preceded by the singing of simple folk hymns. It was in this kind of intense atmosphere that the falling, rolling and jerking took place (see a contemporary account cited in Smith, Handy and Loetscher 1960: I.566-570; McNemar 1968: Boles 1972; Robertson in White, Weeks & Rosell 1986:63-69; also some reflections on the camp meetings and their associated practices from a contemporary professor of Church History in Sprague 1832: Appendix 32-44).

By 1805 the Presbyterians had abandoned the camp meeting, but the Baptists and Methodists continued to make use of it. Methodists described them as 'Methodist harvest time(s)';

four to five hundred were held in 1811, according to Francis Asbury (1745-1816), the great leader of American Methodism, in his Journal (see citations in Smith etc *ibid* 570-576; Johnson 1955; Cartwright 1956: I. 1-108), and around 1,000 in 1820. After 1840 they ceased to be used with any frequency.[16]

Just as in Britain, the Second Awakening in the United States directly resulted in the formation of a large number of societies for the furthering of Christian activity in significant directions. In 1796 discussions began which resulted in the New York Missionary Society being formed, on independent lines similar to the London Missionary Society in England, and missionaries were soon being sent to the Indians in Georgia and west New York State. Other similar societies were formed in 1797, 1798 and 1799. In 1798, when the New York Society was officially inaugurated, it was proposed that the Concert of Prayer be redirected into missionary prayer sessions every second Wednesday of the month for the out-pouring of the Spirit and the proclamation of the gospel to all nations. The American Board of Commissioners for Foreign Missions formed in 1810 as a result of the Williams College 'haystack' prayer meeting in 1806, which sent their first team of eight missionaries to India in 1812, was soon followed by the American Baptist Foreign Mission Society in 1814, the Methodist Episcopal Foreign Missionary Society in 1819, and others in succeeding years.

Notes

[1] The Baptists in Virginia experienced revival over the five years from 1785 to 1790.

[2] This pessimistic assessment has recently been challenged by Stout (1986) and Bonomi (1986). However, Bonomi's figures of around 60% of the adult white population attending church regularly relates to the period between 1700 and 1776 (see Bonomi and Eisenstadt [1982:246-286]).

[3] In a similar way, this assessment has also been challenged. However,

the recent study by Deryck Lovegrove (Lovegrove 1988), which links the revivals we are about to study with the increasing practice of itinerant evangelism and new techniques of theological education on the part of the Dissenters, seems to justify the assessment in broad terms.

⁴ In 1742 Erskine had published his own work on the subjects of revival and eschatology, *The Signs of the Times Consider'd: or, the high Probability, that the Present Appearances in New-England, and the West of Scotland, are a Prelude of the Glorious Things promised to the Church in the latter Ages.* In the same year, Edwards was expressing his own hope in very similar words in *Some Thoughts...* (see above, chapter 2).

⁵ The background to Edwards' *Humble Attempt* is interesting, and shows the connection between the first and second Great Awakenings.

In Scotland in January 1743, a number of prayer societies published their intention of holding a day of thanksgiving for the 'Outpourings of the Spirit from on high on several Corners of this wither'd Church' with petitions to God 'that he would carry on this good and unexpected Word...that all Opposers...may be at last obliged to own that it is the Doing of the Lord'. In the previous year the revivals at Cambuslang and Kilsyth had occurred, and the hope was being expressed that these would continue and spread, and that some who were uneasy regarding the phenomena would be persuaded that they were to be encouraged and not opposed.

In October of the following year, 1744, a group of Scottish ministers, headed by Rev John M'Laurin of Glasgow, agreed to unite in prayer regularly at certain times each week, and also in quarterly meetings, initially for a two-year period, that God would revive his church throughout the world. In 1746, when the initial period had elapsed, they published a 'Memorial' in which they argued for the continuance and extension of the practice.

In New England, Jonathan Edwards, who was already thinking along similar lines, heard of the original proposal in 1745 from his Scottish correspondents, and wrote asking for further details. In his *An Humble Attempt to promote Explicit Agreement and Visible Union of God's People in Extraordinary Prayer* (1747) he printed the Memorial in full, and argued strongly for the adoption of the plan by the churches in America.

Although Edwards did not live to see the fruit of his work in this regard, his work must certainly be seen as a major influence on the Second Awakening and all that flowed from it.

⁶ Lovegrove (1988:182-184) gives the names of seventy-five itinerant societies formed by Calvinistic Dissenting groups between 1776 and 1830. He also prints the journal of Thomas Wastfield, one of the many itinerants (*ibid* 166-181).

⁷ The LMS was interdenominational at its foundation and included Evangelical Anglicans, but Evangelical Congregationalists were prominent from the beginning, and when in 1799 Evangelical Anglicans formed the

Church Missionary Society, Congregationalists became increasingly the dominant group in the LMS.

[8] In this revival the minister, Rev Alexander Stewart came to living faith. Under Stewart's preaching a further awakening took place in 1798 which continued for at least a year. During that time many in the age range from 25 to 35 years were converted, among whom were two young people who later married and whose son Alexander Duff (1806-1878) served with distinction as a missionary educator in India and also introduced a Chair of Evangelical Theology, with an emphasis on missions, at New College, Edinburgh (see Murray 1971:164-165 and notes).

[9] John Venn was the rector of Clapham, and Wilberforce, Macaulay and Thornton were among his parishioners. Venn, whose father Henry Venn had been active in the first Evangelical Revival (see above), served as the virtual chaplain of the group.

[10] See above.

[11] Elias, Evans and Williams were also involved in the new wave of revival which occurred from around 1828 onwards (see below).

[12] The Concert was also observed in the southern states.

[13] In a number of the local revivals in New England, the work began among the young people, before spreading to other age groups.

[14] According to Edward D. Griffin, the President of Williams, in his letter to William Sprague (in Sprague 1832: Appendix 151-165), there were at least nine periods of revival there, in 1805-1808, 1812, 1815, 1824, 1827, 1831, and 1832. The latest one was still in progress as he wrote his letter.

[15] Orr comments

> In the awakening of before and after 1800, the ministers of New England churches called in no evangelists without settled charge to preach for them. They did all the preaching themselves, and helped one another as the occasion required...No protracted meetings were held, use being made of Sunday services and regular week-day lectures. This had the effect of strengthening these set services and made it much easier to integrate new converts...
> Much the same was true of the Middle Atlantic States, except in their western territories where frontier conditions prevailed. There seemed to be no records of emotional extravagance in meetings in New York and Philadelphia, or in lesser towns in the States of Maryland, Delaware, New Jersey, Pennsylvania and New York. Unlike New England, these states possessed considerable numbers of Baptists and

Methodists, particularly prone to demonstrative conduct in the west and the south.

...The Second Awakening was effective from Maine to Maryland. The recording of local movements here and there has served to show that the Awakening in the Eastern States before and after 1800 was without emotional excesses, without the bitter recriminations of earlier movements, that it was fruitful and long-lasting (Orr 1975:55,58).

16 A by-product of the revival in the South was the growth of the Shakers, a group which traced its origins to the 'French Prophets', who had appeared in France during the reign of Louis XIV, had been largely suppressed by persecution, but the remnants of whom had escaped to England. We have already noticed some of their activities in connection with the eighteenth century Evangelical revival in England, but their influence began to grow with the conversion to the group in 1758 of Ann Lees Standerin (1736-1784), also known as Ann Lee Stanley. In 1770, while in prison, she had a vision which convinced her that the 'mystery of iniquity' lay in sexual activity. She was acknowledged by the Shakers as their spiritual mother in Christ, being known thereafter as Mother Ann Lee. Persecution forced Mother Ann and a few of her flock to leave for the New World in 1774. They settled in New York State, but their numbers remained static until 1779, when they gained new members from a revival among New Light Baptists in nearby New Lebanon. They were reorganised three years after her death in 1784 as the Millennial Church, or the United Society of Believers in Christ's Second Coming, with patterns of community living, and with a number of strange beliefs. These included the idea that Mother Ann had been the second appearance of Christ, and the second incarnation of the Holy Spirit whereby the feminine element of God had appeared to continue the work begun by Jesus Christ. In 1805 they began to grow rapidly, especially in the frontier areas of Kentucky and Ohio where the revivals had been effective. A number of conspicuous revival leaders joined their ranks, including Richard McNemar (?-1839) and John Dunlavy (Smith, Handy & Loetscher 1960: I. 586-596: Linder in Douglas ed 1978: 588, 900-901; Garret 1985).

CHAPTER 8

THE SECOND EVANGELICAL AWAKENING (CONCLUDED)

THE SECOND EVANGELICAL AWAKENING: THE SECOND PHASE

THE NAPOLEONIC WARS IN EUROPE from 1803 to 1815, and the American War against Britain (1812-1815) which was the transatlantic outcome of the former, put a brake on the progress of the revival to a certain extent. The peace that followed in 1815 witnessed a renewal of the Anglo-Saxon awakening on both sides of the Atlantic, together with the *Reveil* in Switzerland, France and Holland, and the *Erweckung* in Germany. Those who were involved in the various Concerts of Prayer were urged in that year to pray for a return of peace, a reformation of morals, and a general revival of religion.

The British Isles
Notable revivals took place in 1815 and 1816 among Wesleyan Methodists in Somerset and Dorset, among the Bible Christians (another branch of Methodism which appeared in 1815) in Devon, and among the Primitive Methodists in the Midlands.[1] By 1820 the renewed spiritual impulse had spread to all parts of the country, and all the evangelical denominations were experiencing similar awakenings and growth. Baptists,[2] Congregationalists and Evangelical Anglicans all benefited in growing numbers and increasing influence. In the Church of

England Charles Simeon's influence was at its height, and a number of Evangelicals were appointed as bishops. A new prayer call for the outpouring of the Spirit was issued in 1823 by a number of societies in the various denominations committed to revival and evangelism.

In Wales and Anglesey, powerful awakenings which began in 1817 soon affected both towns and villages. The lower working classes were influenced more in Wales than in England. Baptists, Calvinistic Methodists, Wesleyan Methodists and Congregationalists all saw significant increases.

In Scotland, 1815 was the year that Thomas Chalmers became minister of the Tron Church in Glasgow, where he exercised a powerful and increasingly influential ministry. The Evangelical party in the Church of Scotland were busy in opposing the influence of the Moderates, but also in maintaining Sunday Schools, protesting against the exploitation of the poor, promoting popular education and circulating literature. In the Highlands of Scotland, the Gaelic-speaking evangelist John MacDonald, and John Kennedy, a Congregational evangelist, preached to great congregations. In Glenlyon, crowds assembled day after day and night after night in barns and in woods to hear Kennedy. The work continued even during the winter snows (Orr *ibid* 101-103). The islands of Skye in the Inner Hebrides, and Lewis in the Outer Hebrides also saw significant awakenings.[3]

In Ireland, the work of the Irish Society, the Scripture Readers' Society and the Bible Society resulted in large numbers of Catholics leaving the Church of Rome and joining the Church of Ireland. William Magee, as Bishop of Raphoe and later as Archbishop of Dublin, encouraged his clergy to become active evangelists. The Methodists continued to engage in vigorous evangelism, and revivals were reported regularly in connection with their work.

The *Reveil* in Switzerland, France and Holland

In 1816 Robert Haldane moved to Geneva in Switzerland, where he hired a hall and began to lecture on evangelical doctrines, using especially the Epistle to the Romans. Although he was opposed by professors and clergy of the Reformed Church, his work produced a revival of evangelical religion in Geneva, and a number of men who were to become leaders of Evangelical Free Churches in Switzerland and whose writings were widely read, were influenced, such as Louis Gaussen (1790-1863), Cesar Malan (1787-1864) and Merle D'Aubigne (1794-1872). Revival was experienced in Neuchatel in 1817. A number of pastors in the state Church were converted or renewed, and the effects were seen in a new emphasis on biblical preaching.

In 1817 Haldane moved to southwest France, where he engaged in the same kind of activity as in Geneva, but without either the excitement or the persecution. A number of French-speaking missionaries also moved into France from Geneva; pioneer missionaries were supported from London; Bible societies were formed in Strasbourg and Paris, and a Religious Tract Society was organised. In 1822, the Paris Evangelical Missionary Society was formed to carry the gospel abroad. The revival was beginning to affect French Protestantism.

Het Reveil in Holland was influenced by that in Geneva, notably by Cesar Malan and Merle D'Aubigne. It centred round the poet Willem Bilderdijk (1736-1831) and a number of his friends. Through books, evangelistic missions, Sunday Schools, Bible teaching and philanthropic social action, they influenced many congregations in the Dutch Reformed Church. The Baptists and Brethren especially benefited from the revival (Details on all three countries in Orr *ibid* 107-111; Cairns *ibid* 141-143).

The *Erweckung* in Germany

The impulse for awakening in the German Federation came in part from the Revival in Britain and the *Reveil* in Switzerland. Agents of the British and Foreign Society and the Religious Tract Society distributed Christian literature, preached, and formed other Bible Societies. From German-speaking Switzerland evangelists preached in Bavaria. Revival swept many areas, including the cities of Berlin, Hanover, Bremen, and Hamburg, and the areas of Silesia and East Pomerania. A number of the German nobility were converted.

In Berlin, Johannes Janicke (1748-1827) was pastor of the Bethlehem Bohemian-Lutheran Church, which was a centre of the awakening. He opened a training school to prepare young men for missionary service. Its eighty graduates served with various societies in Africa and Asia. He also formed a Bible Society and a tract society (Pierard in Douglas ed 1978:524). Laymen were also active in the revival, as were two theological professors, August Neander (1789-1850) and Friedrich Tholuck (1799-1877).

The United States and Canada

The years following the War of 1812-1815 were noteworthy for the great numbers of local revivals in various parts of the United States. The Concert of Prayer continued to be observed and the expectation and hope of many were for continued outpourings of the Spirit.

In New England and the Middle Atlantic States, the years 1815 to 1818 were times of widespread local awakenings. Many revivals were associated with the itinerant evangelist Asahel Nettleton (1783-1843), especially from 1812 onwards, until 1820 when his health began to fail. Over a period of ten years he was involved in upward of sixty awakenings in Connecticut, Massachusetts and New York State. The awakening in Saratoga Springs, New York State where he preached in 1819 resulted in the 'hopeful conversion' of 2,000 people. Holding strongly to Calvinist theology in its modified Hopkinsian form,[4] he continued to hold the traditional understanding of the miraculous nature of revival, which was soon to be challenged by his younger contemporary Charles Finney (1792-1875), with his radical rejection of Calvinism, together with his controversial 'new measures' to bring people to conversion (see further below on Finney; also biographies of Nettleton by Tyler 1844 [British ed. Bonar 1854, reprinted

1975], and Thornbury 1977; also Carwardine 1978:4-9; Hardman 1989:82-149).[5]

Nettleton, although an itinerant, never went to a church without the express invitation of the local minister. He laid great emphasis on persistent prayer as a necessary preparation to his evangelistic preaching; he normally used the regular services of the church, visited enquirers in their own homes to counsel them, and invited interested or awakened people to 'inquiry meetings'. These were usually held at a set time in the week, when he gave detailed instruction on the faith to the whole group, and followed it up by speaking to each enquirer personally. He urged on each person the necessity of conversion and faith, but advised them to go home quietly, and pray in the silence of their own rooms (Thornbury *ibid* 111-115). More than once, when he felt that too much attention was being paid to him, and not to the Lord and spiritual matters, he left the congregation and town unannounced in the middle of a mission.

The Baptist churches of New England held special days of prayer and fasting in 1816, which were shortly followed by revival and church growth. The year 1821 was notable in Connecticut for the awakenings among Congregationalists and Baptists. The Congregational Church in Lee, Massachusetts, which had known revival in 1792-1793, 1800 and 1805 continued to experience awakenings in 1820, 1821 (in connection with a visit of Asahel Nettleton), 1827 and 1831. Park Street Church in Boston, where Sereno E. Dwight (Timothy Dwight's son and Jonathan Edwards' biographer) was the minister, experienced revival in 1813, 1814, 1817 and 1827 (see letters in Sprague 1832 Appendix:1-165 for many other local revivals in this period).

The Presbyterians in New York and New Jersey experienced awakening in 1815 to 1818, and again in succeeding years as they held special days of prayer and fasting and other protracted meetings. This was especially true of the Presbyterians of New Jersey throughout 1826.

In 1815 awakenings occurred on a number of college

campuses, notably at Dartmouth College in New Hampshire, Williams College in western Massachusetts, Yale and Princeton. At Williams it was one of a number of such awakenings, which continued for a number of years. At Amhurst College in Massachusetts there were similar renewals in the years that followed (See letters in Sprague 1832 Appendix).

Following the peace of 1815, migrants poured westward into the Ohio valley. Baptists were very active among them and a number of awakenings occurred which brought hundreds and even thousands to saving faith. The same was true in Ontario.

In the Southern states, awakenings frequently took place among the Baptists, Methodists, Presbyterians and Congregationalists in Virginia, North Carolina, South Carolina and Georgia. A Presbyterian evangelist, Daniel Baker, exercised a widespread and effective ministry for forty years beginning in 1816 (Orr *ibid* 124-125).

Charles Grandison Finney (1792-1875), who was to be increasingly prominent from 1830 onwards, began his evangelistic career in 1824, three years after his conversion.[6] He met with a significant response as he preached in small towns in western New York State in 1824 and the first part of 1825. In 1824 he made the acquaintance of Daniel Nash (1774-1831), known popularly as 'Father Nash'. Nash's special ministry of prayer was probably a factor in the increasing success of Finney's ministry (Hardman 1987:55-56).

In 1825 and 1826 Finney preached in larger communities such as Rome and Utica in Oneida County, New York State, with far greater success, but also with an increasing emphasis on his own distinctive theology of conversion,[7] together with the introduction of those measures which, in his view, were theologically and practically suited to persuade sinners to be converted. A convention was held in New Lebanon, New York, from July 18-21, 1827, which brought about a meeting between Asahel Nettleton and Charles Finney, together with a number of other prominent ministers, some of whom sided with Nettleton, and others with Finney. It came to no conclusion, and was seen by Finney and his friends as a vindication of their position (see Rosell in White, Weeks & Rosell 1986:83-93; Hardman 1987:133-149; Finney ed Rosell & Dupuis 1989:216-225).

The second phase of the Awakening produced a flood of societies which sought to apply the benefits of the gospel in different areas of life. They included the American Education Society (1815), the American Bible Society (1816), the American Colonization Society (1816), the American Sunday School Union (1817), the American Tract Society (1826), the American Temperance Society (1826), and the American Home Missionary Society (1826).[8]

Mission Areas

The modern Protestant missionary movement, which began as the direct result of the Second Evangelical Revival which began in 1791, received new impetus from the renewal of the awakening in the years following 1815. Missionaries were sent to new areas, such as Hawaii, the Friendly Islands, Indonesia and Madagascar. Folk movements also occurred in places where missionaries were already working, as in Tahiti and in southern India. In southern Africa similarly new missionary work was opened up, former work which had lapsed was restarted, and significant awakenings took place among the settlers and on a number of mission stations. The Methodists in particular experienced revival; that at Grahamstown in 1822, through the preaching of William Shaw (1798-1872) an immigrant minister from Scotland, produced many converts. Shaw like John Wesley before him itinerated on horseback, organised bands of local preachers, and established new churches, including six missions in the Ciskei and Transkei between 1823 and 1830.

In the West Indies, awakenings were already taking place before the end of the previous century among Baptists and Methodists; these continued, notably in 1802 in St Christopher and Tortola. The Baptists sent out missionaries in 1814 to help in the work, which had been started through the preaching of two American Blacks, George Leile a freed slave from Georgia, and Moses Baker a barber from New York (see Brewer 1990:16-30 and literature cited there).

In 1818 James Thomson, a Scot who was agent of the British and Foreign Bible Society and the English Foreign School Society, arrived in Buenos Aires where he was permitted by the Argentinian government to set up schools on the lines of the 'monitorial' system of Joseph Lancaster. The New Testament was used as the basis for learning, and more advanced students taught the less advanced ones to read. Within three years Thomson had set up schools in Argentina and Uruguay with a total of 5000 pupils. In the years following he did the same in Chile, Peru, Colombia and Mexico. However, much of the work later languished through the lack of teachers, the absence of support from British and American Churches and the hostility of the Catholic hierarchy (Cairns *ibid* 145).

THE RESURGENCE OF 1830 ONWARDS

The year 1830 marked a significant new period of more general revival in many parts of the world. Local awakenings, which had occurred sporadically in the preceding fifteen years, were taken up into a more general period of awakening which continued until the middle of the 1840s.

The American Outpouring

By the late Spring of 1830 revivals were being reported from all over the United States. Boston and New York together with many other cities were experiencing 'great multitudes turning to the Lord' and 'extensive revivals of religion', according to contemporary reports. Smaller towns and rural communities also witnessed awakenings, as did many colleges. Methodists, Baptists, Presbyterians, Congregationalists, Dutch Reformed, German-speaking Lutheran and Reformed and other groups as well benefited from the great numbers of converts. Great numbers of Negroes were won as a result of the awakening.[9]

In at least twenty-five towns and cities in New York State the revival was considered a 'glorious work', notably in the capital Albany, where William Sprague (1795-1876) was a Presbyterian minister.[10]

Charles Finney was closely involved in the large-scale revival in the city of Rochester, New York State which began in September 1830 and continued for six months. This town, which had grown in size and importance on the opening of the Erie Canal, was the scene of a great awakening, as a result of which one thousand out of the total population of 10,000 professed conversion, and 450 joined the Presbyterian churches in one year. The Baptists, Methodists and the Episcopalians in the city also saw large numbers of members joining as a result of the awakening, and many of the surrounding communities also experienced revival (Cross 1950:152ff; Hardman *ibid* 192-211; Finney ed Rosell & Dupuis Ibid 299-327). A more general revival was already under way in New York State and elsewhere when the Rochester revival began, although the results in Rochester were among the most dramatic, and news from there clearly had an effect elsewhere (Finney ed Rosell & Dupuis *ibid* 325 n 114). However, it is not true to say that Finney's 'new measures'[11] *produced* the revival; rather he shared in the harvest which was already taking place. Similar results were obtained in many other places where his methods were not used.[12] However, the Rochester revival brought Finney national fame and secured a sympathetic reception from many, both in the USA and beyond, for his lectures on revival which were published in 1835.[13]

In 1832 he became a pastor in New York City,[14] where he spent the next five years. In 1835 he moved to Oberlin College, Ohio, where he remained as Professor of Theology until his death in 1875, and from where he continued to make preaching tours in the United States[15] as well as trips to England and Scotland in November 1849-March 1851 and December 1858-August 1860 (see Hardman [1987] also McLoughlin 1959:11-165).

In addition to his other activities, Finney worked tirelessly for the cause of social reform. He was particularly concerned to advocate a number of causes which were already being promoted by the various societies which had sprung from the ealier stages of the Second Great Awakening. One of the converts of Finney's campaign in Utica in 1826 was Theodore Dwight Weld (1803-1895), who became one of the leaders of the anti-slavery movement, as well as the temperance movement.[16] Finney himself was involved in both of these impulses, and also strongly supported the rights of women and blacks, the moral reform of society, and other social issues.[17] Oberlin College became a centre for the advocacy of a number of these issues (Dayton *ibid* 15-62). It also became the centre of the 'Perfectionism' which Finney also espoused, partly through contacts with John Humphrey Noyes (1811-1886) and Asa Mahan (d 1889).[18]

In the wake of the revival a new denomination, the Disciples of Christ, was formed under the leadership of Thomas Campbell (1763-1854), mainly composed of groups or individuals who had been squeezed out of their denominations by leaders unsympathetic to revival. Barton Stone (1772-1844), a Frontier Presbyterian evangelist, also broke with his Presbyterian heritage over the subject of unconditional election and together with others formed the 'Christian Church'. In 1832 many from this group joined with Campbell's Disciples (Sweet 1973:232-238).

The British Scene

In England the new wave of revival was experienced in Anglican circles, where a number of notable evangelists such as Robert Aitken[19] and William Haslam were active in promoting evangelistic missions, especially among the poor and dispossessed. The Free Churches also experienced a measure of awakening,[20] but the various branches of Methodism witnessed the greatest growth through a whole series of local revivals up and down the country.

In many places the revivals occurred without the agency of

any notable evangelists, but Methodism also saw great blessing at a later stage through the itinerant ministry of James Caughey (1810-1897). Caughey, an Irish-born immigrant to the United States, was converted in a revival in 1830-1831, was ordained to the Methodist ministry, and felt a call to return to Britain to engage in evangelism. He visited the British Isles from 1841 to 1847 on the first of four trips, and preached in Dublin, Liverpool, Nottingham (where William Booth was converted under his preaching), Huddersfield, Goole, York, Chesterfield and Birmingham. In every place multitudes crammed in to hear him and great numbers were converted. Inns and public houses were left deserted as former customers became Christians.[21]

However, Wesleyan Methodism was becoming more and more 'respectable', and through the influence of Jabez Bunting (1779-1858) increasingly emphasised law-and-order rather than the 'holy disorder' of the revivals.[22] By contrast, the Primitive Methodists, the Bible Christians and the Methodist New Connection continued their outreach to the masses.

The 1830s also witnessed the Oxford, or Tractarian, Movement in the Church of England, which many have described as a revival, but which can hardly be called an Evangelical Revival, emphasising as it did the continuity of Anglicanism with the Roman Catholic Church and arguing for a return to many ritual and other practices which had been decisively rejected by the Protestant Reformers. Certainly, Evangelical Anglicans saw it as a threat to biblical Christianity rather than an ally, although later generations may see things differently.

Two other groups which had closer connections with the Revival but which pursued their own slightly idiosyncratic and eccentric paths were the Christian Brethren, or Plymouth Brethren, and the Apostolic Church; John Nelson Darby (1800-1882) and Edward Irving (1792-1834) were the main leaders of the respective groups. The Open Brethren—with such leaders as George Muller (1805-1898), who were excommunicated by Darby from those who followed his leadership (the Closed Brethren)—were far more positive towards the revival of the 1830s and to subsequent awakenings than were the Closed Brethren.

Among the institutions formed as a result of the revival the Young Men's Christian Association (YMCA), founded by George Williams in the 1840s, and its sister organisation the YWCA, began a work on both sides of the Atlantic which incorporated an evangelistic as well as a social dimension, and did admirable service in helping young people in the burgeoning cities. The Evangelical Alliance, founded in 1846, was a concrete example of evangelical ecumenism which flowed from the revival.

In Wales there were a number of awakenings from 1828 onwards into the 1830s and 1840s which affected various parts of the country. Powerful preachers, such as John Elias (1774-1841), Christmas Evans (1766-1838), and William Williams (1781-1840), saw further fruit towards the end of their long ministries as they were the instruments of awakening and converting many, especially from 1828 to 1830, and from 1832 onwards, following alarm at the threat of a cholera outbreak.

In 1839 a British edition of Finney's *Lectures on Revival* was published. This was soon followed by a Welsh translation, which was eagerly studied by many ministers who were concerned for revival in Wales. A number of awakenings occurred in North Wales in 1839 and 1840, which were followed by others in South Wales over the next three years, which were directly attributed by many to the study of Finney's work. Thomas Rees (1815-1885), who was a Congregational pastor in Aberdare and Llanelli, and later in Swansea, said that the awakening, which was known as 'Finney's Revival' was 'chiefly promoted' by the study of the book. Many of Finney's methods were adopted, with attention paid to those measures which were calculated to produce results. Some Welsh ministers, who had been involved in earlier awakenings felt that the revivals of 1839-1843 were, in contrast to earlier ones, 'of a far more equivocal character, having lost much of [their] spontaneity and irresistible power' (cited in Carwardine 1978b:479).

Sporadic awakenings also occurred in Ireland, where conversions from Catholicism continued and the defeat of Arianism among the Presbyterians brought new life to the evangelical movement in the north (Orr *ibid* 147, 152).

In Scotland the Evangelical party in the Church of Scotland continued to grow in strength under the leadership of Thomas Chalmers, with the Bonar brothers (John [1799-1863], Horatius [1808-1889] and Andrew [1810-1892]), Robert Murray M'Cheyne (1813-1843), W. H. Burns (1779-?) and others in various key parishes. In the summer of 1839 a revival broke out in Kilsyth,[23] near Glasgow, under the preaching of William Chalmers Burns (1815-1868), the son of the minister W. H. Burns, who for the previous seven years had encouraged prayer meetings for revival. The younger Burns also preached at Dundee from where M'Cheyne was absent due to ill health, and where the next three months saw crowded meetings night after night, with over 600 enquirers being instructed in the faith.[24] The revival soon spread all over Scotland, partly under the preaching of Burns,[25] but also independent of him, reaching the Lowlands, the Highlands and the Islands.[26]

In 1842 Chalmers and 473 other ministers left the Church of Scotland as a result of political moves, and formed the Free Church of Scotland. Other smaller Presbyterian bodies came together as a result of the awakening. Baptists and Congregationalists benefited from the revivals, and a number of interdenominational societies were formed both for overseas missionary work and for evangelism and social work at home.

Mainland Europe

Johann Gerhardt Oncken (1800-1884), a German who was converted in England in 1822 and became a colporteur of the Lower Saxony Tract Society which was formed in the same year, was baptised in 1834 in the River Elbe at Hamburg. From then until his death he was a vigorous evangelist, establishing Baptist churches throughout the German Federation and beyond. Baptist churches in Scandinavia, the Baltic States, Poland, Hungary (then part of the Habsburg Empire) and Romania owe their initial impetus to him (Wagner 1978:75-117). The phenomenal success of his work, especially in the first thirty years, is due largely to the spiritual revival which was at work at the time, both in the period we are now considering and also during the mid-century prayer revival (see next chapter).

In 1830 a British Methodist chaplain, George Scott, was employed by the British industrialist Samuel Owen to minister to his workmen in Stockholm, Sweden. He began, in defiance of the Conventicle Act of a hundred years before, to preach to Swedes. By 1832, profound spiritual results were seen, producing a genuine revival of evangelical Christianity. Scott was also active in temperance work and in schools, as well as in publishing an evangelical periodical. He was forced to leave the country in 1842, but the work was carried on by others, including Carl Olof Rosenius and Anders Wyberg. Some of the revival manifestations resembled those on the American frontier; what was referred to as the 'preaching sickness' affected many of the young people, who went into trances and prophesied coming judgment. Doctors and clergy treated it as an epidemic and prescribed various odd remedies, but the movement spread and the results in changed lives were indisputable. The revival continued through the 1840s and on into the 1850s. One notable convert was the internationally famous singer Jenny Lind, known as the 'Swedish nightingale', who gave up her stage career following her conversion.

In Norway, Hans Nielsen Hauge, who had been released from prison in 1814, died in 1824. In that same year the revival in Norway reached its height, as a host of lay preachers, or 'Readers' as they were called, continued Hauge's work. The year 1825 also witnessed revival in the province of Sunnmore. In 1833 a renewal of awakening came all over the country, which continued into the 1840s and 1850s, with a number of key preachers involved, such as Pastor Lyder Brun, Gustav Adolf Lammers and Gisle Johnson. The Inner Mission and other evangelical agencies developed from the awakening and missionary interest was stimulated.

Denmark was also affected by revival, but less strongly than Sweden, Norway and Finland. In the latter country, Paavo Ruotsalainen continued his work until 1857. Revival spread throughout the country in the 1830s, receded in the 1840s as a result of Russian imposition of anti-conventicle laws, but experienced a new surge later in the decade, which continued into the 1850s and had a strong and lasting effect on the national Church (Orr *ibid* 156-158).

There were significant spiritual impulses in Hungary in the late 1830s and early 1840s. Gottlieb August Wimmer (1791-1863), who was influenced by the Moravians, strongly advocated missionary activity by the Hungarian Reformed Church, as a result of which Samuel Bohn went as a missionary to Africa.

The Scottish Mission was set up in Budapest, ostensibly to minister to the Scottish workmen employed on the construction of the bridges over the Danube linking Buda with Pest, but in reality doing evangelistic work among the Jews of Budapest, as well as seeking to introduce a more evangelical emphasis into the Reformed and Lutheran Churches which were controlled by Rationalistic theology. Scottish ministers involved included Dr John Duncan, Rev. William Wingate, Rev. W. A. Allan and Rev. R. Smith.[27]

Spiritual blessing of a marked kind was experienced in both areas of their intended work. Many Jews were converted to Christ, some of whom became missionaries and also achieved prominence as preachers and biblical scholars. Alfred Edersheim (1825-1889) became a missionary to Jews in Jassy, Romania, and later achieved fame with a number of writings including *The Life and Times of Jesus the Messiah* (1883-1890). Adolph Saphir (1831-1891) served as a missionary to the Jews in Hamburg, and later wrote many well-known works. He maintained his interest in missionary work among Jews and other non-Christian peoples of Europe throughout his life. Other Jewish converts who also became missionaries were Alexander Tomorry who worked in Constantinople, and Moritz Bloch who served with the Moldavia-Wallachia mission of the Hungarian Reformed Church.

In 1843 a spiritual awakening took place among ministers of the Reformed and Lutheran Churches in Budapest and other places in Hungary. Many Rationalist clergy came to living faith. This had a number of effects: successful evangelism was undertaken by many in the country; the YMCA was set up in Budapest; foreign missions were stimulated and missions to the Jews received further impetus.[28]

South Africa

In the district of Grahamstown, which had previously experienced revival (see above p 133), a new wave of awakening began in 1831, spreading from the Wesleyan Church in the main town, and moving out to other towns and farms. The same chapel witnessed another extraordinary awakening in 1837, which again spread out to other areas. The 1831 revival produced a large number of ministerial and missionary candidates and resulted in missionary activity among the Bantu and Hottentot tribes.

The Evangelical awakenings in Britain and continental Europe produced a number of ministers who emigrated to South Africa and were very influential in reviving the churches. Andrew Murray from Scotland was one such. His more famous son and namesake was influential in the next period of widespread awakening. Missionaries also came from Britain, Europe (including Germany, France and Norway) and North America to work among the indigenous peoples, once more as the result of the awakenings there, and performed invaluable service which later bore abundant fruit. Among these were Joseph Williams, Robert Moffat (1795-1883), and David Livingstone (1813-1873), all with the London Missionary Society. Moffat witnessed an awakening among the Bantu tribes of Botswanaland, as did the Methodists among the Xhosa people of the Transkei and the Bantus in other areas (Orr *ibid* 168-172).

The Pacific Islands

The evangelisation of the islands of Polynesia was begun by John Williams (1796-1839) of the LMS in 1817. Following his patient work of visiting all the islands in the next seventeen years in which a number of converts were made, especially in Tonga, he returned to the British Isles from 1834 to 1838 to publicise the work and the need for more workers. During his absence a phenomenal awakening took place in Tonga with mass conversions. The revival spread to other islands, and National Tongan missionaries went to all the islands as missionaries. Tragically, Williams was killed and eaten by cannibals in the New Hebrides on his return to the Pacific in 1839. Another revival began in Tonga in 1846. In 1835 an evangelical revival began in Tahiti, and in 1837 a similar work began in Hawaii. Samoa was also affected by a number of outpourings of the Spirit which continued into the 1840s.

In the Fijian islands among the Melanesian people who were cannibals, Methodist missionaries started to work in 1835. Their initial work met with some success, but in 1845 a succession of revival-awakenings began which continued into the 1850s and resulted in the Christianising of the Fijian peoples.

The *Reveil* in Holland affected the Dutch in Indonesia, where missionaries had begun work in 1822, and a folk movement of vast proportions swept Minahassa, the northeastern peninsula of Sulawesi (Celebes) which made the whole area Christian within a couple of generations (Orr *ibid* 159-167).

Asia

In Armenia and Persia, work established by American missionaries among the ancient Eastern Churches, both Orthodox and Nestorian, was visited with revival in the 1830s and 1840s. The Protestant missionary effort in India received substantial accessions of workers from Britain, Europe and

North America as the direct result of the awakenings of the 1800s and following. Much of the work was of a pioneering kind, but there were examples of awakenings and folk movements here, also in Burma among the Karens, and in Ceylon. In Malabar in India, the work of Samuel Hebich (1803-1866), a German Lutheran who served with the Basel Mission, was particularly blessed with awakening (Orr *ibid* 173-177; Neill 1986:277ff).

Conclusion

The Second Evangelical Awakening, including its first and second phases together with the large-scale Resurgence from 1830 onwards, lasted around half a century, and produced major changes in the size, influence, and to a certain extent in the nature of the various Protestant Churches. In the United States, the Baptists and Methodists became the major denominations as the result of the Awakening in its various phases.

Building on the impetus and inspiration of the Great Awakening fifty years before, it made Evangelical Protestantism a significant force at every level in Great Britain, Europe and North America, and established strong churches in many places in the other continents. The Awakening provided the indispensible foundation for the overseas missions thrust of the second half of the century, especially as seen in the Volunteer Student Movement. The social impact, particularly in Britain and North America was considerable, and although the millennium did not arrive (as many in both Awakenings had hoped and prayed that it might) the influence and spread of a strong biblically-based Christianity was no mean achievement.

Notes

¹ Orr 1975:96-98 cites from contemporary accounts and gives the official denominational figures for the period. For an account of the Primitive Methodists in South Lincolnshire from 1817 onwards see Ambler 1989.

² The figures cited by Lovegrove (1988:185-186) for three Baptist Associations seem to indicate a steady growth in the number of churches over the period 1795-1830, with the most spectacular increases in the Western Association (covering the south west of the country).

³ From 1824 to 1835 there was a significant revival on the Isle of Lewis connected with the ministry of Andrew McLeod (see Glasgow Revival Tract Society 1839; also a lecture given by Rev John J. Murray at the Carey Conference 1990 which, hopefully, will appear in the magazine *Reformation Today*).

⁴ Samuel Hopkins (1721-1803), together with Joseph Bellamy (1719-1790) and Timothy Dwight (1752-1817), introduced modifications into the Calvinistic theology which Jonathan Edwards had adopted and slightly adapted before them. According to Hopkins, 'sin was essentially self-love but without legal imputation of Adam's sin to us. Man was responsible to seek a change of heart which would lead to "disinterested benevolence" in the life of the regenerate' (Marsden in Douglas ed 1978:482-483).

⁵ Finney's theology has often been characterised as 'Pelagian' (after Pelagius [c 383-409/410] whose ideas on human free will were condemned by the early Church), but it is arguable that it was not so much purely Pelagian, but rather was influenced by the further modification of Edwardean theology produced by Nathaniel William Taylor (1786-1858 [see Guelzo 1988:28-30]). This may be so, but it seems likely that Finney developed his own ideas independently of Taylor. See Sweet 1976:206-211.

⁶ The impression has often been gained from Finney's 'Memoirs' that the church in Adams, New York, which he was attending and where he was actually choir master, was without any experience of revival at the time, and that the preaching of the minister, George W. Gale, was without spiritual effect. However, the new critical edition of the Memoirs (Finney, ed Rosell & Dupuis 1989:14-15 n 57) shows that a revival was already in progress in Adams and a number of the neighbouring towns when Finney had his conversion experience, partly through Gale's preaching and partly also through that of a young man, Jedidiah Burchard. The conversion of Finney, who was one of the most stubborn opposers of the revival, was the trigger for the conversion of many of the young people with whom he had considerable influence.

In a similar way, the awakenings which accompanied Finney's early evangelistic work in Jefferson County and St Lawrence County in New

York State, on the eastern shore of Lake Ontario, were part of a large movement of the Spirit in the area which affected many other communities (Finney ed Rosell & Dupuis *ibid* 81 n 31).

[7] A sermon preached in 1831, which stirred up the opposition of the orthodox theologians of Princeton, was entitled 'Sinners Bound to Change Their Own Hearts'. The collection of sermons published in 1834, entitled *Sermons on Various Subjects* expounded in detail Finney's theology of human sinfulness and the nature of conversion (see Hardman 1987:275; also Sweet 1976:206-211).

[8] For details on these societies and other initiatives, see Cole (1954); Foster (1960); Griffin (1960). The seven societies mentioned, together with the American Board of Commissioners for Foreign Missions, founded in 1810, comprised the so-called 'Great Eight' benevolent societies, all of whom held their annual meetings in New York City each May. In addition to these, there were innumerable lesser societies promoting prison reform, preventing the desecration of the Sabbath, reclaiming prostitutes, etc.

[9] Details and statistics of the effects of the revival on the various denominations in different states, derived from the primary sources, can be found in Orr *ibid* 132-139).

[10] His volume of *Lectures on Revivals*, published in 1832, remains a standard work on the subject, expounding the classical understanding of the subject against the controversial 'new measures' and new theology of Charles Finney. Another volume also published in 1832 was *The History and Character of American Revivals, 1733-1832* by Calvin Colton. Finney was to publish his own lectures on the subject under the title of *Lectures on Revivals of Religion* in 1835. According to William McLoughlin who edited the modern critical edition of the 1835 *Lectures*, Finney seems to have made considerable use of Colton's work, without any acknowledgement of the fact (Finney ed McLoughlin 1960:lix).

Another volume, by ministers of the Church of Scotland, which also upheld the 'classical' view, was published in 1840 under the title of *The Revival of Religion* (reprinted 1984).

[11] The 'new measures' increasingly used by Finney, which were opposed by the more conservative Presbyterians and Congregationalists, but which Finney made a vital part of his evangelistic methods, were largely taken over from the Methodists. They included (1) public praying by women in mixed audiences, (2) protracted series of meetings (ie daily services), (3) colloquial language used by the preacher, (4) the anxious seat or bench at the front of the church where enquirers were invited to come for prayer and counselling at the close of the meeting, (5) the practice of praying for the conversion of individuals by name when they were present, and (6) immediate church membership for those professing conversion. Other practices which were

also condemned included (7) the invasion of towns by evangelists against the will of local pastors, (8) attacks on such pastors, and (9) too great familiarity with the Almighty in prayer (Carwardine 1978:327-340; Hardman *ibid* 84; Finney's own account of the means used to promote the revival at Rochester and elsewhere are given in his Memoirs, but were omitted from all published editions until the recent one [Finney ed Rosell & Dupuis *ibid* 320-323]).

[12] In later years Finney admitted that revivals had declined in effectiveness and depth since the publication of his *Lectures* in 1835 and the widespread adoption of the methods he had advocated in them. Even in 1836, in a lecture published in the *New York Evangelist*, he stated that, of all the converts of the previous decade of revivals, 'the great body of them are a disgrace to religion. Of what use would it be to have a thousand members added to the Church to be just such as are now in it'.

In 1845 and 1846, he published a number of letters in the *Oberlin Evangelist* which basically were critical of a number of his own methods, particularly as they had been used by others. He also blamed the churches for not nurturing the converts of the revivals and failing to bring them to spiritual maturity (They have been reprinted in book form [see Finney ed Dayton 1979]. Note also Hardman *ibid* 381-384; McLoughlin ed *ibid* li-lii). One of his main criticisms of recent evangelists was that they failed to rely on the power of God, rather than on their own powers of persuasion, to bring people to faith. Evangelism could plod on endlessly, but what was needed was a spontaneous outpouring of God's Spirit which would sweep thousands into the kingdom, as had happened from 1826 to 1831. As Hardman notes,

> Where now was Finney's concept that a 'prayed-down' revival (as opposed to the older ideas that they were sent at God's good time) was possible at any time? His earlier confidence that he could always bring about an awakening by 'means and measures' seemed to be failing him! (Hardman *ibid* 384).

See further below on ideas of 'How to promote a Revival'.

[13] The first 12,000 were sold in two years, but no more were printed in America until 1848, due to the financial crash of 1837 which resulted in the stereo type-plates being lost for ten years! However, many editions were published in Britain and it was translated into Welsh, French and (in 1903) into German. The English editions soon had a worldwide circulation.

[14] This was largely through the influence of Arthur (1786-1865) and Lewis (1788-1873) Tappan, wealthy New York merchants and prominent Christian philanthropists.

[15] In 1842 Finney spent a two-month period in Rochester, during which there was 'Another great revival' there, according to his 'Memoirs' (Finney

ed Rosell & Dupuis *ibid* 432-445). Jedidiah Burchard (1791-1864), through whose preaching the revivals at Adams began during which Finney was converted, was also preaching there at the time. According to Finney, 'Brother Burchard's labors were better calculated to attract the more excitable ones of the community than mine were' (*ibid* 433-434). Finney concentrated more on the upper classes, being especially concerned with members of the legal profession. He also spent considerable time urging his views on 'Christian perfection', which caused some problems (*ibid* 439 n 26).

[16] In his public advocacy of these causes, he adapted some of Finney's 'new measures' and used them to great effect! Sadly, he moved from his Evangelical faith to a broad liberalism when he married Angelina Grimke, a Quaker advocate of women's rights, and he eventually gave up all formal religious profession. He and his wife moved via a 'simple loving and following Jesus' finally into Unitarianism (Dayton 1976:25-34; Finney ed Rosell & Dupuis *ibid* 184-188 nn 67-86).

[17] Among the twenty-four 'Hindrances to Revivals' which he enumerates in Lecture 15 of the 1835 series, he includes 'Resistance to the Temperance Reform' and 'Churches tak[ing] wrong ground [ie not supporting] in regard to any question involving human rights', instancing slavery as an example (Finney ed Harding 1913:324-327).

[18] Both of these men later adopted extreme positions which alienated them from Finney.

[19] Aitken was a Methodist who became a High-Church Anglican. He wrote an introduction to an edition of Finney's lectures on Revival which appeared in 1838.

[20] Among the Congregationalists, John Angell James (1789-1859) of Carr's Lane Church, Birmingham, was a tireless advocate of revival. He introduced William Sprague's book on the subject to the British public, and also wrote a preface to an edition of Finney's lectures in 1838!

Another Congregational minister, George Redford (1785-1860) from Worcester, also supported vigorous attempts to produce revival. He pioneered the use of protracted meetings in England in 1837.

The American Congregational minister Edward Norris Kirk (1802-1874) visited England for an evangelistic tour during this period of spiritual resurgence. It was under his ministry in America that D. L. Moody was converted and as a revival preacher he was judged by one of his contemporaries, Theodore Cuyler, as 'deserv[ing] a place in the triumvirate with Finney and Moody' (cited in Finney ed Rosell & Dupuis *ibid* 561 n 8).

[21] See Carwardine 1978 for a detailed study of the period 1790-1865. He makes use of membership figures of British and American Methodism to plot a number of periods of rapid growth. He also mentions the work of a number of the itinerant evangelists of the time.

[22] It is ironic that Bunting was the product of revival prayer meetings in Manchester. However, after clashing with some of the more radical spirits among the revival preachers, he became a firm upholder of ministerial oversight and control.

[23] This was the site of a revival nearly 100 years before (see above, Chapter 5).

[24] In December 1840, the Presbytery of Aberdeen, which included the parish of Dundee where M'Cheyne was minister, appointed a committee to enquire into the revivals which had recently occurred or were still taking place. A copy of the questions and of M'Cheyne's reply is to be found in M'Cheyne ed Bonar 1844 (repr 1966):543-551.

[25] Burns also preached in Ireland and Canada with great awakening power attending his ministry. In 1846 he went to China as a missionary, where he worked for twenty-two years with a number of encouraging results, but with no repetition of the earlier revival scenes in Scotland. He was a great help to the young Hudson Taylor, who spoke of his help with great appreciation, and also laid the foundation for future Presbyterian work in southern China and in Manchuria (Taylor 1911; 1918; Douglas ed 1978:169).

[26] The lectures on *The Revival of Religion* referred to above (note 10), which were delivered and published in 1840, were given by a number of the ministers directly involved in the revival.

[27] Archduchess Maria Dorothea, who had come from Wurttenberg as the third wife of the Grand Archduke, and who had a strong Pietistic faith, had prayed for more evangelical life in the churches in Hungary. She welcomed the Scottish missionaries as the answer to her prayers and gave them all the support she could.

[28] Information in English on the work in Hungary is very hard to find. I am indebted to Anne-Marie Kool, a Dutch doctoral candidate researching the history of the missionary work of the Hungarian Churches in Budapest for a number of these facts.

CHAPTER 9

THE THIRD EVANGELICAL AWAKENING

THE MID-CENTURY PRAYER REVIVAL (1857-1859) AND ITS EFFECTS

D R J. EDWIN ORR'S original Oxford D.Phil. thesis on the Revival of 1858-1859 was entitled 'The Second Evangelical Awakening in Britain'. Further research by Dr Orr caused him to recognise the the Revival of 1795 and its continuance until the 1830s. Consequently this next Awakening merits the title of the Third Great Awakening.[1]

The awakening began in North America, and spread to the British Isles. News of what was happening in both these places reached South Africa, Australia, India, and elsewhere, and sent Christians to prayer, as a result of which similar scenes to those in the original countries were witnessed.

The years from 1845 to 1855 had seen a spiritual decline in the United States. The apocalyptic excitement aroused by the speculations of William Miller (1782-1849), who predicted that Christ would return visibly in 1843, and then in 1844, was followed by widespread disillusion with spiritual matters, when the prophecies were not fulfilled. Many lost their faith, and the churches were subjected to ridicule and cynicism. The Mexican-American War of 1846-1848 also took up people's attention, and financial and commercial prosperity, following the financial panic of 1833-1837, also diverted attention from spiritual realities. However, a further period of financial panic and crisis in 1856-1857 prepared many for the new awakening which soon followed.[2]

In Britain also, the decade around the middle of the century was one of spiritual uncertainty. In 1846, the Wesleyan Methodist Conference, under the influence of Jabez Bunting, the 'unchallenged leader of the "High Church" party in Methodism', sought to have James Caughey recalled to America by the bishops of the Methodist Episcopalian Church there. Rather than cause a split among the Wesleyans, Caughey returned to America in 1847, but in 1849-1850 a schism occurred anyway (Carwardine 1978:126-133). Caughey's departure brought to an end six years of extremely fruitful evangelistic work which had been attended with revival blessing (*ibid* 107-126).

Charles Finney's first visit to Britain, from 1849 till 1851, was attended with only moderate success. He preached in Nonconformist chapels in Houghton, Huntingdonshire, in Worcester, and in Birmingham. His most successful campaign lasted for ten months at Whitefield's Tabernacle in London, where he preached regularly to crowded meetings, and where thousands professed conversion. However, Finney himself viewed the results of the visit with mixed emotions. There was no tide of revival moving at the time, and his visit failed to produce one (Carwardine 1978:134-155; Hardman 1987:395-423).

Precursors of the Prayer Awakening

Among the precursors of the more general awakening which came at the close of the decade we may mention the ministry of Charles Haddon Spurgeon (1834-1892) in London from February 1854 onwards. The great crowds in New Park Street Baptist Chapel made a move to Exeter Hall necessary in February 1855, which was followed by another move in October 1856 to the Royal Gardens Music Hall in Surrey. Two other large secular halls were used until, in 1861, the congregation moved into the newly-built Metropolitan Tabernacle. In

December 1859 Spurgeon wrote in the preface to the volume of his sermons preached and published in that year,

> The times of refreshing from the presence of the Lord have at last dawned upon our land...In the midst of these new displays of divine love, it is very pleasant to see the spots which have long been favoured retaining their wonted fruitfulness and rejoicing with joy unspeakable in progressing prosperity. Such is the case with the Church to which these sermons were addressed from the pulpit...For six years the dew has never ceased to fall, and the rain has never been withheld. At this time, the converts are more numerous than heretofore, and the zeal of the church groweth exceedingly (Spurgeon 1860:v).[3]

In the United States, a revival began in the autumn of 1855 in the University of Rochester, which had been established by the Baptists in 1850, through the witness of a senior student Kingman Knott. In December, Finney arrived in the city for the third time to begin a series of meetings, in response to urgent requests from a number of citzens, some of whom were not attached to any church. According to Finney, prayer meetings for revival had been held during the previous summer, and many felt that they were on the eve of a great revival. Augustus Hopkins Strong (1836-1921), who was converted at the time and later became president of the theological seminary in Rochester, reckoned that 1,000 people joined the churches as a result of the revival that followed (Strong 1899:365).[4]

A further precursor of what was soon to follow may be seen in the 'Revival Extraordinary' (as a Christian journal described it) which took place in Canada at Hamilton, Ontario, under the evangelistic preaching of Americans Walter and Phoebe Palmer (1804-1883 and 1807-1874)[5] in October 1857. For many years previously they had preached in churches and camp-meetings both evangelistically and proclaiming a 'Deeper Life' holiness teaching. Following a week of meetings in Hamilton, between five and six hundred professed conversion, and in camp-meetings which they held throughout Ontario and Quebec, attendances ranged from 5,000 to 6,000 (Carwardine 1978a:182; Christian History 1989:32-33).

In the same year James Caughey, who had continued to evangelise in Canada and the north-eastern States of America with great success, returned to England to work among non-Wesleyan Methodist churches. A year of preaching in Sheffield produced converts 'by the cart load' (the *Revivalist* of 1859, cited in Carwardine 1978:175). From there he moved on to other towns in the north of England in 1858 and 1859, by which time the awakening was becoming general.

The Prayer Revival: the United States

At a Presbyterian convention held in Pittsburgh, Pennsylvania from December 1 to 3, 1857, ministers and laymen from the synods of Pittsburgh, Allegheny, Wheeling and Ohio met for protracted prayer and discussion on the need for revival and re-awakening. The first Sunday of the new year was used to preach on the subject, and the following Thursday was observed as a day of humiliation, fasting and prayer. A similar convention was held in Cincinatti in May 1858. In December 1857, Baptists in New York State set aside one day each week for an all-day meeting of intercession for an outpouring of the Spirit. Methodists and other evangelical denominations held similar meetings. On July 1 1857, a quiet businessman, Jeremiah Lanphier (b 1809), was appointed as a city missionary in downtown New York City, based in the North Dutch Reformed Church in Fulton Street, Lower Manhattan. In September, he decided to start a noonday prayer meeting once a week, and had a number of handbills printed to advertise the meetings. On the first day, September 23, six men gathered to pray. By October 17 they had increased to twenty and the meetings were being held daily. At this time the revival in Hamilton, Ontario, began. The stock market crash, which left many bankrupt, occurred in the second week of October, but it is not true, as some modern writers have claimed (eg McLoughlin 1959:163), that the subsequent revival was caused by the financial crisis. The crash may have turned many from confidence in material things to an awareness of eternal realities, but the work of prayer, and the beginnings of awakening were already taking place. As Hardman says, 'The panic was the catalyst that triggered the awakening' (Hardman *ibid* 431).

In New York, within six months 10,000 business men were meeting daily to pray in around 150 different groups, and similar prayer meetings soon began to spring up in other cities, such as Philadelphia, and Boston,[6] where Finney was conducting evangelistic meetings. In Chicago, the Metropolitan Theatre was filled every day by 2,000 people meeting for prayer. In Louisville, Kentucky, several thousand crowded each day into the Masonic Temple, and overflow meetings were held around the city. In Cleveland, Ohio, the attendance was around 2,000 each day, and in St Louis, Missouri all the churches were filled for months on end (Smith 1957: 63-72; Christian History 1989:32-33).[7]

The pattern of the prayer meetings was very simple and did not vary from city to city. Meetings had to begin and end on time. Any person, male or female, might pray, give a testimony or an exhortation, or lead in singing as he or she 'felt led'. Although many ministers attended, lay-people provided the leadership.[8]

The awakening which followed soon spread to all parts of the nation.[9] Within two years, over a million people had been added to the churches, at a rate of 10,000 each week. At one time 50,000 conversions were being reported weekly. The northern states from the Atlantic coast to the frontier settlements in the west were all affected, as were the southern states, where slavery was increasingly occupying attention (Candler 1904).

The revival influenced the great cities, but also the towns, villages and rural areas. San Francisco and Southern California were affected, as news from the east reached the West Coast and similar prayer meetings were started there. Colleges and universities were affected, including Harvard, Yale and Princeton in addition to scores of others (Many details in Orr *ibid* 7-30. See also his earlier study [1952], which is entirely devoted to the American phase of the work). At Yale, over 200 of the 447 students were converted; at Princeton, of the 272 students, 102 professed faith and fifty entered the Christian ministry. At Amhurst, nearly the whole student body was converted in 1858 (Cairns *ibid* 150).

Awakenings also occurred in the British West Indies, including the Bahamas, Jamaica, and the Leeward and Windward Islands. Unlike the United States where no fanaticism was reported, among the liberated slaves of the West Indies there were examples of 'unhealthy excitement and religious hysteria' (according to E A Payne, cited in Orr *ibid* 33).

In the United States, the Civil War did not extinguish the Revival. A major revival occurred in the Confederate Army between 1862 and 1864; according to some estimates, 150,000 were converted (Jones 1887).

In 1858, D. L. Moody (1837-1899) began his Christian work in Chicago, and in 1860 gave up his business interests to concentrate full-time on the burgeoning work in Sunday School and YMCA. He made evangelistic trips to the Northern armies, supported by the YMCA.

The decades following the end of the war saw phenomenal growth among the newly emancipated Blacks. In fifty years, Black church membership grew fourfold to 4.5 million, 22 per cent of the Black population (Latourette 1939 IV:452). The new, radically altered social conditions offered a fresh possibility for renewal and revival.

The British Isles

Ulster

As in the United States, where the Revival began through prayer meetings, particularly those held in New York City, so in Europe the same was true. A young Irishman, James McQuilkin, who was converted in November 1856, began to read George Muller's *Narrative* in January 1857. He was so impressed by the record of God's answers to prayer recorded by Muller, particularly in connection with the orphanage work in Bristol, that he began to pray with one, and then three others, for God's blessing on their Christian work. In late Autumn 1857 as the first news of the Revival in America began to reach the British Isles McQuilkin said, 'Why may we not have such a blessed work here, seeing that God did such great things for Mr Muller, simply in answer to prayer?' (see Muller 1906: 448-450).

Throughout 1858, McQuilkin and his friends continued to pray, and increasingly people were converted and added to their prayer meetings. In February 1859 they began prayer meetings in a Presbyterian Church in Ahoghill, where, after initially encountering opposition and mockery, they soon found their meetings attended by crowds. For one meeting on March 14, the crowd inside the church was so great that there was the danger of the gallery collapsing, while outside a further 3,000 were gathered. One of McQuilkin's friends addressed the crowd out in the street, and a profound sense of conviction of sin swept through the people. In April, McQuilkin went to Ballymena, and in May to Belfast; in both places the revival took hold, and soon spread to other towns and out into the countryside. Belfast witnessed united prayer meetings, supported by virtually all the churches and their clergy. Church buildings were filled and crowds of 15,000 and 20,000 met in the open air. Six of the nine northern counties experienced the revival in great power, especially those where the Protestant Churches were strong (Orr 1974:45-51).

Scotland

In Scotland, news of what was happening in the United States and Ulster provoked a deepened desire for a repetition of such events there, together with an increased volume of prayer for such an awakening. The revival began in Aberdeen in the Autumn of 1858, and by the middle of 1859, in Glasgow, where amazing scenes of crowds attending services and prayer meetings were reported in the Christian and secular press. In

1859-1860, the whole of southwest Scotland was affected. In 1861 a new wave broke out in the same area, and spread north to the Highlands, the Western Isles and the Orkneys. Much of the northeast of Scotland was affected in 1859, scarcely a town or village between Aberdeen and Inverness being unaffected, and it continued to spread until the whole country and all the Protestant denominations were affected (Orr *ibid* 52-58).[10]

Charles Finney was preaching in Edinburgh during August, September and October of 1859, when the revival was at its height. From there he moved to Aberdeen, where he reported after some time that 'numbers ha[ve] been converted, and a very interesting change was manifestly coming over [the] congregation and over that city' (Finney ed Rosell & Dupuis *ibid* 596).

Wales
The revival began in Wales in 1858, and reached its height in 1859 and 1860. News of the American Revival stirred up many Christians to pray for a similar visitation to come to the principality. In addition, Humphrey Jones (1832-1895), a Welsh-born Methodist evangelist who had been in America during the outbreak of the revival there, returned to Wales in June 1858. He influenced David Morgan (1814-1888), a Calvinistic Methodist minister, who had been praying for an outpouring of the Spirit for the previous ten years. Under their ministry and that of others, and following increased prayer for revival especially at the Congregational Association meetings at Beaufort on June 29 and 30, 1859, the awakening spread through the whole of the country, affecting every county. The spiritual and moral life of the whole land was profoundly affected; crime decreased dramatically in the year following the revival. Sadly, Humphrey Jones, exhausted through his preaching, travelling and other exertions, suffered a temporary mental aberration which permanently damaged his ministry. He claimed to receive divine revelations, which he passed on to the church in prophecies, in one of which he claimed that the Holy Spirit would descend in bodily form at Aberystwyth on a certain date and at a certain time, which

event would inaugurate the millennium. He eventually came to his senses, but his health and his spiritual effectiveness were permanently damaged (Evans 1959: 49-50).

David Morgan and other Welsh ministers continued to enjoy amazing spiritual results in their preaching, but there were also a number of visits from outside evangelists, especially in South Wales. Walter and Phoebe Palmer, the American evangelists, had arrived from America in 1859, and had spent time in London, Ulster, the north-east of England and in Scotland conducting special revival services. They visited Cardiff in 1862, and for thirty days 'a remarkable work of the Spirit' was experienced there. The following year William and Catherine Booth (1829-1912 and 1829-1890), who were Methodist evangelists and who were later to form the Salvation Army, also visited Cardiff and preached to great crowds.

From contemporary figures, it is estimated that 110,000 were converted and added to the churches as a result of the revival in Wales. The Calvinistic Methodist and Congregational Churches each received around 36,000 new members, the Baptists about 14,000, the Wesleyan Methodists around 5,000, and the Anglican Church about 20,000 (Evans 1959:75).

England

In England, the revival began in the north of the country, and then moved south, first to the Midlands and finally to East Anglia, London, the Home Counties and the South-West. Everywhere it seems that the outbreak of the revival itself was preceded by intercession for the blessing, sometimes in small home prayer meetings, sometimes in great public gatherings, such as that held on January 10, 1860 in the Agricultural Hall in Islington.

The visit of the Palmers to Newcastle in the late summer of 1859 began an awakening which increased in strength and spread to the surrounding area. Across the River Tyne in Gateshead, the New Connection Methodist Church of which William Booth was pastor experienced revival in 1859. William, joined in preaching by his wife Catherine, visited

Hartlepool, where 250 were converted. On the northwest coast, Carlisle, Liverpool and Manchester experienced revival.

Charles Finney had arrived in England with his second wife in the spring of 1959. After preaching for three months in London with moderate success, he had moved to Edinburgh and thence to Aberdeen. He then visited Bolton, where the greatest blessing of his British trip was experienced, and also Manchester, where it was less evident. In Bolton, where the various evangelical churches were already actively seeking revival and where Elizabeth Finney was welcomed in her work among the women, particularly in encouraging women's prayer meetings, a total of 2,000 enquirers and 1,200 converts were recorded (Carwardine *ibid* 179; Hardman *ibid* 439; Finney ed Rosell & Dupuis *ibid* 573-614).

In the Midlands, prayer meetings began to multiply in the summer of 1859 and on into the spring of 1860. The evangelistic phase of the awakening followed in 1861 and reached its climax in 1863 with campaigns held by the Palmers and the Booths in Birmingham, Walsall, and many other places in the area.

In East Anglia, prayer meetings for revival resulted in the quickening of believers, followed by the conversion of outsiders. In Shropshire, on the Welsh border, prayer meetings in 1859 were followed by revival in 1861.

In February 1859, Charles Haddon Spurgeon's congregation at New Park Street Chapel had been forced to move to the considerably larger Exeter Hall. On March 1 he preached to an overflowing congregation at Whitefield's Tabernacle, then to an open-air crowd of 10,000 on Clapham Common on July 10, and to another open-air meeting in Havant on July 12. On July 20 he preached in Wales for the first time, again in the open-air, to a congregation of between 9,000 and 10,000 people. He also preached in the open-air in other places in southern England (Spurgeon 1959:11).

In London in 1860, theatres were used for Sunday evening services, which were attended by vast crowds of people, as were services in Westminster Abbey and St Paul's Cathedral.

Dorset, Bristol, Somerset, Devon and Cornwall (where the Booths laboured with great success) all experienced revival, as did Oxford and Cambridge Universities, from which came many strong Evangelical leaders of the Church of England in the following decades.

James Caughey returned to England from America in August 1860, and preached with great success among the United Methodist Free Churches in the Midlands, Lincolnshire and the industrial North. He also spent three months in Bristol in the south-west. He left England again in August 1862 when his health was beginning to give way, and made his final visit in 1864-1866. According to Carwardine, even in 'the fallow period of the mid-1860s, when most churches experienced only very limited growth...for short periods Caughey was still able to recapture past glories' (Carwardine *ibid* 176).[11]

CONTINENTAL EUROPE

Sweden and Norway benefited from news of the revival in North America and Britain. The Swedish movement affected Norway as evangelists travelled from one country to the other, and the Norwegian Church experienced one of its most fruitful periods of growth. The Danish island of Bornholm was the scene of profound awakening in the 1860s.

Switzerland, France and Belgium were influenced by revival movements, as a result of news from Ulster. Germany experienced many local awakenings two decades later through the influence of evangelists converted in the 1857-1859 Revival in America and Britain. In eastern Bohemia and also in its capital Prague, then part of the Habsburg Empire, there were awakenings out of which a new free evangelical denomination, the Church of Brethren, grew.

In the western parts of the Russian Empire, German settlers experienced awakenings. The 'Stundists'[12] were formed among Russian Christians as a result. Following the visits of Johann Gerhardt Oncken in 1869, they were baptised as believers and became one of the sources of modern Russian

Baptists (Sawatsky 1981:33-35). The evangelistic ministry in St Petersburg during the 1870s of Lord Radstock (1833-1913), followed by the itinerant ministry of the German-born Frederick William Baedeker (1823-1906), produced great numbers of converts among the Russian aristocracy as well as among the ordinary people.[13]

Lord Radstock was converted when he was serving in the Crimea during the war between Britain and Russia (1853-1856). On his return to England, he inherited the title of 3rd Baron Radstock and married two years later. In the wake of the Prayer Revival, he began preaching and found his efforts meeting with amazing results. Dr Baedeker was converted through his preaching in Weston-super-Mare in 1866. He was also involved in a healing ministry (Trotter n d 22-26). He preached in Holland in 1867 and made three visits to Russia, in 1874, 1875 and 1878. As a result of his preaching in the drawing rooms of the Russian nobility, many of the aristocracy were converted and a spiritual awakening resulted. Among the converts were Princess Catherine Galitsin, Princess Natalie Lieven, Count Korff the Lord Chamberlain of the Czar's Court, Count Brobinsky the Minister of the Interior, and Colonel of the Guard V. A. Pashkov. At the height of the revival, forty aristocratic homes were open to Radstock for his preaching. He also introduced Dr Baedeker to many in positions of authority, which later made it possible for Baedeker to traverse Siberia, visiting prisons in order to preach, and distributing vast numbers of Scriptures. Pashkov continued the work when Radstock left Russia after his first visit, and when he was expelled in 1878.[14] He continued to hold evangelistic meetings in spite of Orthodox opposition (between 1,000 and 1,300 were often present at services held in his palace [Muller 1906:546][15]) and he engaged in philanthropic work, using his great wealth. However, he and Korff were banished in 1884 and died in exile. The Pashkovites continued in spite of severe persecution (Dr Baedeker found some of them in his visits to prisons in Siberia and elsewhere), and they eventually became part of the modern Evangelical Christian-Baptist group which is still active in the Soviet Union today (On Radstock see Trotter n d: Fountain 1988. On Radstock, Pashkov and the movement which resulted, see Heier 1970. On Baedeker see Latimer 1907).

The South Seas

In Australia in mid-1859, news of the revival in the United States and in Britain caused the formation of united prayer meetings for revival in Melbourne, Sydney and elsewhere. Revivals soon followed in many cities as well as in the gold-fields. The movement of revival associated with prayer meetings had passed its peak by 1861, but a new, evangelistic phase began in 1863, particularly associated with the visit of William Taylor (1821-1902), an American Methodist. From 1863 to 1865, he preached with great success in many places in Australia, as well as in Tasmania and New Zealand. In 1860 revival had already been felt in New Zealand.

In Tonga and Fiji, there was steady growth throughout the decade 1854-1864, but the years 1859-1863 were particularly fruitful (Methodist statistics in Orr *ibid* 92). In Hawaii, the years 1860-1861 were times of revival and great ingathering, which also affected the Hawaiian missionary work in Micronesia. Indonesia experienced revivals and folk movements in different places.

Southern Africa

News of the American Revival reached American missionaries in Natal in 1858, spread to British Wesleyan missionaries, and soon produced an awakening among the Zulus which continued for a number of years and was followed by a new wave in 1866, associated with a Zulu chief, Pamla, who became an evangelist. Revivals occurred in 1857 at Grahamstown, but, most notably, in 1860 at Worcester, where Andrew Murray Jr (1828-1917) was the minister, through a Fingo servant girl (See the story in Orr *ibid* 96-98). Other places also experienced awakening at the same time or soon after, and eventually the revival reached all parts of the country. The visit of William Taylor produced a spiritual movement, especially among the black population, beginning with the Xhosa. He preached all over the country among black and white with great effect and with thousands of converts resulting.

Asia in general and India in particular

In 1860 revivals took place in Shanghai among the missionaries and in a number of places among the small groups of Chinese believers. In the same year there was an awakening in Beirut, Lebanon. In 1859 a new awakening took place among Nestorian Christians in Iran, and in 1861 among Armenians in Central Turkey.

In India, as in other places, news of the revivals in the United States and Britain produced a prayerful concern for awakening there. Prayer movements among English-speaking people in Calcutta, Bombay and Madras produced spiritual blessing in the communities there, but in 1860 an amazing revival took place among the indigenous people in Tamilnad, which was accompanied by public agony over conviction of sin, tongues, visions and prophecies. Twelve years later there was a similar awakening in Kerala, out of which the Mar Thoma Church developed. People movements also occurred in a number of places. In 1870, William Taylor visited India, and once more his ministry was attended with remarkable results (Details in Orr *ibid* 102-110).

Effects of the Prayer Revival

The 1859 Revival was in many ways *a lay revival*. Certainly, lay people were prominent in many aspects of it, as well as in much that resulted from it. Many movements in which lay people were active developed or grew as a result of the Revival, notably the YMCA, particularly in its growth in America, the Salvation Army, the Keswick Movement (although ministers were also prominent here), Christian Unions in universities, and the Sunday School movement. The *missionary movement* received a new injection of candidates at a time when, in various parts of the world, the political situation made new thrusts possible.[16]

A number of itinerant evangelists came to prominence in the Revival, notably the Palmers, the Booths, William Taylor, and Dwight L. Moody,[17] together with many others whose spheres of influence were less widespread. Itineracy had begun in the Great Awakening, had continued in the years preceding the Second Awakening, and had further grown in the Second Awakening itself. In America, following the Resurgence of 1830, the numbers were further added to with men like the Presbyterians Jedidiah Burchard and Daniel Baker, the Congregationalist Edward Norris Kirk (through whom D. L. Moody was converted), the Baptists Jacob Knapp and Jabez Swan, and Methodists like John Newland Maffitt, James Caughey (who visited Britain a number of times) and John S. Inskip. Their numbers were further swollen following the mid-century Prayer Revival with such men as Absalom Earle, Emerson Andrews, Edward P. Hammond, and Orson Parker, and even the occasional woman, like Maggie Van Newton (Weisberger 1958:135-137). In Britain there were men such as Humphrey Jones, Richard Weaver, Reginald Radcliffe, Brownlow North, William Carter, Robert Aitken, and many others (Kent 1978:passim).

THE RESURGENCE OF 1882 ONWARD

Edwin Orr, in one of his last publications (Orr 1981:33-40), distinguishes a 'Resurgence' in the years 1882 onwards, which grew out of the mid-century prayer revival, and which continued its influence.

Moody's British campaign of 1881-1883 has already been mentioned. D.P.Thomson, a Church of Scotland missioner, has pointed out that, unlike Moody's previous British visits, the revival spirit was less evident at the time of this trip, although great blessing did attend the campaigns.

Moody's influence was also felt in many places beyond Britain and America in the ministries of others whom the Lord used. Many countries in Europe and Africa were profoundly affected by the evangelistic ministries of those who were themselves influenced by Moody, such as Fredrik Franson (1852-1908) and August Skogsbergh in Sweden, and Professor Theodor Christlieb (1833-1889) in Germany.

Moody's Cambridge mission in 1882, while he was in England, was the beginning of a worldwide interdenominational student missionary movement. Christian Associations in the USA, and Christian Unions in the UK had been formed as a direct outcome of the 1858-1859 Revival, the former affiliated with the YMCA. Moody's influence was the catalyst which made this movement into a world missionary movement. It was also through his influence that 'the Cambridge Seven', which included the England cricketer C.T.Studd (1862-1931), went to China as missionaries in 1885. In 1912 Studd also founded a missionary society to reach parts of Africa. Wilfred Grenfell (1865-1940), who later became a missionary to Labrador, was also converted through Moody, at a tent mission in East London in 1885.

Moody began to preach in American universities in 1885, and the following year held a conference at Mount Hermon, Massachusetts for 250 students from 100 colleges and universities, at which 100 volunteered as missionaries following an address by Robert Wilder, the son of one of the 1806 Haystack prayer meeting missionaries. In 1886, the Student Volunteer Movement for Foreign Missions was formed, with John R. Mott (1865-1955) as chairman. In the academic year 1887-1888 there were 3,000 volunteers for mission, and the numbers multiplied each year. The movement spread to Britain, and then around the world, and the resulting World's Student Christian Federation provided the source for a large proportion of the outstanding leaders of twentieth-century Protestant Christianity.

In 1883 D. L. Moody formed the Moody Bible Institute, with the training of missionaries as one of its main aims. Reuben A. Torrey (1856-1928) was its first superintendent. In 1886, A.B.Simpson (1844-1919), who had been converted in the 1858 Revival, called a summer convention out of which the Christian and Missionary Alliance was formed.

The modern Christian Endeavour movement began as a result of a period of revival in Portland, Maine, in 1880-1881, where Francis E. Clark (1851-1927) organised the converts into societies for training and growth. By 1895, there were 38,000 societies with 2,225,000 members in many places throughout the world.

In the United States and Canada, men like Samuel Porter Jones (1847-1906), known as 'the Moody of the South',[18] and J.Wilbur Chapman (1859-1918), and a little later William Ashley 'Billy' Sunday (1862-1935), rose to prominence as evangelists during and after the period of resurgence.

In South Africa, Andrew Murray (1828-1917) and Spencer Walton were instrumental in awakenings and accompanying evangelism. In Australia and New Zealand, the ministries of John MacNeil and George Grubb were similarly blessed.

The 1880s witnessed revivals in many missionary areas, such as Japan, where it was reported in 1883 that 'a spirit of religious revival bringing times of refreshing from the presence of the Lord is spreading in Japan', resulting in five years of rapid growth, with adult membership increasing from 4,000 to 30,000. In China, the CIM work grew with the arrival of considerable numbers of missionaries, many of whom had been converted or called to missionary service as a result of the Resurgence. Denominational societies likewise benefitted. Missionary work began in Korea in the same period. In India, the number of medical evangelists, which had grown from seven to twenty-eight between 1859 and 1882, had increased twenty-fold by 1895, with 168 Indian doctors assisting them. Revivals were reported in Kerala and Tamilnad, and forward movements in many other places.

In Africa, many missionary societies made great advances after years of difficulty and slow growth. In 1884, the British Livingstone Inland Mission saw a remarkable movement of the Spirit in the Congo. At one station, Banza Manteke, where the missionary was Henry Richards, 1,000 converts were added to the church by 1887 and a total of 2,000 by 1889, during which year 950 were baptised. Similar work was seen at other stations, and it soon spread to American Baptists in the area. In East Africa, the Anglican mission experienced opposition and martyrdom, particularly with the murder of Bishop James Hannington (1847-1885). However, in 1893, as one of the missionaries sought a new empowering by the Spirit, revival and awakening broke out which in the ensuing fifteen years caused remarkable growth. The number of lay teachers grew from 75 to 2,032, communicants from 230 to 18,041, those baptised from 1,140 to 62,716, and catechumens from 230 to 2,563 (Orr 1981:38-39).

In Southern Africa, Madagascar and Australia there were revivals and awakenings among the indigenous peoples. In Nicaragua and Chile, alone among the Latin American countries, there were awakenings. In Armenia there was an evangelical revival in 1889 attending the evangelistic work of Haroutune Jenanian of Tarsus.

The Resurgence of the 1880s was thus the continuation of the mid-century Prayer Revival of the 1850s, and secured a worldwide missionary outcome to the initial impulse.

Notes

[1] It is a little surprising that Orr spoke of the 1859 Revival as the Second Evangelical Awakening in the first place, because the Revival of the 1790s was already generally recognised.

An English writer, John Kent, disagrees with Orr that the movement in England in 1859 deserves to be called an evangelical awakening. In his chapter '1859: The Failure of English Revivalism' he says of Orr's book; 'Though widely known, Orr's book did not make a convincing case for the view that what happened in the 1860s was comparable in size and significance to the eighteenth century evangelical revival' (Kent 1978:72 note). He also goes on to say

It is a fundamental weakness of J. E. Orr's *The Second Evangelical Awakening* (1949) that the author gave no attention to the way in which the campaign to work up an English revival in 1860-1 split the

Evangelical world, though one ought to expect such a division in view of the growth of the 'new evangelicalism' after 1830. But Orr's book is committed to a unitary view of 'evangelicalism', and his chapter on 'Opposition to the Revival' was concerned entirely with defending the reputation of the Ulster Revival against the criticisms which were in fact made by contemporaries on the proper ground that it encouraged hysterical phenomena. Orr, however, would have found it difficult to talk about a 'second evangelical awakening' if he had first had to admit that the main body of evangelical Anglicans remained either indifferent or hostile to the English lay revivalists, and that on theological as well as on more personal grounds (*ibid* 111-112).

While Kent is correct to stress the differences among evangelicals, particularly the attitude of more conservative-minded evangelical clergymen who frowned on the itinerancy and unusual methods of men like Reginald Radcliffe (1825-1895) and Richard Weaver (1827-1896), he is wrong in dismissing the revival movement of the period as less than a genuine movement of awakening. He also overstates Orr's contention about the 1859 Awakening. Orr was concerned to establish that it was a genuine revival movement, which ought to be seen as the same kind of revival as the eighteenth-century one, not as being equal to it in significance.

Similarly on the Awakening in America, William G. McLoughlin says that 'the religious excitement of 1857-1858 scarcely deserved to be called the Third Great Awakening' (McLoughlin 1959:163), although earlier in the same book (*ibid* 10), as well as in his more recent volume (1978), he refers to the 'Third Great Awakening', which had three phases.

A more sympathetic verdict is given by Keith Hardman who says:

> Historians have almost ignored the Awakening of 1858...Even several of the standard histories of awakenings hardly mention it, or they discount its effects, partially because it was so lacking in fanaticism or sensationalism and was largely led by laymen (Hardman 1987: 496 note 18).

[2] Timothy Smith has a chapter on 'The Resurgence of Revivalism 1840-1857' (Smith 1957:45-62), but the chapter deals with the divisions among the churches over the adoption of the 'New Measures' of Finney, rather than with accounts of revivals taking place. He does, however, cite two articles by Robert Baird written in 1849 and defending the thesis that a state of continuous awakening was the normal condition of the Church, together with references to accounts of revivals in *The Christian Union and Religious Memorial* of 1848 and 1849 (*ibid* 45 & note).

[3] Preaching on Revival on January 11, 1874, he mentions with approval the evangelistic missions of D. L. Moody and Ira D. Sankey, and expresses his belief that 'At this time...there are manifest the most pleasing signs that God is about to work among his people'. He then says,

As a church we have always felt a delight in any work which has to be done for God of this kind, and we have enjoyed for many years a continuous visitation of grace. That which would have been a revival anywhere else has been our ordinary condition, for which we are thankful. By the space of these twenty years, almost without rise or fall, God has continued to increase our numbers with souls saved by the preaching of his truth (Spurgeon 1875:13-14).

[4] He also notes that forty of the converts of the 1830 revival there entered the Christian ministry, and that 1,000 were converted in the 1842 revival there. Another of Strong's works, his *Systematic Theology*, first published in 1886, is still in print.

[5] On Phoebe Palmer, see the new biography by White (1991).

[6] In Boston, a daily prayer meeting for revival had been held from 1840 onwards in one of the Congregational churches. In 1850, it was joined by all denominations, and was held daily at 8.00 am for an hour. New prayer meetings sprang up in 1857 and 1858, including a ladies' prayer meeting begun by Mrs Finney. By March, 1858, there were eight major prayer meetings in different churches in Boston (Hannah 1977:66; see also Finney ed Rosell & Dupuis *ibid* 563-564 and nn 19-23).

[7] The *Congregationalist* of April 2, 1858 reported:

A gentleman from Ohio, recently in Boston, stated that...from Omaha City, in Nebraska, to Washington, *there was a line of prayer meetings along the whole length of the road;* so that wherever a Christian traveler stopped to spend the evening, he could find a crowded prayer meeting, across the entire breadth of our vast republic (cited in Finney ed Rosell & Dupuis *ibid* 563 n 17).

[8] *Christian History* (*ibid*) reproduces a sign used in a New York City prayer meeting, which read:

Prayers and Exhortations
Not to exceed 5 minutes
in order to give all an opportunity

———

Not more than 2 consecutive
prayers or exhortations

———

No controverted points
discussed.

[9] Finney criticised the account given by Samuel Irenaeus Prime (1812-1885), in his *The Power of Prayer* (1859), of the causes of the revival

and its linkage with the Fulton Street prayer meeting of Jeremiah Lanphier. He felt that the tide of revival expectation had been growing for some time in a number of places, and believed that the revival in Rochester, with its united morning prayer meetings, was the real precursor of the Prayer Revival of 1857-1858 (Finney ed Rosell & Dupuis *ibid* 555 n 77;573 n 4).

[10] At Portassie in Banffshire, for nearly three days and nights there was continuous praying, singing and exhorting of neighbours. A contemporary report states 'Labour is totally suspended. Even the cooking of victuals is much neglected'. Revival was general in the Isle of Lewis, and at Greenock in Renfrewshire 1,000, most of whom were working people, were converted in six months. Fishing communities were particularly affected (Bebbingdon 1989:117).

[11] Kent speaks of the 'Failure of English Revivalism' during this period (Kent 1978:71-128). However, this was a failure of the work of the revivalists to convert the nation by their methods, not the failure of divinely given revival in answer to prayer to quicken the churches and bring many into the Kingdom.

[12] The name comes from the devotional Bible study hours (Stunden) conducted by a German Reformed pastor Bohnekamper for German settlers and Russian peasants in Russia during the 1840s. Under his son Karl, the religious movement called 'Stundism' appeared around 1862, which freed itself from all foreign connection and became purely Russian in character.

[13] Dr Baedeker was the cousin of Karl Baedeker who produced the famous series of guides. From his wide travels he contributed material for some of the guidebooks. In 1877, he settled in St Petersburg for three years with his family and played a prominent part in the awakening which was in progress there. Following this, he continued his evangelistic journeys, first in the universities and prisons of Scandinavia, then in Russia from the Caucasus to Siberia. Later journeys took him to a number of other European countries. In Slovakia, Christina Roy, the daughter of a Lutheran pastor, was converted in a local revival accompanying his preaching. She was responsible for beginning the 'Blue Cross' movement in Slovakia with a strong involvement in social and temperance work.

[14] On his way back home from Russia, Radstock spent time preaching in Sweden and Denmark, where awakening was taking place, and where his ministry met with great response.

[15] George Muller (1805-1898) made a twelve-week visit to St Petersburg in 1882-1883. He stayed at the home of Princess Lieven and preached over 120 times in drawing room meetings to the nobility, in Colonel Pashkov's palace, as well as in other places. He experienced some police harassment as the authorities tried to contain or stamp out the spiritual movement that was

going on. After leaving St Petersburg, he visited the industrial city of Lodz in Russian Poland (southwest of Warsaw), where a local revival took place in connection with his preaching (Muller *ibid* 546-547).

16 Stephen Neill lists a number of significant events occurring at the time of the mid-century Prayer Revival which opened new areas for the gospel. The Christians who were revived together with the many new converts were thus available for missionary work at a time of new opportunity. The main events were (1) The acceptance by the British people, through its government, of responsibility for rule and administration in India, and the end of the life of the East India Company as a quasi-sovereign power. (2) The end of the second war between the European powers and China in 1858, and a series of treaties which granted permission to foreigners to travel in the interior of China together with toleration and protection of missionaries and Chinese Christians. (3) The opening of Japan to the West. (4) The publication in 1857 of David Livingstone's *Missionary Travels and Researches in South Africa*, which generated a new missionary enthusiasm to penetrate to the heart of Africa with the gospel (Neill rev O. Chadwick, 1986:274-276).

17 D. L. Moody made a number of visits to Britain, during which revival impulses were experienced. This was particularly true of his visit in 1873-1875. Spurgeon, in a sermon of that year already quoted, speaks of the missions of Moody and Sankey to Newcastle and Edinburgh and of the divine blessing attending. He notes 'a very notable ingathering of converts' which had taken place in Newcastle, and feels that 'the gracious visitation which has already come upon Edinburgh is such as was probably never known before within the memory of man' (Spurgeon 1874:13-14). Andrew Bonar notes in his diary for 1874 'the tide of real revival in Edinburgh', which then spread to Glasgow as Moody and Sankey moved on there. He compares it with 'the days of 1839-1840 and onwards', and says 'but there is more now than then' (Bonar 1893:301; see also Moody n d 164-186 on 'The Awakening in Edinburgh' [ch 16] and in Glasgow and other Scottish towns [ch 17]).

The American evangelists spent most of 1874 in Ireland and in the north of England with similar results attending their preaching, and in March 1875 began their London campaign which lasted for four months and was attended with great results. Meetings were held in large secular halls, such as the Agricultural Hall, Islington and Exeter Hall, as well as in Spurgeon's Metropolitan Tabernacle (see Bonar *ibid* 308-310; Moody *ibid* 201-227).

Moody returned to Britain in 1881-1883, and again in 1892. Andrew Bonar notes that there was great blessing in all the meetings of the trip in the 1880s, but of the later visit says 'This is the *third* [emphasis added] great wave of revival in my life' (*ibid* 391), presumably referring to 1839-1840, and 1859, although it is strange that he should exclude the revival of 1873-1875. (On Moody's evangelistic work in general see Weisberger 1958:175-219; McLoughlin 1959:166-281; Kent 1978:132-235; Hardman 1983:189-208.)

[18] 'Sam' Jones was an alcoholic before his conversion. As a result he combined his evangelistic ministry with a strong emphasis on Prohibition. Another evangelist of the period, Benjamin Fay Mills (1857-1916), attempted to combine evangelism with the Social Gospel. Finding it impossible, he left the itinerant ministry in 1895 to preach Christian Socialism. In 1899 he became the minister of the First Unitarian Church, Oakland, California. He eventually repented of his heterodoxy, and returned to itinerant preaching in 1915, a year before his death.

CHAPTER 10

THE WORLDWIDE REVIVAL OF 1900-1910

THE FIRST DECADE of the twentieth century saw a number of revivals in various parts of the world. Some were related to one another, others were apparently independent; some manifested characteristics similar to those seen in previous revivals, others manifested phenomena which, while not completely new, were at least unusual when judged by revivals which had taken place in Protestantism during the previous four centuries; some dissipated after a comparatively short time, others initiated new movements and denominations which still manifest great potential for further growth and influence. When taken together, they justify us in speaking of a worldwide revival in the first decade of the present century.

Although we are rapidly approaching the end of the twentieth century, the revival we are now considering has a modern 'feel' about it, especially as a number of those who experienced it are either still living, or have only recently died. Certainly, eyewitnesses of the 1904-1905 Welsh Revival have been interviewed by present-day writers on revival (see eg Edwards 1990:243-247), as, of course, have those who have experienced later twentieth-century revivals (see again Edwards *ibid* ch six 'I was there—eyewitness accounts').

PREPARATIONS AND BEGINNINGS

The Revival seems to have been prepared for by the appearance of multitudes of small prayer meetings in many parts of the world, arising spontaneously and often independently. In America at the Moody Bible Institute (Torrey 1924:47-48), in England at the Keswick Convention and elsewhere, in Wales at the Llandrindod Wells convention, in Scotland, in Australia and New Zealand (Torrey *ibid* 8, 48-49), in India, China, Japan, Africa and Latin America, Christians were praying for God to quicken and revive his work.

There were a number of awakenings in Wales in the three decades between the mid-century Prayer Revival and the Revival of 1904 (Evans 1974:9-21). Among these were local revivals in Tredegar and Aberavon in 1866, an awakening in 1871 which affected several towns in Glamorgan as well as villages in the Rhondda Valley (Robert Aitken and Lord Radstock were involved in Cardiff and Newport), visitations in the west and north of the principality in 1887, and various 'stirrings' in the 1890s. The ministry of Richard Owen (1839-1887) in various places in North Wales in the 1880s resulted in at least 13,000 being won for Christ, according to Owen's own estimate.

In 1900, a revival began among South African Boer soldiers, who had been captured by the British during the Boer War (1899-1902) and transported to various places around the globe including Bermuda and Ceylon. According to Orr,

> The work was marked by extraordinary praying, by faithful preaching, conviction of sin, confession and repentance and lasting conversion and hundreds of enlistments for mission service (Orr 1981:42).

The spirit of revival spread to South Africa with the return of the prisoners after the conclusion of the war in 1902. The 1904 evangelistic campaign conducted by Rodney ('Gypsy')

Smith (1860-1947), known as the 'Peace Mission', reaped the benefits of this.

In Japan, an awakening occurred in 1900 among the churches, which had not experienced growth for a number of years. It began with prayer and was followed by evangelism, which attracted great numbers of urban dwellers, with the result that the total membership of the churches almost doubled in a decade.

In 1902, Reuben A Torrey (1856-1928) and Charles M. Alexander (1867-1920) conducted an evangelistic campaign in Melbourne, Australia, where the ground had been well prepared by 1,700 small prayer meetings for revival. As a result of four weeks of the mission, 8,642 persons professed conversion and the news spread throughout Australia, as well as to India, England, Scotland and Ireland, resulting in increased prayer and expectation for a similar work, which was, in time, fulfilled (Torrey *ibid* 48-49).

In 1904, Torrey and Alexander were in Cardiff in Wales, to conduct a month's mission. A year earlier, when it was first learned that they were to come, prayer had begun to be offered by many in England, Scotland and Wales, that God would revive not only Cardiff, but the whole of Wales. Halfway through the week of the mission, when there was little evidence of response, the evangelists called for a day of prayer and fasting. The results in Cardiff were amazing, and when the Americans had to leave to conduct a mission in Liverpool, the meetings continued without them. In fact they continued for a whole year, with thousands being converted (Torrey *ibid* 49-50).

According to Torrey, it was as the day of prayer and fasting was being observed in other parts of Wales that Evan Roberts received his baptism of power, at a meeting conducted by W.W.Lewis and Seth Joshua (1858-?) of the Calvinistic Methodist Forward Movement,[1] and the Welsh Revival began (Torrey *ibid*). Certainly, Evan Roberts' experience of September 22, 1904, empowered him for the amazing ministry which followed (Riss 1988:32-33), but it does not seem to be true that the meeting was one which was called in response to Torrey's call for prayer and fasting. The meeting in question was one of a series that Seth Joshua was conducting at the time in Blaenannerch, near Newcastle Emlyn. Orr shows that although the Revival began soon after Torrey's Cardiff mission, it was not caused by it (Orr 1973:45). Indeed, the first movements of awakening had begun six months earlier at New Quay, a small town on the west coast of Wales, twenty miles south-west of Aberystwyth.

THE WELSH REVIVAL

Rev Joseph Jenkins (1859-1929), the minister at New Quay, was very concerned about the level of spiritual life among the young people in his church. One Sunday morning at a young people's prayer meeting he asked for testimonies of God's work in their lives. Few spoke until a young girl, Florrie Evans, who had been converted a few days before, stood up, and with a tremor in her voice, said: 'If no-one else will, I must say that I love the Lord Jesus Christ with all my heart.' This simple testimony began a movement of spiritual blessing in New Quay, which soon spread as Joseph Jenkins took teams of young people to chapels in the surrounding area.

In September, when Seth Joshua arrived in New Quay to conduct a week of meetings, he found a remarkable 'revival spirit' there. On Sunday September 4 he reported that he had 'never seen the power of the Holy Spirit so powerfully manifested among the people as at this place just now'.

He moved on to Newcastle Emlyn, where the work was more difficult, although a number of students at the Welsh Calvinistic Methodist Academy were spiritually quickened. One of them was Sydney Evans, the room-mate of another student, Evan Roberts. From there, Seth Joshua moved on to the nearby village of Blaenannerch for further meetings.

Evan Roberts (1878-1951) was a young man who had worked in the coal mines and then been apprenticed to a blacksmith, but in 1904 had given up this profession in order to enter the ministry of the Welsh Calvinistic Church. For the previous eleven years he had devoted himself to intense prayer for an outpouring of the Holy Spirit, both for himself and for Wales. His prayers for himself were answered on September 22 in the meeting at Blaenannerch, when he had an intense spiritual experience which he interpreted as a new infilling of the Holy Spirit,[2] and those for Wales were also to be answered shortly.

He returned to Newcastle Emlyn, where he was enrolled at the Academy to study for the Welsh Calvinistic Methodist ministry, but spent much of the next month praying with his friend Sydney Evans and planning for a number of evangelistic teams who would take the gospel throughout Wales. He believed, on the basis of a vision which he had received, that God was going to give them 100,000 converts to Christ.

At the end of October, in response to another vision, he returned to his home in Loughor, near Gorseinon. With his minister's permission, he began to speak, first at youth meetings, then at after-meetings and prayer meetings, about his own experience and of the need of all Christians to be filled with the Spirit. His 'four points' soon became famous:

1. If there is past sin or sins hitherto unconfessed, we cannot receive the Spirit... 2. If there is anything doubtful in our lives, it *must* be removed... 3. An entire giving up of ourselves to the Spirit [is necessary]. We *must speak* and *do* all He requires of us. 4. Public confession of Christ [is required].

On Sunday evening, November 6, in Libanus Chapel, Gorseinon, as Roberts spoke at the after-meeting, there was an overwhelming sense of divine awe; many were prostrated with conviction, others cried for mercy, many rejoiced as they were filled with the Spirit, some cried out, 'No more, Lord Jesus, or I die!'

Soon the Revival spread to other places throughout South Wales, as Evan Roberts, Sydney Evans, Seth Joshua, Joseph Jenkins and others preached, and as teams of young people also spoke in the churches. On November 8, Rev R. B. Jones (b 1870) began a ten-day mission in Rhos, near Wrexham in North Wales, during which revival phenomena overwhelmed the meetings. Soon the Revival was spreading through North as well as South Wales.

Often Evan Roberts would not preach in the meetings where he was present, but the overwhelming sense of the divine presence would take hold of the people as he prayed. The absence of preaching, which was a feature of much of the Revival, underlined the fact that God rather than man was at work. On the other hand, many observers felt that it may also have contributed to the way in which the revival died out after a few years and left many places which had been divinely visited even more spiritually dry than they had been before the Awakening. Others, however, would dispute this and point to the fact that the worldwide effects were felt for years to come (see the very fair and balanced assessment in Evans 1974:176-177, 182-186).

Certainly, the Revival soon attracted attention in many parts of the world, and many Christians came to Wales to observe, to experience the blessing for themselves, and to take the effects of the Revival back with them. We shall note this shortly. Within Wales, the effects on the churches and on society were marked. Drunkenness and crime were drastically reduced, stocks of Bibles were sold out, prayer meetings were held in coal mines,[3] in trains and trams, and in places of business.

In February 1905, Evan Roberts withdrew from public activity for seven days to rest,[4] and in April 1906, he withdrew permanently, suffering from complete exhaustion from his arduous labours. For a long time he lived at the home of Mrs Jessie Penn-Lewis and her husband, and in 1930 moved to Cardiff, where he died in 1951.

The Revival in Wales itself reached its height in 1905, but began to decline soon after, although Seth Joshua and many others continued to reap the benefits of the heightened spiritual awareness in their evangelistic preaching. The news of the Welsh Revival continued to spread and to have great effects for good elsewhere.

THE REST OF THE BRITISH ISLES

While the Welsh Revival hit the headlines and was reported throughout the world, with awakenings occurring in many places as a result, revival was also experienced in other parts of the British Isles, often in response to news of what was taking place in Wales, although not in every case.

In Ireland news of the Welsh Revival was greeted by some with suspicion, but soon special prayer meetings were being held in various places which were followed by great blessing. In Lurgen, Dublin and Belfast, and shortly after in a multitude of other places in the North, many converts and enquirers were being reported. Seth Joshua from Wales, evangelists from England, and local preachers, saw great response to their preaching. The Isle of Man was also affected (Orr 1973:29-32).

In Scotland the news of what was happening in Wales had the effect of stirring Christians to pray. Teams of Welsh evangelists conducted meetings in Glasgow, Motherwell and elsewhere in the industrial heartland. From these places the awakening spread to many other towns and villages in the surrounding areas. Joseph Kemp, the pastor of Charlotte Chapel in Edinburgh, visited Wales at the end of 1904 to observe the revival for himself. On his return he reported to his church, and the resulting prayerful expectancy was soon answered in an awakening there. The Highlands and Islands were also markedly affected by awakening. At the same time, Reuben Torrey and Charles Alexander were conducting missions in Edinburgh, Aberdeen, Glasgow and Dundee, with considerable response (Orr *ibid* 33-35).

In England, those areas close to the Welsh border were the first to be affected, but soon there were evidences of unusual spiritual response in all parts of the country, including the country areas, such as Durham, Northumberland, Bedfordshire, Devon and Cornwall, but also the great cities, like

Manchester, Liverpool, Bristol and London itself. The Archbishop of Canterbury called for a nationwide day of prayer,
and at least thirty bishops declared their support for what was
happening in Wales. All the main Free Churches were enthusiastic at what was taking place, and benefited greatly in terms
of membership increases. Torrey and Alexander campaigned
in many cities, in addition to many native evangelists, including William Booth and his Salvation Army. Evan Roberts
preached in Liverpool and Bristol, and R. B. Jones addressed
the Keswick Convention (Orr *ibid* 36-49).

SCANDINAVIA AND CONTINENTAL EUROPE

In Norway, special prayer for revival was already in evidence
in 1901, and awakening followed in the next two years. News
of the Welsh Revival was received with scepticism by many in
the state Church, who preferred to emphasise the regular
preaching of the Word and the administration of the sacra-
ments by the properly ordained clergy. However, much devotional literature from England and America was being
translated and published, including works by C. H. Spurgeon,
F. B. Meyer, D. L. Moody and R. A. Torrey. An earthquake
which occurred on October 23, 1904 seemed to produce a
greater openness to spiritual matters, and the beginning of
1905 saw an increased prayerful expectancy.

The evangelist who was particularly used in the awakening
which followed was Albert Gustav Lunde. Born in 1877, he
had become a sailor and later worked as a customs official in
the USA, where he was converted in a Salvation Army meeting in Chicago. He began preaching in the USA, returned to
Norway in 1901 and engaged in an itinerant ministry. After a
short trip back to America, he returned in 1904 and devoted
himself to praying and preaching for spiritual awakening. His
preaching in Oslo was attended with remarkable results, and
he was supported by clergy as well as by government officials.
He preached all over Norway, and was joined by other evangelists. The awakening spread throughout the country, in
state church parishes, Inner Mission prayer halls and Free

Church congregations. The revival was free of excesses. Laymen were prominent in the work, and the state church adapted its structures to allow for this.

In Denmark the awakening was channelled through the Inner Mission, but the Bible Society and the Free Churches were also used. The state church clergy largely ignored what was happening. However, great numbers of young people were converted through the work. In Sweden, a visit by Lunde sparked off an awakening, which soon became widespread. All classes were affected and missionary interest boomed in Sweden for many years after the revival. Finland was also affected, Frans Hannula being particularly influential in his ministry, especially to young people.

In Germany, visits by R. A. Torrey and Charles Inwood to the Blankenburg Conference, and by Jakob Vetter to Wales, resulted in heightened prayer and resulting blessing. Christian Endeavour societies, which had begun ten years before in Germany, were greatly blessed; and the German Tent Mission held large meetings in many places where remarkable numbers of conversions took place. The revival spread from Berlin, Mulheim in the Ruhr and Hanover to all parts of the country and beyond. The mining district of Teschen in Silesia (part of Austrian Poland) was greatly affected, Christian Endeavour societies being particularly strong; Bohemia, Moravia, and Slovakia, then parts of Austro-Hungary but now comprising Czechoslovakia, were stirred by news of the Welsh Revival, Slovakia in particular experiencing an extraordinary movement of the Spirit. Dr Frederick Baedeker, who continued to engage in itinerant evangelism until shortly before his death in 1906, was involved in a number of these awakenings. Hungary, the Balkans and Bulgaria experienced awakening in 1905, as did the Baltic states of Latvia and Estonia.

In Russia, the Russo-Japanese War of 1904 and the edicts of toleration of Czar Nicholas in 1905 and 1906 resulted in a new situation of freedom for the persecuted Stundists, Mennonites, Baptists and Evangelical Christians, which was followed by revival and growth. Ivan Prokhanov became the leader of the groups which had multiplied through the ministries of Lord Radstock and Dr Baedeker, and which included many aristocrats, such as Princess Lieven.

The Netherlands experienced a measure of awakening, although the hyper-Calvinist and the rationalist wings of the churches were unsympathetic. The Free Churches, especially the Baptists, were most affected. The tiny Protestant minority in Belgium was affected by news of the Welsh Revival.

In France a second *Reveil* occurred as various French observers visited Wales and reported back to their churches. All parts of the country were affected, including the holiday resort of Cannes on the Riviera. The various Evangelical churches were quickened and co-operation developed between the groups as a result. In Valentigny, 'bitterness, remorse, tears, confessions and repentance' were followed by an outbreak of spiritual power. French cantons in Switzerland were affected by what was happening in France, and German-speaking cantons were similarly affected by events in Germany (Orr 1973:50-64).

AMERICA

At the turn of the century in the United States there was considerable hope and expectation of a new outpouring of the Spirit. Prayer meetings were proliferating and much evangelistic activity was being undertaken, both by nationally known evangelists such as J. Wilbur Chapman (1859-1918), Benjamin Fay Mills (1857-1916) and Samuel Porter Jones (1847-1906), as well as by lesser known evangelists, pastors and circuit-riders. Blessing was experienced in many places, but nothing to compare with the Revival of 1858.

In 1905, news of the Welsh Revival stimulated further prayer and caused many to realise the difference between the 'revivals' that were really evangelistic campaigns, and what God was doing in Wales and elsewhere. Large conferences of ministers met in New York, Chicago, and in many other cities in the United States and Canada to discuss and pray for a nationwide revival. Very soon their prayers began to be answered as churches in all parts of the country began to experience crowded meetings and many applications for membership. Evangelism continued to be undertaken as before, but with far greater response. The same results were experienced in Canada. Orr, who as usual supplies scores of examples culled from official reports, cites two accounts written in 1905, one from a Methodist editor, the other from a national Baptist journal:

> A great revival is sweeping the United States. Its power is felt in every nook and corner of our broad land. The Holy Spirit is convincing the people 'of sin, of righteousness and of a judgment to come'. There is manifested a new degree of spiritual power in the churches. Pastors are crying out to God for help, and not a few of them are finding that help right at hand. The regular prayer-meetings and public services seem to be surcharged with convicting power, so that cries of penitence and prayers for mercy have been heard in places unused to such demonstrations. In several of our Detroit churches great throngs have attended the meetings, and the converts have been so numerous that the membership rolls will be increased by hundreds. It is a real revival.

> The tidings of revival come from every side. There is a quickening of spiritual impulse and life in the churches and in our own educational institutions: evangelism is no longer in the air, it is in the active realm of Christian experience. There is a remarkable responsiveness to the presentation of the claims of Christ upon the hearts and consciences of men...

The reference in the second quote to educational institutions is interesting, and is abundantly borne out by the facts. Spiritual awakenings were reported on campuses nationwide, with YMCA, Bible classes and missionary activities

benefitting. In 1896, 2,000 students were engaged in missionary studies; in 1906, 11,000 were enrolled. From the outbreak
of the awakening onward, 300 missionaries a year were sailing
for foreign fields. E. Stanley Jones (1884-1973), a student at
Asbury College, was one such. William Borden and Kenneth
Scott Latourette (1884-1968) were others (see Orr *ibid* 65-100
for a great number of facts and figures).

The modern Pentecostal Movement began in a series of
meetings held in a Methodist Church hall in Azusa Street in
Los Angeles starting in mid-April 1906, through the preaching
of W. J. Seymour (d 1923) from Texas. Seymour was one of
the converts from a school in Houston, opened by Charles
Parham (1873-1929), following his own 'Spirit baptism' in
Topeka, Kansas at Bethel College, where he taught.[5]

Los Angeles had already experienced a number of local
revivals in 1905, as prayer meetings were started following the
arrival of reports from Wales. The meetings in Azusa Street,
which were held continuously every day for a period of three
years, were the scene of the new phenomena of speaking in
tongues which became a prominent feature (although not the
only prominent feature) of the movement that quickly
developed. In the early days, some felt that they were speaking in foreign languages, including Chinese; however, subsequent experience, including missionary work, convinced
them otherwise.

Sporadic, unsought outbursts of glossalalia had been
experienced during the Revival at Mukti in western India in
1905, and at Dholka in the Gujarati area among CMA missionaries and church members in 1906, but the emphasis on
the experience as an essential accompaniment and proof of
Spirit-baptism, which soon became the hallmark of Pentecostalism as well as the cause of separation from existing
denominations, marked a significant difference from other
such manifestations.

The message was carried to Toronto and Chicago, and,
through a visit to the USA by Thomas B. Barratt (1862-1940),
an Englishman working in Oslo, it was taken to Norway, and

thence to Denmark, Sweden and England, where an Anglican vicar, A. A. Boddy, introduced it into his church in Sunderland, following a visit to Oslo. Subsequently, the Pentecostal message was taken to Wales, where George Jeffreys, Stephen Jeffreys and Donald Gee became influential leaders in the newly emerging denominations, and to Scotland and Ireland.[6]

In Latin America, Evangelical missionary work, which had been introduced in the nineteenth century, made steady but unspectacular progress, encountering a great deal of opposition from the Roman Catholic authorities.

In Chile, the 1880s and 1890s had witnessed awakenings in a number of places. In 1902 the Methodist Church in Valparaiso had experienced a local revival. However, in 1907 there was a more widespread awakening, which began a period of phenomenal growth affecting all the denominations, but also producing the Inglesia Metodista Pentecostal which developed from the Valparaiso Methodist Church. In Argentina there was an awakening among the Welsh colonists in Patagonia at the end of 1905, and soon after Baptists and Brethren began to grow, although, as elsewhere, they were later overtaken by the Pentecostals. In Ecuador, Peru, Mexico and in the Caribbean islands there were revivals which initiated periods of growth in various denominations, especially the Methodists. The figures for Evangelicals in Latin America and the Caribbean indicate a seven-year growth from 132,388 communicants in 1903 to 369,077 in 1910 (Orr *ibid* 101-106).

AUSTRALASIA AND THE SOUTH SEAS

The campaigns of Torrey and Alexander in Australia and New Zealand have already been mentioned. They were followed by waves of revival in 1905, which were triggered by news of the Welsh Revival and which were harvested by Australian evangelists and by visiting preachers such as J. Wilbur Chapman and Charles Alexander in 1909.

Hawaii, Micronesia, the Marshall Islands, the Philippines and Indonesia all experienced awakenings in the first decade of the century, the movements in Borneo among the German missionaries and among the Bataks in Sumatra being marked. The island of Nias, off the coast of Sumatra, experienced what were among the most significant effects. The island had been evangelised in the period of revival in the 1860s. After 35 years, there were 5,000 Christians. A new awakening came in 1908, and by 1915 20,000 had been baptised and were being instructed in the faith.

AFRICA AND MADAGASCAR

News of the Welsh Revival again acted as a catalyst in South Africa, affecting both Afrikaner and British churches. Among the latter, Baptists, Congregationalists and Presbyterians shared in the blessing, although it was the Methodists who experienced the greatest growth. Growth in the Dutch Reformed Church is harder to estimate, as most converts would already have family affiliation to the church. However, a deep spiritual work was evident. There were also awakenings among the African peoples of the country over the next two decades. In Transkai, Zululand, Natal, Swaziland, and in other areas, awakening and renewal were evident. Madagascar had already experienced revival in 1894, but a remarkable movement of awakening began in 1905, stimulated in part by news from Wales, which continued in force until 1907.

In German South-West Africa, in Northern Rhodesia and in Nyasaland, revival came to the national Christians and to the missionaries in 1910. In that year the visit of Charles Inwood to the convention at Loudon resulted in amazing scenes of repentance, confession and joy, which were then followed by fruitful evangelistic activity. Conventions in the years leading up to 1910 had been times of increasing blessing, and for the months preceeding the convention, over a hundred special prayer meetings had been held.

In the Congo, there were local revivals in 1901, 1902, 1906, 1907, 1908 and 1912 in different parts of the country. In Uganda, 1906 was a year of revival; in southern Cameroon, revival in 1906 continued and grew until 1909; in Nigeria, awakenings in 1905 were followed by a significant people's movement. In the Ivory Coast and Gold Coast, spiritual renewal also produced an indigenous movement associated with William Wade Harris. Awakenings in Liberia continued for a number of years.

Even in North Africa, under the sway of Islam, there were spiritual awakenings, notably in Egypt in 1903 and 1906, and in Algeria in 1905 and 1906 (for more detail concerning Africa, see Orr *ibid* 116-130; also Orr 1975).

INDIA

Revival came to the churches of India in 1905, although for the previous ten years there had been a rising tide of expectancy accompanied by special prayer for a spiritual infilling. In various parts of the country different leaders, both men and women and both missionary and national, were used to prepare the Church for revival and to lead when revival came. Pandita Ramabia, an Indian woman around Poona; R. J. Ward, an Englishman in North India; John 'Praying Hyde' Hyde (1865-1912), an American in South India; Amy Carmichael (1867-1951), an English missionary at Dohnavur in the south; John Roberts, a Welsh missionary in Assam; Sadhu Sundar Singh (1888-1928?), a converted Sikh, in North Punjab, and itinerating in India, Afghanistan, Tibet, Nepal, Burma, Ceylon, Singapore, China and Japan—these and many others were the Lord's instruments before and following the revivals which moved through many parts of India from 1905 onwards (Orr *ibid* 131-157; Cairns *ibid* 198-200; Evans *ibid* 153-160).[7]

CHINA

The first twelve years of the twentieth century in China saw events of extreme political significance, beginning with the Boxer Uprising in 1900 in which hundreds of missionaries and thousands of Chinese Christians were murdered, and concluding with the Hsin-Hai Revolution in 1911, which brought the Manchu dynasty to an end. The same years saw amazing movements of revival and spiritual awakening.

In 1900 two college revivals brought a large number of students to Christ, many of whom were martyred in the bloodbath later in the same year. In 1903 there were revivals in Canton in the south and Manchuria in the far north. 1906 and 1907 were years of widespread awakening, and in 1908 and 1909 there were further waves of extraordinary awakening in many places, including Manchuria, where Jonathan Goforth (1859-1936), a Canadian Presbyterian missionary, was the prophet and evangelist of a movement which swept the length and breadth of Manchuria and spread from there into the six neighbouring provinces in China. From these and other awakenings in other parts of the country, a number of national evangelists and leaders arose, such as John Sung (Goforth n d; Orr *ibid* 158-154; Cairns *ibid* 200-202).

KOREA

During the first decade of the twentieth century the Church in Korea experienced three periods of revival: a limited one which began in 1903 and continued till 1905, associated with a group of seven missionaries; more general awakenings in 1906, stimulated in part by news of the Welsh Revival; and the explosive awakening of 1907, when public confession of sins was widespread. In all these revivals, prayer was a key feature (Kim in Carson ed.1990:231-233; Orr *ibid* 165-172: Cairns *ibid* 203-204). The membership of the churches quadrupled during the decade.

The turn of the century was a time of profound change and crisis in Korean society, with Japanese invasion and annexation, and the opening up of Korea to Western influences. The North-Western Province where the revivals began was particularly open to such tensions and changes.

In August 1903, a group of seven Methodist missionaries met together in Wonsan for a week of Bible study and prayer. Their leader was Rev R. A. Hardie, a Canadian. As he studied the subject of the Holy Spirit and prayer, he was led to see his own spiritual poverty and lack of faith. Following a profound spiritual experience, he confessed his sins of pride, hardness of heart and lack of faith to his colleagues, and later to his Korean congregation. This led to public confessions by others and the beginnings of spiritual awakening. Two months later Frederick Franson, the director of the Scandinavian Missionary Alliance, arrived to conduct a series of meetings, which resulted in a significant development of spiritual concern and public confession of sins. After he left, the revival grew and spread to many other parts of Korea, affecting other denominations and continuing until 1905.

The revival of 1906 was an interdenominational movement, associated with Bible conferences held in three places, Wonsan, Pyongyang and Seoul. These events, known in Korean as *Sa-Kyung-Hai*, had begun in 1890. In the summer of 1906, early morning prayer meetings beginning at 4.30 am, and modelled after the traditional Korean animistic prayer method, were started in connection with the Bible conferences. News of the Welsh Revival stirred up prayerful expectation, which was soon answered in a new wave of revival affecting many parts of the country.

The 1907 Revival occurred against the background of national hopelessness and despair following the Korean-Japanese Agreements of 1904 and 1905, and the forced dethronement of King Ko-Jong. Many people responded by flocking to the churches. At the same time, Methodist and Presbyterian missionaries and national Christian leaders began praying for a new manifestation of the power of the Holy Spirit on the churches in general, and especially upon the members of a ten-day Men's Theology and Bible Training Class due to meet at Pyong-Yang in January 1907. The total attendance was around 1,500. The day before the course ended, the evening meeting seemed full of the presence of God, many broke down confessing their sins, and the whole congregation wept, confessed, prayed and praised at the same time. According to those present, what might appear to be chaos was actually a beautiful expression of the work of God's Spirit. Within two months 2,000 were converted, and by the middle of 1907 there were 30,000 converts connected with the

Pyong-Yang centre. Women were also profoundly affected by the revival. Soon the awakening was spreading to the whole of Korea.

The revival and the accompanying awakening within Korea as a whole resulted in the renewal of the Church and its awakening to a new devotion, evangelistic, social and missionary zeal, as well as a profound moral renewal of the national life. Korea has continued to experience further significant periods of revival.[8]

JAPAN

In 1900 the Protestant Churches in Japan held a number of prayer conferences, following which they engaged in a united evangelistic campaign in 1901. The continuing spirit of prayer, together with the great response to the evangelistic message, caused missionaries to speak of 'Pentecost in Japan'. The movement of evangelism was continued in the following years and was resumed after the Russo-Japanese War of 1904. News of the Welsh Revival stimulated a further awakening, as did news of the Korean Revival. The number of Japanese Christians doubled in the decade (Orr *ibid* 173-177).

The series of revivals in the first decade of the twentieth century was soon to be followed by the Great War of 1914-1918, which involved all the major European nations together with their colonies and allies in many parts of the world, as well as the United States of America. Not only were hundreds of thousands killed in the conflict, but the whole world scene was profoundly altered. This, together with other factors, may account for the fact that, thus far in our own century, no further world-wide revival has yet taken place.

Notes

[1] The Forward Movement developed from the evangelistic work of Rev. John Pugh (1840-1897). His open air work met with some opposition but

also enjoyed much blessing. From his extensive experience he crystallised the strategy necessary to reach the unchurched for Christ: firstly the initial campaigning, conducting militant evangelism, often in the open air; then the establishment of more permanent worship centres for the converts. Within thirty years, forty-eight centres of worship had been established with a total seating capacity of over 42,000 (Evans 1974:22-24).

[2] At the meeting in Blaenannerch, Seth Joshua closed the meeting by praying loudly in Welsh, 'Lord, bend us'. Evan Roberts, who had been deeply moved during the whole meeting, went out to the front to kneel, cryng out in great agony of spirit, 'Lord, bend me.' This was accompanied by a new sense of the Spirit's power and a renewed burden for the salvation of lost souls (Evans 1974:68-70).

[3] G. Campbell Morgan wrote at the time of the effect of the Revival on the miners and the way they treated the pit ponies:

> The horses are terribly puzzled. A manager said to me, 'The haulers are some of the very lowest. They have driven their horses by obscenity and kicks. Now they can hardly persuade the horses to start working, because there is no obscenity and no kicks' (cited in Riss *ibid* 40).

[4] A bitter attack on Evan Roberts by the minister of the Bethania Congregational Chapel in Dowlais, Rev Peter Price, appeared in a secular newspaper, the *Western Mail*, on January 31, 1905. The writer claimed that there were two revivals going on in Wales at the time, a real one and a sham one. His own church had experienced something of the true revival with hundreds of conversions, but the other revival was 'a sham Revival, a mockery, a blasphemous travesty of the real thing', the work of 'its chief figure' Evan Roberts, whom he censured for his claims to be under the immediate control of the Holy Spirit, and for the excesses of the revival. The attack hurt Roberts, although he never replied to it. It may have contributed to his premature retirement from his position of leadership in the awakening.

[5] Parham later faded from the movement, especially following his indictment on charges of sodomy made by fellow-Pentecostals who were engaged in a power struggle with Parham for leadership of the new movement (see Goff 1988:128-146, esp 138-142 & notes).

[6] The origins and subsequent history of Pentecostalism are now the subject of a number of properly-researched works (E. G. Bloch-Hoell 1964; Hollenweger 1972: Synan ed 1975; Riss 1988; Dictionary of Pentecostal and Charismatic Movements 1990), although not all of these set it fully within the context of the world-wide revival which was taking place at the time. The Pentecostal phenomenon, which eventually became a worldwide movement, was initially a very small part of the revival in the first decade of the century,

the vast majority of which took place with no occurrence of the distinctive activities which are the *sine qua non* of classical Pentecostalism.

[7] One example may be given among many possible ones. Amy Carmichael described the awakening which began in October 1905 at Dohnavur among the unemotional Tamil people:

> It was at the close of the morning service that the break came. The one who was speaking was obliged to stop, overwhelmed by the sudden realisation of the inner force of things. It was impossible even to pray. One of the older lads in the boys' school began to try to pray, but he broke down, then another, then all together, the older lads chiefly at first. Soon many among the younger ones began to cry bitterly, and pray for forgiveness. It spread to the women...Soon the whole upper half of the church was on its face on the floor crying to God...oblivious of all others...I had never heard of such a thing as this among Tamil people...Nothing disturbed those who were praying, and that hurricane of prayer continued with one short break of a few minutes for over four hours.

The effects were felt over the next seven months with the hopeful conversion of all the children in the schools, the revival of the Christian workers, national and expatriate, a remarkable spirit of oneness, the restoration of backsliders, and successful evangelism in the surrounding area (Houghton 1955:146-148).

[8] I am indebted to two Korean students, John I. Moon and Joseph Yooshik Kim, who attended the course which I gave at Fuller Theological Seminary School of World Mission in August 1991. They both produced good papers for me which harvested the research done by a number of other studies on the Korean revivals. The general reader may consult Blair 1957; Shearer 1966; Orr 1975.

CHAPTER 11

LATER TWENTIETH-CENTURY REVIVALS

THE REVIVALS OF 1900-1910 were the last worldwide awakenings to take place in this century. There have been a considerable number of more localised awakenings, some of which have been comparatively shortlived, others of which have lasted for many years, and some of which are still in progress. In order to complete our survey, we will briefly refer to those which have occurred, or are still in progress, in the present century.[1]

While there is a considerable amount of agreement among Christians who are sympathetic to revival on what occurred in past awakenings and whether certain movements should be included in the history of such awakenings, vested interests—whether they be theological or denominational—will cause some groups to include and others to exclude certain modern movements in the account. This is true of a number of those we shall mention in this chapter and is especially true of the Healing and the Latter Rain movements which took place in North American Pentecostalism soon after the close of the Second World War (see Riss;1988:105-124), and also the Charismatic Renewal movement which began in the USA in the early 1960s, and which has subsequently spread throughout the world.[2]

BETWEEN THE WORLD WARS

The Great War of 1914-1918, in which a whole generation of young men of the European nations engaged in the conflict were killed, also saw the end of much spiritual life and activity in the churches. In Britain, Europe and North America, Liberal Theology caused divisions in denominations and societies as many saw it attacking the vitals of the Christian faith, cutting the nerve of evangelism and blunting the edge of all spiritual activity, including prayer. In Britain and in much of Europe church-going ceased to be the accepted practice in society in general.

However, a number of spiritual awakenings also occurred in the two decades following the Great War.

The British Isles

A notable revival movement, which began in 1921 in the fishing port of Lowestoft in Suffolk, spread to other parts of East Anglia including the nearby port of Great Yarmouth, and from there reached fishing ports on the east coast of Scotland.

The revival began in London Road Baptist Church, Lowestoft, where the minister, Rev P. E. Fergusson, concerned about the lack of conversions, had called the church to special prayer. For six months around sixty people had met every Monday evening to pray for revival. Rev Douglas Brown from Balham in London, who had come into a new spiritual experience in February 1921, and in whose church ninety-six people had come to faith in Christ during a single service, was invited to preach at a special week of meetings in Lowestoft. Halfway through the week the church building was packed to overflowing and an extraordinary work of conviction and conversion began which resulted in hundreds professing faith. Soon Douglas Brown was being invited to preach in many other churches in the town and the surrounding area. He preached in Yarmouth and here many of the fishermen were converted, both local men and many from the fishing ports on the north-east coast of Scotland. It was these who told of their new-found faith when they returned home to Scotland, and this had the effect of bringing spiritual blessing there also. Jock Troup, a Scottish evangelist who took up the work which had begun in Yarmouth, returned to Fraserburgh (north of Aberdeen) in response to a vision. There he was involved in the deep spiritual work which followed (Richie 1980). This revival also brought to prominence D. P. Thomson, who later became an official evangelist of the Church of Scotland (Edwards 1990:248-252).

In Ireland, in the midst of 'the troubles', as the IRA sought by guns and bombs to bring Ulster into the newly-created Republic of Ireland, W. P. ('Billy') Nicholson evangelised in the 1920s with packed meetings and lasting results.

In Aberavon in South Wales, the ministry of D. Martyn Lloyd-Jones (1899-1981), a highly qualified medical specialist with a promising career in prospect, who forsook his profession to become the pastor of a declining Forward Movement of Wales mission church, was marked by revival during the 1930s (Murray 1982: 131-227, esp 203-227).

The island of Lewis in the Hebrides, which had experienced revival a number of times in the nineteenth century, saw another series of awakenings between 1934 and 1939. Even these were not the last, as we shall see.

North America

In North America, during the period between the Wars there were many evangelists who continued the kind of large campaigns popularised by Moody, Torrey and Chapman. Torrey continued his nationwide and worldwide evangelistic missions until he died in 1928. Billy Sunday, who had begun his itinerant evangelistic activities before the Great War, continued until his death in 1935. The use of the word 'revival' to describe such activities, which became increasingly popular following the work of Charles Finney, became almost universal in the USA at this time. However, in spite of many coming to faith in Christ through the work of these men, their ministries were not, by and large, accompanied by revival in the classical sense of the word. Some of the lesser men who engaged in this kind of work brought it into disrepute through their methods and their financial dealings.

J. Edwin Orr visited North America in 1935 and 1936, seeking to bring the classical message of revival to the churches, but sometimes encountering opposition from Dispensationalists who believed that the End was near and that apostasy, rather than revival, was to be expected. Significant local revivals occurred in 1936 at Wheaton College, Illinois, at Columbia Bible College, South Carolina, and at Eastern Nazarene College, Massachusetts,[3] in connection with his visits (Appasamy 1964:72ff; Orr 1971:153-157). The revival at Wheaton actually began three weeks after he had left to conduct meetings in Texas, but prayer meetings for revival had been started the previous year and his visit heightened the sense of expectancy that something significant was soon to happen. The breakthrough came when a number of students made public confessions of sin in a meeting which lasted for around ten hours. In the resulting awakening, a number of students came to faith in Christ for the first time, hundreds put wrongs right in their lives and relationships, and scores dedicated themselves to missionary service. Twenty-five senior students became outstanding missionaries in Europe, Asia, Africa and Latin America.

A later revival occurred at Wheaton in 1943 in which Billy Graham, a senior student at that time, was deeply moved and soon became an evangelist with Youth for Christ. More than forty students who graduated that year became overseas missionaries (Cairns 1986:210-212).

Europe

Extraordinary revival and evangelism occurred in the Soviet Union following the revolution of 1917, and continued until 1929. The two main evangelical groups in nineteenth-century Russia, known respectively as 'Baptists' and 'Evangelical Christians',[4] arose from groups within the Orthodox Church and from Mennonites, who also came under German influence (Wagner 1978:107-108; Steeves 1982:149-152). Ethnically, they were Russian, Ukrainian and Byelorussian. Their growth was rapid, in spite of periods of persecution, and by 1914, only fifty years after the first baptism, they numbered well over 100,000. They had begun in the Ukraine, in the Caucasus in the south, and in St Petersburg in the north. Following the Bolshevik Revolution the previous restrictions on non-Orthodox activity were lifted, and remarkable growth took place (see Sawatsky 1981:38-43). Growth among the Ukrainian Baptists was particularly vigorous; from a few thousand members in 1917, they had increased to 100,000 by 1927 (Bordeaux 1987:117 citing Russian Baptist sources). The Stalinist repression of the Churches began in 1927 and lasted till 1941, when the German invasion meant that the attention of the authorities was diverted elsewhere, and also patriotic support was needed from every quarter.

In East and South-East Poland there were revivals in the 1920s, and considerable growth, both among Polish and Ukrainian Baptists. This was particularly marked in 1927 (Keim 1983:14).

The situation of the Christian Church in Romania, which for most of this century has been one of oppression and persecution, has also been one of revival and amazing growth. Throughout the present century, the Baptists and other Free Churches have been attacked and repressed, firstly by the state under the influence of the Romanian Orthodox Church, and since the Second World War by the Communist authorities, as part of their attempt to eliminate all opposition to their totalitarian rule. A renewal movement, the Lord's Army, has existed within the Orthodox Church since the 1920s, and has been persecuted during the whole time of its existence. Despite this, it continued to grow, and at its height before the Second World War its membership was as high as 2,000,000. Because of sustained opposition from the leadership, persecution from the state, and the death of key leaders, it now numbers around 500,000. The Baptists in Romania have experienced extremely rapid growth throughout the century in what should probably be seen as a series of waves of revival. In 1919, when the Romanian Baptist Union was formed uniting Baptist churches in Moldavia, Wallachia and Transylvania (newly acquired from Hungary, although the Treaty of Trianon did not finalise the transfer until 1920), the total number of members was 18,751. In 1921 there were 633 churches with 21,193 members (14,000 Romanian, 6,223 Hungarian, 670 German and 300 Russian). In 1931 there were 1,525 churches with 47,205 members. In other words, over a ten year period the number of churches and of members had more than doubled. In 1936, the last year for which figures were available before the war, the number of members had risen to 65,880. Clearly, revival continued, probably up to the outbreak of hostilities (Davies 1990:265-274).

A young Scottish evangelist, James A. Stewart (1910-1975) was involved in significant revivals in the Baltic States of Latvia and Estonia in 1934 and 1935. In Riga, the Latvian capital, he preached in the churches where two brothers, William and Robert Fetler[5], were pastors. In both churches there were already prayer meetings for revival, and the prayers were abundantly answered in the evangelistic missions in which Stewart preached. Over 2,000 people packed the buildings for the meetings, which often went on till the early hours of the morning. According to Stewart's own testimony, 'The heavens were opened and the floods descended... Mighty movements of the Spirit were witnessed.' He commented later that it was not only the large crowds who attended the meetings, which went on for five months, nor the number of conversions, but 'it was the awful sense of the majesty and holiness of God: it was the liberty of the Spirit' (Jenkins 1989:16-17).

He left Latvia for Estonia to regain his strength, but was moved to prayer for the spiritual state of the people in that country and soon made contact with a Baptist pastor in Talinn who was praying for revival. The meetings which began in the Baptist church soon had to move to a larger Lutheran church, but this also proved too small, and finally a large public hall seating several thousand was rented. Even this was inadequate, in spite of the fact that three or four meetings were held each day.

In 1935 and 1936 Stewart conducted meetings in Poland and Czechoslovakia, which were also attended with revival. In Poland, he preached in many country towns along the border with the Soviet Union, including some Jewish communities which were especially large in the east of the country. He described the blessing as even greater than what he had seen in Riga and Talinn. In Czechoslovakia, he preached in the towns of Kutna Hora and Kolin as well as in the capital Prague and the capital of Moravia, Brno.[6] In Kolin, he established a pattern of work which he continued wherever possible elsewhere. In the mornings he ministered in prayer meetings which he had called to pray for revival, and where he encouraged believers to holiness, prayer and faithfulness in service, and where he told what God had done in other places; in the afternoons he led them in visiting homes to distribute Scripture portions and to invite people to the evening meetings; in the evening meetings, which were primarily evangelistic in content, 'evangelistic outreach merged into scenes of revival, with the blessing continuing long after the evangelistic meetings had ended' (Jenkins *ibid* 32).

In 1937 Stewart moved on to Hungary, where the spiritual blessing on his ministry reached its climax.[7] Hundreds of ministers professed conversion and great crowds thronged his meetings, which were held in the largest concert hall in Budapest, as well as in Debrecen. Even the Regent of Hungary supported the work. Stewart returned to Hungary in 1938, and again in 1939 and in 1940, just as the nation was entering the War. Once more, signs of great spiritual concern were common in his meetings. When he made a return visit in 1946, evidences of revival were still present (Jenkins *ibid* 33-45).[8]

Edwin Orr has suggested that the Revival of 1904ff brought in a harvest of souls and thus prepared men who were soon to die in the Great War to meet their Maker. The revivals in Eastern Europe in the 1930s may also have been a divine

or what was to follow in the Second World War,
people to face the suffering which was soon to
s may also have been the case in Norway, where an
ng took place which lasted from 1934 till 1941, par-
ly associated with a Swedish Finn, Frank Mangs, who
conducted a series of remarkable campaigns in Oslo and other
Norwegian towns in 1934 (Orr 1981:53).

Africa

The 1920s and 1930s saw a number of notable revivals in
Africa, one of which has continued to a certain extent up to
the present time. In Congo, an awakening took place in the
1920s which affected the mission-related churches, but also
produced an indigenous movement led by Simon Kimbangu.
The next decade saw more spiritual awakenings; as a result,
Protestant communicants increased in twelve years from
below 10,000 to nearly 200,000 (Watt 1939). In Cameroon,
Nigeria, the Gold Coast, the Ivory Coast and in other parts of
West Africa there were awakenings, and also in Nyasaland
(Westgarth 1946).

In South Africa, campaigns by Lionel B. Fletcher brought
thousands into the churches, and in 1936 revival meetings
conducted by Edwin Orr were also greatly used. In Ethiopia,
when the missionaries were forced to leave the country in
1937 following the Italian invasion, they left a church among
the Wallamo tribe with only forty-eight believers. When they
returned in 1942, they discovered that from the one church
there were now over a hundred assemblies with around 10,000
believers as the result of revival.[9]

The most widespread and longest-lasting of the awakenings
in Africa was undoubtedly what is known as the East African
Revival, which began at Gahini in Ruanda in 1934, spread to
southern Uganda by 1935, and also profoundly influenced
Burundi, Kenya and Tanganyika, mainly among Anglican
churches. The men whom God particularly touched at the
beginning were Dr Joe Church, a missionary doctor, and
Simeoni Nsibambi, an African Christian. Repentance and

open confession of sin were the hallmark of the revival, which was influenced by the distinctive teaching of the Keswick Convention. Through visits by Joe Church and others, the influence of the awakening spread to southern Sudan, Congo and South Africa. From 1947 onwards, through the visits of African leaders involved in the revival, England was influenced, although the effects were largely confined to individuals and small groups. The effects of the Revival have been renewed periodically up to the present time.[10]

Asia

In India, nationalism and the desire for independence absorbed the attention of most people in the twenties and thirties, but there were a number of movements of revival in various places, especially in the south, one of which was associated with a converted Sikh, Bakht Singh, who became a powerful evangelist and Bible teacher.

In China there was a revival in Shanghai, beginning in 1925 and continuing until the following year. The Bethel Bands, formed by Andrew Gih and other young Chinese evangelists, toured all the provinces of China with revival accompanying their work in many places. In 1931 they were in Manchuria, where awakening was experienced, and also in Peking, Shanghai, the peninsula province of Shantung and throughout central China, as well as in the south and the west. John Sung, one of the band members, went off on his own tour of evangelism, not only in China but also among the Chinese dispersion throughout South-East Asia (Lyall 1954). In the north of China, there was revival from 1927 to 1937, involving Marie Monsen of the Norwegian Lutheran Mission, together with indigenous Christian evangelists (Monsen 1961).

Korea experienced local revivals in 1927 and 1928, during the time when the country was suffering under the power of Japanese militarism (Kim 1990:234). A series of revivals in Vietnam from 1938 till 1942 increased the communicant membership of the Protestant Churches from 8,748 to 12,618 (Orr 1981:62).

Latin America

A grave political situation in Mexico in the mid-1930s produced a prayer movement, which resulted in revival followed by evangelism. In the ten years from 1936 to 1946, evangelicals grew from 50,000 to 250,000 (Orr *ibid* 56).

THE LAST FORTY-FIVE YEARS[11]

The British Isles

Compared to other parts of the world, which we shall look at shortly, there have not been many instances of revivals in the period since the end of the Second World War.

The island of Lewis in the Hebrides, which has been the scene of revival a number of previous times, was once again visited with awakening in 1949, when Rev Duncan Campbell was on the island conducting a two-week mission. 'It seemed as if the very air was electrified with the Spirit of God...There was an awesomeness of the presence of God', according to one witness. The revival continued with great power for at least two years, with effects continuing for a longer period (Campbell 1954; Edwards 1990:253-257).

In the view of many, the time of Billy Graham's 1954 London Crusade at Harringay Arena was a time when revival seemed imminent. The spiritual interest evident at all levels in the capital was unique. The campaign was the topic of discussion in the media, as well as among ordinary people travelling to work on buses and Underground. The London churches, at least, received a new impulse of spiritual life. Many of those who professed conversion at the time, later entered Bible and theological colleges to train for full-time Christian ministry.

It is also possible to see evidence of spiritual revival in a number of local churches which have grown remarkably in a comparatively short time. One example of this is the dramatic story of the Anglican church in York, where the late David Watson was the vicar, and where a dying church faced with closure was revived and became a centre of life and witness, not only in the area, but nationwide. A less well-known example is another Anglican church in High Wycombe, Bucks, where the congregation has grown from 40 to around 700 in fourteen years, with the growth coming largely from conversions, rather than transfers from other churches.

North America

In the United States, a prayer movement began in 1948 among pastors of churches, especially in Southern California but also in other parts of the country. In March 1949, a prayer conference was organised by Rev Armin R. Gesswein, a Missouri Synod Lutheran pastor, at the Pacific Palisades Presbyterian Conference Grounds in Los Angeles. J. Edwin Orr and Harold J. Ockenga from Boston spoke on the subject of Evangelical Awakening. According to an eye-witness report in the British weekly The Life of Faith (May 25, 1949), entitled 'First Signs of Revival: Unusual Stirrings in California',

> More than 400 ministers and their wives attended, and half of these continued in penitence and prayer until the early hours of the mornings. There was a great moving of the Spirit, with the spirit of Revival being carried out from the conference to many areas (cited in Orr 1971:166).

Following the conference, a tide of expectancy began to rise in Southern California, mid-week prayer meetings and Sunday services saw large increases in attendance, and a number of new church buildings were begun with a view to accommodating the large numbers.

At the same time, another conference was held in late August 1949 at the Forest Home Conference Centre belonging to Hollywood Presbyterian Church, which proved to be of lasting spiritual significance. Two years before, there had been a spiritual stirring among Christian students at the conference centre, when Miss Henrietta Mears, the Hollywood Presbyterian Church's Sunday School Director, had been speaking. At the Student Briefing Conference of 1949 J. Edwin Orr and Billy Graham were the speakers. At this conference,[12] Billy Graham himself received a new experience of empowering by the Holy Spirit, which was evident in the evangelistic campaign which he conducted later in the year in Los Angeles. The campaign, first scheduled to last for three weeks, eventually continued for a total of three months, due to the unprecedented interest shown. Ministers and young people, many of whom had themselves been spiritually blessed at or through the conferences earlier in the year, threw their energies into the mission. Billy Graham's subsequent evangelistic campaigns around the world, while not in themselves evidence of revival, are the results of a significant personal experience of revival for one man.[13]

Also in the United States, there were a large number of significant revivals which occurred on the campuses of Christian Colleges, Bible Schools and seminaries, beginning in 1949, reaching a peak in the following year, and continuing for some time after. At Bethel College, St Paul, Minnesota in 1949, J. Edwin Orr began a series of lectures on atheism and faith, and then moved on to cover the history of Evangelical Awakenings, together with the prerequisites of revival. Soon the whole student body was involved in meetings for prayer, confession of sin, restitution and commitment of life. Students from the nearby St Paul Bible College visited the Bethel campus and soon Edwin Orr was preaching at meetings there, with similar results. At Northwestern College and Seminary, which was also in the same area, a visit by the President of Bethel College was the means of the awakening spreading there. In total, six college campuses in the Minneapolis-St Paul area were affected, with more than 2,000 students testifying to personal quickening.

Later in 1949 at North Park College in Chicago, a revival began as a result of the visit of J. Edwin Orr and Armin Gesswein. News of this awakening and those in Minnesota eventually caught the notice of the national press, and seems to have resulted in revivals on scores of campuses from coast to coast. Notable were the revivals at Wheaton College (Willard 1950), at Asbury College in Kentucky (Hoffman 1956), which experienced a further awakening in 1970, at Seattle Pacific College in Washington State (in connection with a visit of Armin Gesswein, J. Edwin Orr and others, Orr 1971:175), and Baylor University in Texas.[14]

The 1960s saw the development of the Charismatic Movement in the mainline denominations, following the birth in the 1950s of the Full Gospel Businessmen's Fellowship International under the leadership of Demos Shakarian, a friend and disciple of Charles Price and Oral Roberts, two Pentecostal healing evangelists. The movement spread rapidly among Episcopalians, Lutherans, Roman Catholics, and eventually among all denominations and throughout the world (see various articles in Burgess & McGee eds, 1988). It has undoubtedly brought spiritual life and awareness to millions, but even among its leaders there are those who doubt that it actually constitutes revival. Many of them feel that it is hopefully the precursor of a worldwide revival, which will itself herald the Parousia of Christ.

The 1960s also saw the birth and growth of the Jesus Movement among the hippies in California in 1967, which bore the hallmark of genuine awakening and was the means of rescuing thousands from the effects of drugs and winning them to Christ (Plowman 1971). According to one of the leaders in the movement, who was the minister for college students at Hollywood Presbyterian Church, it began spontaneously over a wide front on the West Coast of the United States from Los Angeles in the south via San Francisco to Seattle in the north (Don Williams in *Christianity Today* [Aug 27, 1971], cited in Jensen 1986:3-4). The movement had its excesses, notably that associated with David Berg and his Children of God, also Jim Jones and the mass suicide at Jonesville.

Broadly parallel with the Jesus Movement, a series of awakenings took place on the campuses of various Adventist colleges, beginning with Walla Walla College in Washington

State in 1967-1968 and extending in 1968-1969 to Pacific Union College, Angwin, California (about 75 miles north of San Francisco), and in 1969-1970 to Loma Linda University, La Sierra, California (east of Los Angeles). Andrews University in the state of Michigan, Columbia Union College in Washington DC, and Atlantic Union College in Lancaster, Massachusetts were affected in 1970-1971 (Jensen 1986:5-13). There were different causes which seemed to spark off the various awakenings; at Walla Walla College it began through a visit of workers from Campus Crusade, Inter-varsity and Navigators; at Pacific Union it started with a spontaneous prayer movement; at Columbia Union it came about through the visit of students from Andrews University. At the same time, the 'classical' marks of revival were evident in each place, including: 'Deep conviction of sin, confession and repentance; large numbers of conversions; a drop in crime rates and discipline problems; an infusion of compassion for unbelievers, resulting in spontaneous evangelism and ministries of social compassion; the emergence of leaders who have become prominent in Christian organizations; and the emergence of new ministry organizations to provide channels for evangelism and service for new believers' (Jensen *ibid*).

More recently, there have been a number of local revivals on other university campuses and at Christian schools. In 1978 a quiet movement of growth began at Stanford University, Palo Alto, California, south of San Francisco, which bears the hallmarks of genuine revival. Attendance at the main meetings grew from 30 in 1978 to 180 in 1984; the daily prayer meeting increased from 5 in 1979 when it began to 60 in 1984; Bible study groups which were started in the same year multiplied. Large numbers of students became involved in summer mission programmes. The movement spread to other universities and colleges in northern California. Those who were involved in the movement have scattered since graduation and are in positions of leadership and influence in IVF and other Christian groups where they have seen dramatic growth (Lamb 1991).

A much more dramatic revival took place at Whittier Christian High School in Los Angeles from 1987 to 1989. It had been preceded by fifteen years of secret prayer for revival by the mother of one of the students who had attended in the early 1970s, and by four parent/teacher prayer groups who were similarly praying through the early part of 1987.

The first stage of the revival began when one of the teachers, who was also a staff worker with Campus Crusade, spoke at a school assembly at three minutes notice when a scheduled speaker failed to turn up. Against his normal practice, he invited students to come forward at the end of an evangelistic message which he gave. To his surprise, scores responded, repented of their sins and began to follow the Lord. A meeting was begun for teaching and encouragement and soon 100 were regularly attending.

The second stage which began in the following autumn was marked by deep conviction of sin expressed in weeping, followed by genuine repentance and sound conversion. The sense of the presence of God was overwhelming. An earthquake measuring 6.1 on the Richter scale occurred during the second stage of the awakening, which gave those involved the idea of a movement called 'Youthquake', which organised prayer meetings for revival and sought to influence youth groups and other campuses in the area.

The third stage, which followed the launch of this movement, saw the most dramatic signs. 'The Spirit would "fall" spontaneously upon students in prayer meetings and even in the middle of classes. Just like in Jonathan Edwards' church some would fall to the ground overwhelmed by the love of God, some trembled under the power of the Holy Spirit like the early Quakers, and some, much to our dismay, would break out into ecstatic tongues of praise' (Stratton 1991:17). The revival spread to some of the other colleges in the area, and also to two campuses on the other side of the United States in Pennsylvania as one of the leaders spoke in his home state about what had happened in California. A prayer movement for God to send out 100,000 missionaries in this generation has grown out of the awakening (Stratton *ibid* 26-27).

A similarly dramatic but much more short-lived awakening took place at Dominion Christian School in Kansas City in September 1989. Weeping, fainting (or 'being slain in the Spirit'), ecstatic praising and tongues characterised the meetings, as children came under profound conviction and were counselled by older students.[15]

Two spiritual renewal movements, which many see as the precursors of awakening, are under way in the United States, the first among Southern Baptists and the second among ministers of many denominations in the Pacific Northwest.[16] The movement among Southern Baptists began in September 1989, when six Southern Baptist leaders issued a call for corporate prayer and public confession of sin. The 'solemn assemblies', which are a feature of the movement, have been times of confession and repentance, accompanied by many tears, and have resulted in the resolution of bitter church conflicts and increased attendances, among other things. They are being taken up by other denominations. In the 'Northwest Renewal', pastors' prayer conferences are being held in the states of Oregon and Washington, marked by confession of sin, the removal of denominational barriers, and a deep sense of fellowship. Charismatics and non-charismatics are confessing their antagonisms and criticisms, and are finding a new spiritual oneness.

In Canada, a significant revival took place in Saskatoon, Saskatchewan, in the early 1970s through the ministry of the Sutera brothers (Koch 1975; Lutzer 1976).[17]

Cuba

On the island of Cuba, there was a wave of revival beginning in 1950 which affected all the churches, but was mainly pentecostal in manifestation. The advent of the Castro regime brought it to an end. There is evidence of a new wave of revival at the present time, in spite of repression and persecution. It is estimated that 200,000 Cubans have made professions of faith over a period of fifteeen months. Thousands of others have expressed curiosity (Open Doors May 1990:6). The temporary openness at the time of the Pan-American Games there in August 1991, which also meant that import restrictions on Bibles were lifted, resulted in thouands coming to faith in Christ (Open Doors November 1991:5).

South America

South America has witnessed amazing growth in the last three decades among evangelical churches, but especially among the Pentecostals.

In Brazil, a prayer movement began in 1951 which was followed by significant movements of the Spirit of God under the ministry of J. Edwin Orr in the early 1950s. Local awakenings occurred in a number of places, there were large numbers of people professing conversion and the number of seminary students in the Presbyterian Church increased greatly.[18]

A remarkable revival is in progress in Argentina at present. This country lagged behind other lands of South America in seeing dramatic church growth, but this has changed since the Falklands War in 1982. A number of pastors and evangelists, including Omar Cabrera, Carlos Annacondia, Edgardo Silvoso and Hector Gimenez have seen remarkable success in their ministries, which have often been accompanied by exorcisms, physical healing and other miracles (Whittaker 1990:17-18,45; Wagner 1991:28-30).

There are reports of similar phenomena in Chile at present, but it has not been possible to obtain any more information on this.

Europe and the Soviet Union

In the Soviet Union, following the cessation of hostilities with Germany there was a period of comparative freedom and two remarkable waves of revival, the first in the late forties in the western borders of the Soviet Union, the second during the early and mid-fifties in central and eastern parts of the USSR (Sawatsky 1981:55-77).

Similarly, from 1945 till the end of 1947, in spite of the communist take-over, the Baptists in Romania enjoyed complete freedom and experienced great revival. For the next seven years also the churches were not subject to state pressure or control and growth continued, although this situation eventually changed, and from 1959 onwards the communist authorities turned their full attention to the task of controlling, and if possible, destroying the witness of the Christian Church. In 1974, at a time when the authorities were forced by external political pressure to make a number of concessions, revival broke out in the Western Transylvanian town of Oradea among the Baptists (Davies 1989/90:3-5). The preaching of a minister whose licence had been taken away, but later restored by the authorities, was accompanied by signs of deep repentance, and resulted in hundreds being converted and added to the church. In one year the number of people baptised in one church jumped from 42 to 356, with the membership increasing from around 700 to over 1,000. This church, where the revival began, continued to grow in spite of repression and persecution by the authorities, and the current membership stands at over 2,700, with 210 having been baptised in 1990 and a further 235 in 1991.[19] The revival soon spread to other areas and other denominations, and continues up till the present. The overthrow of the tyrannical Ceausescu regime in December 1989 has increased the opportunities for witness and evangelism on the part of those associated with the revival. The greatest danger to its continuance comes from the influx of extreme charismatic groups, some preaching Prosperity Theology, as well as the invasion of all kinds of well-meaning Christians who want to help, but whose presence is in danger of hindering the work (World Evangelization Information Service 9/9/91).

Revival is taking place in Bulgaria at the present time (World Evangelization Information Service 9/9/91). Forty years ago, there was also revival, mainly among the Pentecostal churches, who were generally bolder than the other denominations. However, in 1956, a member of the security police was converted in a Baptist church. He was dismissed from his position, but the news of his conversion spread. The Baptist church which he joined soon grew from five to one hundred members. The church was closed by the authorities and the members were scattered, some going to the capital Sofia. They maintained a quiet witness and eventually their children were converted and formed the core of a young people's group which secretly studied the Bible with the help of materials supplied from the West. In 1970, a team of seven evangelists was formed from this group, which took the Bible study material to small groups all over the country. From this work, much of the growth which began in 1984 has continued and, in the last two years, has developed into full-blown revival. In 1984, the Baptist Union of Bulgaria had a total of between five and six hundred members. The figure today is around 3,000, with 180 baptisms having taken place in three months, one pastor having baptised 44 in one month, and another 42. There is similar growth among the Pentecostals and an increasing number of independent charismatic churches. In Sofia alone, there are ten such churches, with an average of 200 members each. One of the newest, which only began in 1989, now has a membership of around 800. A spiritual awakening is also beginning among the Gypsies in Bulgaria. There are seven new Gypsy churches; 44 Gypsies have been baptised recently, and more baptisms are imminent.[20] There is also evidence of a revival movement in the Bulgarian Orthodox Church. It is a grassroots movement, led by priests and laity. It does not have the approval of the hierarchy (Open Doors November 1991:8).

A spiritual awakening has been going on for some time among Gypsies in France, where the Gypsy Evangelical Church is one of the country's largest evangelical denominations. The first Gypsy church was established by Clement le Cossec, an Assemblies of God pastor and the founder of the Gypsy Evangelical Mission. From France the work has spread to Gypsy communities elsewhere in Europe and to other parts of the world. In Romania, a flourishing work among Gypsies was savagely persecuted by the authorities under the late President Ceaucescu, but now there are new opportunities. In June 1991, 4,000 Gypsies attended evangelistic meetings in Romania (Mumper 1991:4).

Africa

In Africa, a notable revival occurred in Congo in 1953, which many have seen in retrospect as a preparation for the suffering and martyrdom which followed during the troubles which followed independence in 1960 (CLC 1954: Edwards 1990:258-262). On the island of Madagascar, an awakening occurred in 1946 and soon spread throughout the island through a national Christian Daniel Rakotozandry. In at least one West African country, there is an awakening in which many Muslims are coming to faith in Christ. However, there is the need to restrict the amount of information given because of the danger of reprisals from the fanatical Muslim Brotherhoods. The same is true in at least one North African country in remote rural areas. There is a revival reported in the Coptic Church in Upper Egypt through the preaching of an Orthodox priest. People have been coming from far and near to hear his preaching, but the meetings have recently been stopped by the ecclesiastical authorities (Open Doors November 1991:6).

Asia

In India, following independence from the British, the evangelical churches engaged in evangelism, and Indian Christians increasingly developed their life and witness. The Evangelical Fellowship of India was formed to promote evangelism, the deepening of spiritual life, and to encourage prayer for revival. In Kerala, a measure of revival was experienced at its conferences in 1954 and 1955. Revivals and ingatherings took place in the north-east states of India. In recent years, the Friends' Missionary Prayer Band and other indigenous groups have formed missionary societies for the further evangelisation of India, with most encouraging results.

The church in Nepal, which until recently suffered state persecution, has grown from 2,000 to 50,000 in ten years. According to Rev Robert Karthak, one of the most respected pastors there, the pouring out of the Holy Spirit on the first day of Pentecost is being relived in Nepal at the present time (Open Doors July 1991:7).

Although it has not received much publicity because of the sensitive nature of the situation, there is an awakening in progress in Bangladesh, where many Muslims are coming to Christ. In East Asia, there have been a number of notable revivals in the last forty years. In Borneo, awakenings occurred in 1953 and 1973 (Lees 1979:141-155,185-198; Lees 1987:105-122) and in Timor, Indonesia in 1965-1966 (Tari 1971; Koch 1972; Crawford 1972; Peters 1973; Cooley 1973).[21] In Korea awakenings have taken place in 1945, 1947, 1950 and continue on to the present time (Kim 1990:235,243-246).[22]

Perhaps the most amazing revival is that which has taken place since 1978 in China, and which is still going on, even under the renewed persecution which has followed the official suppression of the student democracy movement (Lyall 1985; Lambert 1991:142-174). 'Christianity fever' is the phrase coined by the Communist Party to describe the phenomenon, which it is powerless to stop. Accurate figures are impossible to obtain[23] (see Lambert's careful estimates) but the greatest growth has been in the central coastal provinces around Shanghai and in some of the southern provinces (see the map in Lambert *ibid* 158). Prayer seems to be an outstanding feature of the life of Chinese believers (see Wang *ibid* 247-254 on 'Lessons from the Prayer Habits of the Church in China').

This survey shows that, although the twentieth century has not seen revival on the scale witnessed in previous centuries, movements of the Spirit of God have been far from absent.

Among the subjects to which we now turn, we shall be asking the question: 'What, if anything, can we do to bring about a worldwide awakening?'

Notes

[1] Accounts of the best-known of recent revivals, eg those in East Africa, China, Korea, Borneo and Indonesia, are readily available. A number of these accounts are referred to in the text of this chapter. The reader is referred to them for more detail.

[2] Even among those deeply involved in the Charismatic Movement there is disagreement on this, many believing that, while the movement is a significant evidence of God at work among his people, real revival is still to come (see Matthew ed, 1990, where Bryn Jones and other leaders of the Harvestime movement [now known as Covenant Ministries] write of their hopes of a future revival on a large scale).

[3] This occurred six years after what was described at the time as 'the greatest revival in its history' which happened at Eastern Nazarene College in the late Spring of 1930 (Orr 1971:157).

[4] The Evangelical Christians developed mainly from the revival in St Petersburg under the ministry of Lord Radstock, which was continued by Colonel Pashkov (see above).

[5] William Fetler had been trained in Spurgeon's College in London.

[6] In Hungary, the next country he visited, he met an American missionary, Ruth Mahan, whom he married. After his death, his widow married a Czech pastor, Vladimir Fajfr, who was one of the converts of Stewart's work in Czechoslovakia. Although in their eighties, they are both still active in Christian work and live in the town of Zilina in Czechoslovakia. Ruth Fajr's book *James Stewart, Missionary* provides a connected account of Stewart's various visits.

[7] In Hungary between the Wars there was a considerable amount of spiritual activity already in existence, far more than in the other countries he had visited. Some of this was influenced by the Scottish Mission, which continued to work in Budapest, some showing more general influences from Evangelicalism abroad. Among the movements introduced into Hungary in these years, we note Christian Endeavour (known as the Bethania Union), an Evangelical Student Movement (F. F. Bruce and Godfrey Buxton were involved from Britain), YMCA, the Blue Cross Deaconess movement, and a number of foreign mission initiatives.

[8] The present writer, who has visited Hungary a number of times, has been told of a revival in some parts of the Lutheran Church in Hungary in 1938-1939, and again in 1946. Many of those who were influenced at the time left the Lutheran denomination and joined the Baptists. It has not been possible to discover whether these revivals were connected with the ministry

of Stewart, or whether they were independent of him. If the latter is the case, it would show that there was a more widespread movement of revival in operation at the time.

[9] The information in this paragraph derives from a series of statements in Orr 1981:55 which have no sources given. Possibly the evidence is contained in his unpublished papers.

[10] For accounts of the East African Revival by those who were personally involved, see Smith 1938; 1946; 1951; Church 1981; for assessments see Warren 1954; Taylor 1958; Stanley 1978: Gehman 1986. The book by H. H. Osborne (Osborne 1991), with a foreword by the present Archbishop of Canterbury, is basically a history of the Ruanda Mission of the CMS, although it does include an account of the Revival and its effects as an integral part of that history.

[11] In this section in particular there is a clear unevenness in the amount of space devoted to the various instances of revival. Where books describing such occurrences are readily available, the reader can refer to the fuller accounts. Contrariwise, where the author has only been able to obtain scant information, a brief reference is all that has been attempted. Most space has been given to events where information is not widely available and where the writer has been able to elicit facts and figures from those who were personally involved.

[12] A further result of the conference was the formation of the Hollywood Christian Group, dedicated to work for the conversion of those involved in the giant (at that time) film industry. The group continued for twenty years.

[13] See above on Billy Graham's London Crusade of 1954, which many felt was a time when revival was imminent. It is likely that others of his campaigns have manifested certain characteristics of revival, or have been the beginning of new spiritual movements.

More recently, Billy Graham said on a television programme in connection with his Edinburgh Crusade in 1991, that the Evangelists' Workshops which he had conducted in Moscow as part of the Lausanne Committee's Conference on Evangelism in 1990 was the nearest he had ever been to revival in the whole of his ministry.

[14] J. Edwin Orr was involved in a number of the college awakenings in the 1950s. In his account, he either talks of himself as 'an Irish evangelist' or 'an evangelist-historian', or uses the reports of others which mention his name! In most cases, the revivals were also reported independently by others (eg Willard 1950; Hoffman 1956), so there seems no reason to doubt the accuracy of his accounts.

[15] I owe this information to Miss Carrie Glanville, who attended my

course on Revivals at Fuller Seminary in August 1991, and who was present when the events took place. She also showed me a report on the events in a local Christian newspaper.

[16] They are described in a special study prepared by 'National and International Religion Report' which was reprinted in *Today* magazine (December 1990) pp 4-5,46.

[17] This was drawn to my attention by Rev Josif Tson of Romania. However, I have not seen either of the books mentioned.

[18] I owe this information to Dr Paul E. Pierson, Dean of the Faculty of Fuller Theological Seminary School of World Mission, who served as a missionary in Brazil.

[19] This revival is described in detail in *Revival in Romania* (forthcoming).

[20] The majority of this information was gained in November 1991 through conversation with a Bulgarian Baptist pastor, Vasco Vassilov, who was converted in 1962, worked in the semi-clandestine operations in the past, has been involved in the present revival and is now a full-time itinerant evangelist concentrating on work among the Gypsies. The most recent reports (March 1992) are even more encouraging.

[21] A number of writers have expressed reservations regarding some aspects of Kurt Koch's and Mel Tari's accounts of the Timor awakening. See eg Peters and Cooley *op cit*.

[22] Kim and others have expressed serious reservations regarding the kind of gospel being preached by some Korean church leaders, notably Paul Yonggi Cho, which was a mixture of the 'Possibility Thinking' of Robert Schuller and Prosperity Theology. According to Kim (*ibid* 246). Yonggi Cho has recently declared his rejection of the gospel he had formerly preached and committed himself henceforth to preaching the biblical, Reformed gospel. See also Douglass 1991:16-34.

The Yoido Full Gospel Central Church, where Paul Yonggi Cho is pastor, has received world-wide publicity. However, in Korea the requests of Western visitors to see the church are greeted with amusement (usually polite!) by Korean Christians. They feel that the church, which has around 250,000 members, in a city where the total church membership is around 3,000,000, is nothing exceptional!

[23] David Wang says, 'By conservative estimates, there are about fifty million Christians in China today. These are not Christians by birth or by tradition…These are people who have made a personal decision to follow Christ, and they are fully aware of the price they may have to pay' (Wang in Carson ed 1990:247).

CHAPTER 12

CONSTANTS AND VARIABLES OF REVIVAL

F ROM OUR SURVEY of the revivals and awakenings that have taken place in the Church over the centuries it is clear that there are a number of factors that constantly recur, and others that appear on some occasions and not others.

Among those features which constantly appear in revival we would include (1) persistent prayer, (2) powerful preaching and testimony, and (3) a deep awareness of the presence and holiness of God leading to a strong sense of conviction of sin and repentance followed by extreme joy when peace with God is received.

Among more variable factors are (1) physical manifestations of conviction of sin, (2) miracles of healing and the exercise of spiritual gifts such as supernatural knowledge, prophecy and speaking in tongues.

CONSTANTS IN REVIVAL

The most constant of all factors which appear in revivals is that of *urgent, persistent prayer*. This fact is acknowledged by all writers on the subject, and is usually made the basis for strong encouragements to pray for revival in the present (see Edwards [1742] Goen ed 1972:515-521; Edwards [1747] Stein ed 1977:309-436; Finney [1835;1868] Harding ed 1913:49-113; Church of Scotland 1840:132-159; Smeaton 1889:287-290; Torrey 1924:41-55, 174-191; Wallis 1956:113-175; Ravenhill

1959:6-10, 152-158; Lloyd-Jones 1986:174-198, 212-224, 278-316; Tippit 1987:25-46; Roberts 1988:66-69; Edwards 1990:72-85, 124-129; Hughes 1990:78-86 Hulse 1991).

Such prayer is both part of the preparation for revival, and also a characteristic of churches and Christians who are revived.

Luke, in both his Gospel and the Acts of the Apostles, makes a strong connection between prayer and the power of the Holy Spirit. Alone among the Gospel writers, he makes the point that Jesus himself was praying when he received the Holy Spirit at His baptism (Lk 3:21–22). In the power of the Spirit Jesus then triumphed over Satan in the desert (Lk 4:1) and began his public ministry in Galilee (Lk 4:14–15, 18–19). Luke also tells us that 'Jesus often withdrew to lonely places and prayed' (Lk 5:16), and that after one such occasion 'The power of the Lord was present for him to heal the sick' (Lk 5:17).

Similarly, the disciples after the ascension of Jesus 'joined together constantly in prayer' before the Holy Spirit came on them on the Day of Pentecost (Acts 1:14; 2:1–2). In a similar way Luke records the new enduement with the Spirit experienced by the church in answer to prayer (Acts 4:31). The promise of Jesus which he also records (Lk 11:13) assures the church that the heavenly Father continues to give his Spirit in answer to the prayers of his people.[1]

On many occasions in the history of the Church, the outpouring of the Spirit has been preceded by persistent, united prayer, as groups of Christians have joined together in beseeching God to act in a decisive way in the life of his people. Concerts of prayer, begun in the eighteenth century in Britain and North America, have often been the means by which believers have sought and received God's blessing. This was particularly noticeable in the awakening at the end of the eighteenth century with the Prayer Call, and also the Prayer Revival in the middle of the nineteenth century. Similarly the 1904 Revival was preceded by the formation of thousands of prayer groups, large and small, in many countries around the world. At the present time, there is a growing movement for prayer for revival, both nationally and worldwide.

When we were looking at the Old Testament we noted the key verse in 2 Chronicles (7:14), which according to at least one commentator (Williamson 1982:32, 225-226) is of central significance in the structure of the book. This verse, which is often appealed to by Christian writers and preachers in connection with revival (eg Hughes 1990:78-86), speaks of the need for God's people to 'humble themselves and pray and seek [God's] face and turn from their wicked ways', thus emphasising the paramount need for prayer. As God's people truly seek his face, humbling themselves before him and acknowledging their complete dependence on him, earnest and urgent in expressing their wholehearted desire for his presence and blessing together with their determination, like Jacob (Gen 32:26), not to give up until he answers, he will 'hear'. They will find that he reveals to them their secret sins which up to that time they have cheerfully committed and tolerated, but which now become hateful to them as they have a glimpse of how he views them, and their praying will itself 'prepare for the way of the Lord' as he comes to bless and save (Lk 3:4-6).

John Wesley's dictum that 'God does nothing but in answer to prayer' would lead us to the conclusion that, even where there are no records of Christians praying before revival, such prayer was nevertheless offered. Those who have been earnest and persevering in prayer, either alone or with others, have not always left records of the fact, especially if they are concerned that God, and not they, should have the credit for what subsequently happens.

In the case of the First Great Awakening, there were Christian leaders such as Cotton Mather (1663-1728), who over the course of his life spent hundreds of days in prayer and fasting for revival,[2] even though he did not live to see the answer to his prayers, at least not in his own church.[3] His contemporary Solomon Stoddard (1643-1729) experienced five local awakenings in his congregation at Northampton. We have no record of special prayer being offered by Stoddard, although presumably he, and possibly his congregation also, regularly sought God's blessing upon the work at Northampton. Jonathan Edwards, who was Stoddard's successor at Northampton, experienced revival in the church in 1734 and 1735, as well as in the 1740s as part of the large-scale awakening in the Thirteen Colonies. He was a very prayerful man, who, as he tells us in his 'Personal Narrative', at the age of nineteen,

> had great longings for the advancement of Christ's kingdom in the world; and my secret prayers used to be, in great part, taken up in praying for it (Hickman ed 1834:I.xiv).

In his *Faithful Narrative* he records that, shortly before the outbreak of the revival in 1734, the young people in the congregation had followed their pastor's advice

> that they should agree among themselves to spend the evenings after lectures in social religion, and to that end divide themselves into several companies to meet in various parts of the town; which was accordingly done, and those meetings have been since continued, and the example imitated by elder people (Goen ed 1972:148).

In these home-meetings, prayer was a feature, which would therefore have supplemented the private and public prayers of Edwards himself for awakening.[4]

During the Great Awakening in the American colonies also, David Brainerd's experience of awakening among the Indians was preceded by months of fervent wrestling in prayer both for worldwide revival and for the success of the gospel through his own preaching (see his *Diary* edited by Edwards [many editions. In the most recent (Pettit ed 1985), there are nearly two full columns of references to prayer in the 'Index' pp 607-608]).

We have already seen that George Whitefield attributed

much of the blessing which attended his ministry and that of others to a daily prayer meeting which he and his friends began in October 1737. We also saw that, on his return from Georgia in December 1738, he regularly attended the Fetter Lane Society, where 'sometimes whole nights were spent in prayer', and where, on more than one occasion, the power and presence of God were experienced in an overwhelming manner.

More than ten years earlier, the Moravian Church was renewed at Herrnhut in August 1727. This was preceded by weeks of prayer and spiritual counsel on the part of Count Zinzendorf and his fellow leaders. It was also preceded by nearly a century of prayer for renewal by the persecuted remnants of the Unity of Brethren in Bohemia and Moravia from whom the refugees at Herrnhut had come. The twenty-four hour prayer watch which soon became a distinctive feature of the Moravians, and which continued for another hundred years, provided much of the moving power which sent the Moravian missionaries to all corners of the globe.

Examples could be multiplied, but the 'Prayer Revival' of the mid-nineteenth century above all others is an encouragement to all Christians who may feel that if there is nothing we can *do* to bring revival, what is the point of even reading about it?

The experiences just mentioned serve to show the need for prayer,[5] while at the same time they show that there is nothing automatic or mechanical in the way that revival comes. 'Though it linger, wait for it; it will certainly come and will not delay' (Hab 2:3). God is sovereign; he is the One who inspires all true prayer; in *his* time, he will answer true, Spirit-inspired prayer. There is no need to further emphasise this point; the need is rather to do it!

A second factor which constantly recurs in revival and awakening is *powerful, urgent, relevant, Christ-centred, preaching*. On the Day of Pentecost, the 120 disciples were filled with the Spirit, and immediately began to speak in various languages about the wonderful works of God. This was followed by Peter's preaching, which was accompanied by such spiritual power that 3,000 were convicted and converted (Acts 2). The work continued and spread, as the Christians preached publicly and testified personally to the great saving acts of God in Christ (Acts 3ff).

Often in revivals an individual, or a small group, have experienced powerful awakening and renewal as they have waited on God in prayer, and then their personal testimony and public proclamation have been the means of communicating that blessing to other believers as well as awakening and converting non-Christians. This is such a constant feature that it is not necessary to repeat examples from what we have already considered.

The nature of the preaching and testimony needs to be noted. Powerful, urgent, relevant, Christ-centred communication of the gospel, emphasising the holiness and grace of God and the need for personal response is the kind of proclamation that has normally been a feature in revivals. In other words, 'awakening' preaching is what God has used at such times.[6] This is not to say that such preaching of itself can produce revival, nor even the conversion of one individual. But it does mean that when preachers themselves have been revived and quickened in times of revival, the content of their preaching as well as their method of presentation bear evidence to what has happened.

The preaching God uses at such times is not an emotional, manipulative, contentless ranting,[7] although a genuine awakening often produces its own crop of spurious counterfeits, those who think that imitation of the genuine article will produce the same results. Even preaching by genuinely revived preachers will produce some counterfeit conversions, but these are added to by the counterfeit preachers.

Preachers in revival are never flippant. They know they are the servants of the Most High God; they are aware of their awesome responsibility and of the seriousness of their task. They have a sense of the awfulness of men dying without Christ, and are extremely concerned to communicate the gospel faithfully. They have an urgent desire to bring men and women to repentance and faith before it is too late. They are concerned to make the truth plain and to show to each person its relevance for them. They are also concerned to avoid superficial, and therefore false, conversions.[8]

The twin activities of public preaching and personal testimony provide the ideal combination which has so often been the way that awakening and revival have spread. Even when the preaching has been limited to 'properly ordained ministers'[9] the witness of 'ordinary Christians' has been a major factor in the spread of revival. Again, the example of the early Christians in the Acts of the Apostles is relevant (Acts 8:4).

At times of spiritual awakening there is a paramount need for sound teaching and instruction. When those who are revived are themselves soundly taught in the truth of God's Word, they can properly interpret their own experience, adequately proclaim the truth to others, and also correctly instruct new converts. When this is not the case, or when they fail to properly instruct converts of the revival, there is a strong possibility that there will be dangerous extremes of belief and practice, and that the whole movement of awakening and revival will not produce lasting fruit. In the case of the 1904 Welsh Revival, many believe that Evan Roberts' neglect of preaching and instruction was the cause of the awakening's failure to achieve its full potential (Evans 1974:183-185).

The twin needs of warm, convinced, evangelistic preaching and testimony, and sound instruction of those awakened, revived, and converted are emphasised by many writers on the subject (Sprague 1832:115-214; Finney [1835, 1864] Harding ed 1913:155-249; Church of Scotland 1840:111-131; Smeaton 1889: 278-280,286-287; Ravenhill 1959:52-57, 68-74; Edwards 1990:100-111).

Revival often spreads through contact, almost like a contagion. Individuals or groups who have experienced God's power are the means of bringing it to others. In some cases, it seems that a preacher brings revival with him as he moves on from place to place. Edwin Orr's experience seemed to be of this nature in his many campaigns around the world between the two World Wars, and others have also had this experience. However, this is different from the teaching that it is possible to produce a revival by the use of means.

A third factor which constantly occurs in times of revival is *an unusual sense of the presence and holiness of God*. This produces a deep conviction of sin which overpowers, and, at times, seems to threaten to drive people to despair and distraction. Those who are touched by the Spirit of God in revival are often overwhelmed with a conviction of their own sin and guilt before God; they have a sense of God's holiness and hatred of sin, and often feel they are too bad ever to receive God's forgiveness. They may remain under such conviction for some time—days or weeks, and may come near to despair and distraction. As we shall see, this is the cause of some of the unusual physical behaviour which manifests itself on many occasions: fear of God's wrath and judgment on sin producing shaking, weeping, crying out, prostration etc. The joy which comes flooding into the hearts and minds of those who move from such fear and terror to the sense of God's forgiveness and acceptance may also produce highly emotional behaviour with physical accompaniments.

The people of God in revival are joyful and serious at the same time. They know they are unworthy recipients of God's choicest blessings; they have been humbled themselves as they have been convicted of their previous superficiality; they are overwhelmed with joy in their knowledge of the Lord; they are careful not to forfeit the Lord's presence through grieving the Holy Spirit. They are concerned for outsiders that they come from sin and alienation to faith and joy. Many of them have felt the awfulness of estrangement from God and want to warn others of the terrible nature of life and death without Christ.

Those present in times of revival testify to an unusual sense of God's presence, which at times pervades a whole community. Jonathan Edwards says of the awakening in Northampton in 1735, 'The town seemed to be full of the presence of God' (Goen ed 1972:151).

According to a contemporary witness of the 1904 Welsh Revival, 'The Spirit was in the pits [the coal mines]...it was as pleasant to go to work as it was to go to a place of worship....The presence of God was everywhere' (cited in Edwards 1990:246). The experience of a Christian man and his daughter from the north of England who wanted to visit Rhos in North Wales where the revival was especially evident is worth quoting:

> They caught the Sunday midnight slow train and arrived in Chester station at 6.00 a.m. Not knowing where to go from here, they enquired of a porter: 'How can we get to the place where the revival is?' They were told there would be a train at 8.00 a.m. to Wrexham and from there they would catch a local train to Rhos. 'But how will we know when we are near Wrexham', they asked. 'Oh', replied the porter, 'You'll feel it in the train.' And they did! There was an unmistakeable expectancy in the air. Two miles outside Rhos they enquired again and were told, 'Go down that road and you will feel it down there'(*ibid* 247).

In the 1949 Revival on the island of Lewis in Scotland, as a prayer meeting in a cottage in a village where there was a lot of opposition was concluded, 'the whole granite house shook like a leaf', according to Rev Duncan Campbell, who was present. He goes on to say that, although it was 2.00 am, 'the whole village [was] alive, ablaze with God'. Men and women were carrying chairs and asking if there was room in the church for them! (*ibid* 257). Many further testimonies can be given to the same effect.

The absence of such a sense of the holiness of God and of the overwhelming consciousness of his presence is an indication that at present the Church stands in great need of revival. Whatever experiences we may have of God's gracious presence in our lives, ministries or meetings, we all need to pray for a new, significant visitation of God.

Notes

[1] Note the present tense of the verb 'ask', ie 'keep asking', emphasising the need for perseverance in prayer, as illustrated also by the parable in Luke 18:1–8. See also Luke 11:9 lit 'Keep asking…keep seeking…keep knocking'.

[2] At times Mather was guilty of self-advertisement in declaring his piety to others. However, in this case, he records it in his private diary (which he left for his sons to read, and which has in fact been published for the first time in the twentieth century [Mather ed. Ford 1957]).

[3] Mather first began to urge prayer for revival in 1692 and set himself to do this seriously in 1696. In 1726 he proposed regular, synchronised days of prayer for revival by all evangelical Christians (see Lovelace 1979b: 244, 275).

[4] It seems that as Edwards' experience grew he saw increasingly the value of united prayer for revival. In *Some Thoughts…* (1742) he mentions private prayer and fasting, but also canvasses the possibility of a day of fasting and praying to be observed by 'all God's people in America', and makes some suggestions for ministers 'without a great deal of trouble' to organise this (Goen ed 1972:513-521). When he wrote his *Humble Attempt* in 1747, the major part of the work is taken up with exegesis of biblical texts (notably Zech 8:20–22) which speak of united prayer, together with exhortation and detailed suggestions for regular prayer of this kind for awakening (Stein ed 1977:312-436).

[5] Because this is not primarily a book on praying for revival (although the author's hope is that it will stir up Christians to pray), there is no space to deal in any detail with the content of such prayer. What can be gleaned from reading, discussion and experience is that in prayer for revival as well as in prayer during revival there is an urgent desire for fellowship with God, for holiness individually and among the people of God, for a demonstration of the glory of God, and for the vindication of the Name of God.

[6] Charles Finney, in the letters which he wrote on revival in 1845, considered that the preaching which was common at the time compared unfavourably with that which God had used fifteen years before. He says, 'There is much less probing of the heart by a deep and thorough exhibition of human depravity, than was formerly the case…I fear that stress enough is not laid upon the horrible guilt of this depravity.' He also comments that

'stress enough has not been laid upon the necessity of divine influence upon the hearts of Christians and of sinners' and acknowledges 'I am confident that I have sometimes erred in this respect myself...I have laid too much stress upon the natural ability of sinners to the neglect of showing them the nature and extent of their dependence upon the grace of God and the influence of his Spirit' (Finney ed Dayton 1979:17-18).

[7] Finney devotes no less than six of his letters (see previous note) to this subject of 'encouraging an unhealthy degree of excitement' in revival preaching, and cites an amusing example at a camp meeting in New York State which he had himself witnessed (Finney *ibid* 38-63 esp 50-51).

[8] The sermons that Jonathan Edwards preached when the revival of 1734-1735 broke out were published in 1738 under the general title, *Five Discourses on Important Subjects, Nearly concerning the Great Affair of the Soul's Eternal Salvation...Delivered at Northampton, chiefly at the Time of the Late Wonderful Pouring Out of the Spirit of God There*. They include one on 'Justification by Faith' which is strongly doctrinal, and considerably enlarged for publication, others on 'Pressing into the Kingdom of God',· 'Ruth's Resolution', and 'The Justice of God in the Damnation of Sinners', all of which contain urgent calls to conversion, and 'The Excellency of Jesus Christ', a sermon which he preached away from Northampton, but which was well received, focusing on Christ as the Lamb and the Lion in Revelation 5:5-6 (in Hickman ed 1834: I. 620-689). His famous sermon on 'Sinners in the Hands of an Angry God' was preached at Enfield, Connecticut, in 1741 'at a time of great awakenings; and attended with remarkable impressions on many hearers', and contains urgent appeals to 'flee from the wrath to come' (in Hickman ed 1834: II. 7-12).

[9] As men like Jonathan Edwards, Gilbert Tennent and George Whitefield wished. See further below.

CHAPTER 13

CONSTANTS AND VARIABLES OF REVIVAL (CONCLUDED)

VARIABLES IN REVIVAL

WHEN OUTSIDE OBSERVERS look at revivals, they often focus on the outward and unusual phenomena, rather than concentrating on the inward experience which is causing the external and exceptional. This is certainly true of non-Christian observers, but it is often also true of unsympathetic Christians, who view the whole movement with suspicion or distaste. At times, it is also true of those who are actually involved in the revival, but who are not sufficiently discerning to distinguish the essential from the peripheral.

Jonathan Edwards showed a masterly discernment in his assessment of the Great Awakening in the eighteenth century, but his example has not always been followed in later revivals, as it was not even in his day. This is not to claim that his assessments were always right, but he does point the way to us in the assessment we make of certain phenomena which have sometimes been evident in revivals.

Physical accompaniments of conviction of sin and the sense of joy following the experience of conversion have often been evident in times of revival. The Great Awakening in Britain and North America saw all kinds of physical manifestations, especially under the preaching of George Whitefield, the Wesleys, Edwards, Gilbert Tennent and others. The attitude of the various leaders towards these differed in part from each other, although no radical division was caused by these differences.[1]

John Wesley initially seemed to be more favourably disposed to them than was his own brother Charles, George Whitefield or John Cennick. When people fainted or writhed on the ground under his preaching, he initially took it fairly uncritically as a genuine manifestation of the work of God's Spirit in conviction and even encouraged it.[2] However, his enthusiasm for such phenomena eventually declined, and by the end of his life he felt it was Satan who pushed people to such 'extravagance' (*Journal* ed Curnock 1938: VII.153).

Even in the early days when he was more favourably disposed to the strange behaviour of those under conviction, his encouragement of the practice was limited to praying such prayers as 'Lord! where are thy tokens and signs?' (Dallimore *ibid* 326). Unlike some modern practitioners, Wesley did not seek to produce such experiences as 'being slain in the Spirit' by physical contact with the converts.[3]

His brother Charles called the strange phenomena 'the fits' and virtually made fun of them (Dallimore 1988:94). His remedy was to have those who were manifesting this behaviour (often young women) carried outside into the fresh air where, he says, they immediately recovered! Whitefield accepted the unusual manifestations as being possibly genuine accompaniments of conviction, but also recognised the possibility of counterfeit.

Edwards made the profoundest assessment, arguing that it is only to be expected that the sight of one's own sin as God sees it is likely to cause bodily accompaniments of spiritual distress, just as an intense experience of the love of Christ may have physical effects (Goen ed 1972:230-234). In the case of the latter, he describes in some detail the experience of his own wife, although he does not mention her by name (Goen *ibid* 331-341). However, he makes the point strongly that the genuineness of the experience is not to be judged one way or other by the outward accompaniments.[4] As we shall see, he also introduces the possibility of counterfeit experiences, either psychologically induced or satanically inspired. (For a discussion of the phenomena in the eighteenth-century awakening see Dallimore 1970: I.321-331.)

Subsequent revivals have often, but not invariably, seen physical manifestations of different kinds. When they have appeared they have sometimes been bizarre. We have noted a number of these in our historical review, especially in the camp meetings in the Second Great Awakening in the American South. Some of the preachers definitely encouraged such manifestations, which occurred among rough frontiersmen. Critics of that revival and similar critics of all revivals have often exaggerated what actually took place. As a modern writer says:

> These grossly exaggerated revival exercises, which have been cited widely to discredit the revival, were probably restricted to a comparative few…Except at the very start, they were never a significant factor in the camp meetings (Boles 1972:68).

We shall be wise if we follow Edwards's example in concentrating on the spiritual message and assessing the genuineness of the experience by its spiritual results (see especially his positive criteria in *The Distinguishing Marks…* [1741] in Goen *ibid* 248-260; see above Chapter II).

The continuance of *miracles and spiritual gifts* in the Christian Church after the close of the Apostolic Age up till the present time is a difficult subject. Our concern at present is with the possibility that, in times of revival, whatever is the case in other times, there have been occurrences of this kind. The evidence for such occurrences in the centuries before the present one is quite sparse. This could be accounted for in different ways, but it does seem to be the case that, while times of revival are exceptional times, this does not necessarily mean that miracles of healing, and the exercise of other spiritual gifts, will inevitably take place. The evidence of previous centuries is that usually they do not; the evidence of the present century is that quite often, but by no means always, they do.

From time to time revivals have produced *claims* to revelation and gifts of prophecy, but these have often proved spurious. We have already noted in the eighteenth century, during the time of the Evangelical Revival in England, that the small sect of 'French Prophets' or Camisards who had fled to England from persecution in France were claiming the gift of prophecy. In France, children had been prominent in claiming visions and prophecies, being known as 'the Little Prophets of the Cevennes'. Initially, some of the revival leaders in England were sympathetic to their claims, but extravagances and prophecies which failed in their fulfilment caused them to reject their claims.[5]

Whitefield himself at one time gave considerable credence to impulses and impressions on his mind which he understood to be God-given. However, Edwards gently chided him concerning this when they met, and Whitefield later changed his understanding on the matter (Dallimore 1970: I.342-344; Murray 1987:489-490).

Among the Primitive Methodists who were formed at the beginning of the nineteenth century in the Second Evangelical Revival (see above Chapter VII), there were frequent claims to visions and dreams from God. Hugh Bourne, Lorenzo Dow and others recorded various dreams and visions they had received, calling them to ministry, guiding them regarding the holding of camp-meetings, giving a 'Visionary Ladder' of leadership order, confirming the doctrine of Christian Perfection, warning them of plots against them, among other things.[6] In the visions there was a highly developed symbolism which indicated 'the spiritual condition of individual leaders, whether they were living holy lives and engaging fully in their ministries'. They included trumpets, cups, a standard with an eagle above, a shining breastplate, crowns and stars. The visionary leaders ceased to be trusted after Mary Dunnel, one of the leaders as well as one of the main visionaries, was found guilty of immorality and fell away.

We have already noted the sad case of Humphrey Jones, a Welsh Methodist evangelist who was greatly used in the 1858 Revival in Wales. Exhaustion from his labours produced a mental aberration which caused him to claim the gift of prophecy, with bizarre, and ultimately tragic results on his ministry (see above Chapter IX).

In our own day, the preacher who was initially used by God in the revival which broke out in Romania in 1974 eventually left the country for the USA, believing that God had told him that he would be a new Billy Graham through whom the Lord would convert America. The result has been a tragic end to his effectiveness.[7]

While some would claim that such occurrences do not negate the possibility of genuine prophecies, they do serve as a warning concerning the dangers inherent in such claims, and should warn us of the possibility of self-deception, especially at times of heightened spiritual activity and awareness. Such claims seem to involve all kinds of danger and the possibility of abuse and deception.

In the matter of miracles a large number of quite staggering claims have been made concerning the work of the lay evangelists involved in the revival in Timor in Indonesia, including raising the dead, turning water into communion wine, team members walking on water, and many examples of healing the blind, the deaf and the dumb (see especially Tari 1971, but also Koch 1970: Crawford 1972).

However, doubts have been cast on the accuracy of some of Tari's statements. According to one writer (Roberts 1988:185), 'Tari's works are seriously questioned by thoughtful Christians'; compare also Cairns (1986:363), who says, 'Other writers claim he exaggerates the miracles in Indonesia in 1966'. Frank L. Cooley, a staff member of the Institute for Study and Research of the Indonesian Council of Churches, visited Timor in 1972, and reported his findings in a long letter, reprinted in the *Southeast Asian Journal of Theology*

(1973:78-93). He reacts quite coolly (!) to some of the claims regarding miracles, but found it impossible to check the validity of what was said. Mel Tari's statement that water had been turned into communion wine over 60 times he finds too much to accept!

Other twentieth century revivals have been accompanied by healings and exorcisms, according to the witness of those involved. The remarkable revival in China over the past thirty years has been marked by all kinds of miracles as God has vindicated the faith and perseverance of his suffering people.

However, such happenings also bring their problems and the possibility of their misuse. The revival in Western Romania which the writer has observed first-hand has not been accompanied by miracles of healing,[8] with two exceptions, both of which have had unfortunate consequences, which have persuaded the leaders that prayer for healing should be kept strictly separate from the evangelistic activity of the church. In one case, a man whose lower body was burned by acid after he fell into a pit at work was completely healed, even to the extent that his flesh and muscles grew again. However, he has now set himself up as a sort of 'guru', does not attend church, claims to receive visions and prophetic messages, and is creating a cult-following for himself. Similarly, a woman who was healed of a brain-tumour as a result of the prayers of the church engages in an itinerant programme, demonstrating her own intellectual prowess and does not ascribe her healing to the Lord.

In the matter of miracles and spiritual gifts, Jonathan Edwards followed the general Reformation and Puritan understanding of the disappearance of such activities as prophecy, working miracles, tongues etc. at the close of the New Testament canon at the end of the first century[9] (see *Charity and its Fruits* [Ramsay ed 1989:153]; *History of the Work of Redemption* [Wilson ed 1989:365]). Edwards was not a man to follow any tradition, however venerable, without good reason, but neither was he an iconoclast. He was probably predisposed to accept the Reformers' views, and this was reinforced during the awakenings by the extreme claims made by some to new revelations, guidance by impulses and from texts of Scripture taken out of context (see *Some Thoughts*... [Goen ed 432-444).

In addition, his high view of the ordained minister and his preaching office possibly disposed him against the exercise of any spiritual gift which would threaten the position of the minister.[10]

Finally, his own deep experiences of fellowship with God led him to value these infinitely more than any 'immediate revelations' which some who were involved in the revival were claiming. Speaking of the ideas of some to the effect that the coming millennium would witness a return of the spiritual gifts which were present in the Apostolic Age,[11] he says:

> I don't expect a restoration of these spiritual gifts...nor do I desire it...it appears to me that it would add nothing to the glory of those times, but rather diminish from it. For my part, I had rather enjoy the sweet influences of the Spirit, shewing Christ's spiritual divine beauty, and infinite grace, and dying love, drawing forth the holy exercises of faith, and divine love, and sweet complacence, and humble joy in God, one quarter of an hour, than to have prophetical visions and revelations for a whole year (Goen ed 1972:281).[12]

How many of those today who oppose the continued use of spiritual gifts do so for this reason?

In the view of the present writer, we are not justified biblically in rejecting *a priori* the possibility of miracles and other spiritual gifts today,[13] especially in times of revival. However, we do well to treat claims to such powers with some caution, to be aware of the dangers which even genuine experiences can bring as well as the possibility of counterfeits, and to concentrate on the relationship with God which is the aim of the work of the Holy Spirit at all times.

When miracles appear to be taking place in connection with

a work of God, either in a time of revival or at any other time, it is worth asking a number of questions:

> Do they contribute to the work of the Gospel? Do they distract from the spiritual work? Is Christ glorified as a result? What is the spiritual character of those manifesting these gifts and powers?

These may help us to assess the genuineness or otherwise of what is claimed.

Notes

[1] Modern writers often make sweeping statements about physical manifestations in past revivals and about the attitudes of the revival leaders to the phenomena. Those who are unsympathetic to the whole idea of revival often use such phenomena to discredit the genuineness of the movements (eg Davenport 1917, whose book bears the title *Primitive Traits in Religious Revivals*). On the other hand, some modern Charismatic writers make broad generalisations about such phenomena in past revivals and the attitudes of leaders at the time, together with comparisons with the present, which need to be severely qualified. For example, to state that the phenomena of 'being drunk in the Spirit' or 'being slain in the Spirit' (phrases with little, if any, biblical precedent) were common in past revivals and were welcomed by the leaders in those revivals makes a number of unwarranted assumptions and begs a number of important questions.

[2] See the various entries in his journal for April and May 1939 cited in Dallimore 1970: I.321-322, taken from the time of his extended visit to Bristol.

[3] A brief, but helpful, comment on the *differences* between the historical examples and the modern appears in the *Church Growth Digest* [UK] (Meredith 1989/90:10-11).

[4] In his *Distinguishing Marks...* he gives a total of nine 'non-signs', factors the presence or absence, of which say nothing as to whether a movement is, or is not, the work of the Spirit of God (Goen *ibid* 228-248). The second of these deals with 'effects on the bodies of men; such as tears, tremblings, groans, loud outcries, agonies of body, or the failing of bodily strength'. He argues that the presence of such signs do not of themselves

authenticate the work, neither do they necessarily negate it. He is certainly not surprised when they do appear, and gives a number of scriptural arguments to justify them.

[5] See the note to Chapter V above.

[6] The writer is indebted to Rev David Morrell of Abbots Langley, Herts who loaned him a copy of his M.Phil. thesis on *Some Aspects of Revivalist and Charismatic Movements in England, 1800-1862* (University of Manchester, 1987). Chapter 7 on 'Phenomena' was particularly helpful.

[7] Some of the 'Kansas City Prophets' who visited England with John Wimber in 1990 prophesied that a revival would break out in Britain by the end of July of that year. John Wimber was so convinced of the genuineness of the oracle that he brought his family with him to the UK in order not to miss the event. The set date passed without any revival taking place (Wright 1991b:20-21).

[8] This is true at least of the Baptist church of Oradea where the revival began. The writer is not able to say whether or not it is true in other places or in the Pentecostal churches, which have also been touched by the revival.

[9] The Reformers' rejection of the possibility of new revelations in the present arose partly from their reaction to the Zwickau prophets and other Anabaptist groups who subordinated Scripture to the immediate guidance they claimed to have from the Spirit, and partly from their opposition to Roman Catholic claims to the infallible guidance of the Spirit in the Church's *magisterium*. They did not all, however, reject all spiritual gifts apart from the gift of preaching, as is sometimes claimed. See, for example, Martin Luther's 'Letters of Spiritual Counsel' (Luter ed Tappert 1955:) for references to prayer for people for their release from the power of the devil.

The Puritans followed the Reformers' views partly because of the appearance of the Quakers and other left-wing prophetic groups in England and New England who repeated the extreme claims of the radicals of the sixteenth century. They, too, did not all reject all spiritual gifts, although they defined many of them in such a way as to exclude the claims of such groups as the Quakers. See John Owen's work on Spiritual Gifts (Owen ed Goold 1854:).

[10] Edwards' view of the pastoral ministry was, like that of his forbears and contemporaries (Hall 1972:4-10; Westerkamp 1988), a very high one. In a number of the ordination sermons that he preached, some of which were published soon after being delivered, he articulated the classic Puritan attitude to the ministry, which he made his own to a marked degree. 'A faithful minister is to be joyfully received and beloved by the people under his care as a precious gift of their ascending Redeemer' (*The Church's Marriage to Her Sons, and to Her God* in Hickman ed 1834: II. 17-26), and is 'the greatest

blessing of anything in the world that ever God bestows on a people' (*The True Excellency of a Gospel Minister* in *ibid* 955-960). As the minister is to follow Christ in his example, so the people are to 'esteem him very highly in love for his work's sake', seeing his work 'is in some respects the same with the work of Christ' (*Christ the Example of Ministers* in *ibid* 960-965). As he said in his farewell sermon

> Ministers are his messengers, sent forth by him; and, in their office and administrations among their people, represent his person, stand in his stead, as those that are sent to declare his mind, to do his work, and to speak and act in his name (*ibid* I. ccxlv).

Similarly,

> in administering the sacraments, the minister represents the person of Christ; he baptizes in his name, and in the Lord's supper stands in his stead. In administering church-censures, he still acts, as the apostle expresses it, in the person of Christ (*ibid*).

Edwards' ideas on lay ministry were also those of classical Puritanism. The clergy-centredness of such an approach required that the life of the church focused on the Sunday meetings for worship, the climax of which was the (lengthy) sermon delivered by the minister, with a week-night 'lecture' thrown in for good measure. The place of the laity was to listen, and then to put the teaching of the sermon into practice in their various 'callings'. The days when laymen were allowed to preach were long past; the only exceptions were those who had been duly licensed to do so by an official body (as was David Brainerd [Pettit ed 1985:174]), and who usually were later ordained to the ministry (see above Chapter VI n 9).

By contrast, the Separates and Baptists who developed from the Great Awakening made lay exhorting and lay preaching a major part of their strategy in establishing and building up new churches. In their subsequent growth they, to a certain extent, hijacked the results of the revival from the control of the Congregationalist clergy (Goen 1962; McLoughlin 1967; Stout 1986: 209-211). Like the Moravians and Methodists, they mobilised the membership of their churches, and, together with the latter, led the way after the Revolutionary War in opening up the new territories to the gospel (Sweet 1973: 215-221).

11 On this, see further below on 'Revival, History and the Millennium'.

12 This quotation is taken from *Distinguishing Marks....* The whole section (Goen ed 1972:278-282) is worth reading both by those who affirm the continuance of spiritual gifts, as well as by those who deny such continuance. Also worth reading (by both groups!) are two of the sermons in the series *Charity and Its Fruits*, based on 1 Corinthians 13. Sermon 2 is on 'Love More Excellent Than Extraordinary Gifts of the Spirit', and Sermon 14 on

'Divine Love Alone Lasts Eternally' (in Ramsay ed 1989: 149-174, 351-365; also in Edwards ed 1852, modern repr). The comparisons and contrasts which Edwards makes are invaluable.

[13] The question of the nature of prophecy today is a difficult one, and this is not the place to enter into a discussion of this subject. See a review article by Mark Cartledge of a number of different positions adopted on the subject in recent writings (Cartledge 1991:17-19). Also see Wright 1991b:20-21 for an assessment of the 'Kansas City Prophets'.

CHAPTER 14

ABERRANT ACCOMPANIMENTS OF REVIVAL

IN THE TWO PREVIOUS CHAPTERS we have already mentioned some of the problems associated with revival. In the present chapter we will pursue this a little further, mainly by reference to two excellent treatments of the subject, the first by Jonathan Edwards in Part IV of his *Some Thoughts Concerning the present Revival of Religion in New-England* (1742; Goen ed 1972:409-495), and the second that of Richard Lovelace, who makes conscious use of Edwards' analysis, but also develops his ideas (Lovelace 1979:239-270; Chapter 8 'How Revivals Go Wrong').

In studying what Lovelace calls 'the pathology of awakenings', we need to be aware of the various effects of the world, the flesh and the devil, which divert and distort the work that is going on in revival.

The effects of *the world* will be seen in the opposition and caricature suffered by those involved in revival from the hands of outsiders. When the church is alive and active and forcing the outside world to pay attention, rejection of the message is accomplished by misrepresentation of it and its advocates. Faults and imperfections in Christians, especially in those who are leaders in the church, are magnified and used as a reason for rejection of what is happening in revival. This often comes through the media, and in the present day the influence of television can have a tremendous influence in distorting the popular conception of Christianity.

Opposition can also come from those inside the professing

church who reject the message of the revival, especially when much of the Church is at a low ebb of spiritual life. They ostensibly focus on the excesses, but in fact they may be reacting against the challenge of a revived Christianity. In the eighteenth century, one of the most articulate opponents of the Great Awakening in New England was Charles Chauncy, a Congregational minister in Boston. He wrote his famous *Seasonable Thoughts on the State of Religion in New-England* in 1743, professedly to defend the true Puritan nature of New England church life from the innovations of the revivalists. He appealed to the Orthodox writers of the past to make his case, but he was increasingly Rationalistic in his faith and eventually embraced Universalism.

Over-reaction against such opposition or caricature on the part of those experiencing revival has its own potential for distortion. Revived Christians can develop a ghetto mentality or a persecution complex when faced with opposition from the outside world or from the 'world in the church'. They can also develop a sense of superiority and pride, and manifest a critical spirit towards those who attack them. Being convinced of the rightness of what they are doing, and believing that God is on their side, they may doggedly persevere in their chosen patterns of behaviour, and unwittingly go to extremes. They may also separate overhastily from those in the church who are attacking them, rather than remaining in the church group or denomination, seeking humbly to learn from the criticisms and seeking to maintain a winsome testimony to what they believe God is doing in and through them.

The world can also have a bad effect on revival when those involved in it are overly influenced in their ideas and methods by society around them. Techniques of mass-communication adopted from the world can easily become means of mass-manipulation which will produce many spurious converts, whose presence will adversely affect the purity of the revival and whose subsequent behaviour will discredit it. Some of the techniques which were introduced into revival activity by Charles Finney in the nineteenth century come into this category, with adverse results for subsequent periods of revival and a general muddying of the waters for a Christian understanding of the nature of revival. Revivalists who followed in Finney's footsteps introduced even more techniques learnt from the world, with even more disastrous results.

The world, ie the society around, can also subtly influence the forms, goals and ideals of the revived church, particularly when the church is moving away from its old forms of expression etc, as happens in revival. A culturally appropriate Christianity can too easily become a culturally-conditioned Christianity.

Finally, the world can be the source of direct temptation to revived Christians, especially leaders, in times of heightened emotion, activity and success, in the areas of money, power and sex. When emotions have been profoundly stirred, and when God is bringing unheard of blessing and 'success' to his people, worldly temptations along various lines can be a real source of danger.

The flesh, that is the fallenness that remains even in the most advanced Christian, and which is especially powerful in new converts, can and does adversely affect revivals when they occur. New converts in particular, overwhelmed with a sense of their new experience, can easily imagine themselves perfect and infallible. They can easily feel that they have arrived, that there is no more work to do other than to enjoy their new-found blessings, that the Spirit within them will infallibly guide them in their opinions, decisions and behaviour, and that other Christians who oppose their behaviour are 'dead', unregenerate and tools of the devil in opposing the genuine work of God. Examples can be brought from the Great Awakening of the eighteenth century down to our own day. Edwards says that spiritual pride

is the main door, by which the Devil comes into the hearts of those that are zealous for the advancement of religion. 'Tis the chief inlet of smoke from the bottomless pit, to darken the mind, and mislead the judgment:

> this is the main handle by which the Devil has hold of
> religious persons, and the chief source of all the mischief
> that he introduces, to clog and hinder the work of God
> (Goen ed 1972:414).

And spiritual pride is a sin which closes the mind to correction or instruction from others, and so prevents the person from learning the error of his ways.

The flesh can also be responsible for perpetrating excesses of emotion and behaviour which are the merely natural, and, perhaps, idiosyncratic accompaniments of genuinely spiritual experience. These excesses are mistaken, both by outsiders and insiders, as essential parts of the spiritual experience itself. The flesh can cause those involved in revival to concentrate on those features which pander to human desires, majoring on emotional and physical expressions (eg hugging, kissing and excessive physical contact) which have potential for misuse.[1]

A further effect of the flesh is in the degeneration of spiritual experience, the spiritual law of entropy, which causes the 'decay' of spiritual experience and its hardening into a new formalism, which preserves the outward expressions of revival, but has lost the inner heart.

As we have already hinted, especially in the citation from Edwards on spiritual pride, *the devil* is extremely active in times of revival, throwing up smokescreens, causing misunderstanding and misrepresentation, driving to excess, etc.

Lovelace suggests three lines of attack employed by Satan in times of revival which we may develop further:

> (1) to destroy the work either by persecution or by
> accusation which will discredit it and limit its growth,
> (2) to infiltrate the work and reinforce its defects in
> order to provide more evidence for accusation, and (3) to
> inspire counterfeit revival which may deceive the elect
> and further confuse and alienate the onlooking world
> (Lovelace 1979:257; the whole section [pp. 257-261] is
> worth reading).

The devil diverts attention from the spiritual nature of what is happening in revival to the peripheral behaviour, especially of the 'lunatic fringe' who always appear at such times. Indeed, Satan has a hand in the excesses of such people. He inspires counterfeit revival, 'false fire' to deceive those desiring revival and to discredit genuine revival.

As 'the accuser of the brethren' (Rev 12:10) he provokes rumours, accusations and false charges, especially against the leaders in revival. He causes misunderstandings between individuals and groups involved in revival, seeking to divide those who are genuinely revived from each other. He magnifies genuine differences between those involved, so that they feel they must emphasise their differences rather than the points on which they agree—cf the disagreements of John Wesley and George Whitefield. He seeks to cause the revived and the unrevived to mutually exclude each other, causing new divisions in the Church.

Finally in this chapter, we may note the effect of what Edwards terms 'wrong principles' (Goen ed 1972:432ff), and what Lovelace refers to as 'Theological Factors in Aberrant Revival' (Lovelace 1979:261ff). Wrong theological ideas, held in particular with reference to the experience or conduct of those affected by revival, can cause grave problems in the progress of revival and in its long-term effects. Edwards mentions, among other things, claims to immediate inspiration or revelation, the adoption of new methods to arouse people's interest and concern without thought of the long-term consequences, arguing from God's blessing on a preacher that everything he does is right and not in need of checking and correction from Scripture, the neglect of external order and of the use of the means of grace (*ibid* 432-458). All of these are relevant today, and we might also add defective views of conversion, wrong views on sanctification, the Christian life etc. These ideas can adversely influence the further development of the communities formed or strengthened by revival, and can, in many cases, carry within them the seeds of their own destruction. This is true of the subject we are to consider next.

More could be said on a number of these points and illustrations given, but perhaps enough has been said to give notice that if God favours his people with revival, it does not bring an end to all problems, rather it brings a whole new set!

Notes

[1] This is not only a modern practice! Jonathan Edwards in *Some Thoughts...* says

> The mutual embraces and kisses of persons of different sexes, under the notion of Christian love and holy kisses, are utterly to be disallowed and abominated, as having the most direct tendency quickly to turn Christian love into unclean and brutish lust, which won't be the better, but ten times the worse, for being Christened by the name of Christian love (Edwards ed Goen 1972:468).

CHAPTER 15

CAN REVIVALS BE PROMOTED—OR ABORTED?

IDEAS ON 'HOW TO PROMOTE A REVIVAL'

WE NOTED AT THE VERY BEGINNING of this book the modern confusion over the meaning of the word 'revival'. This confusion has its source in the radical change proposed by Charles G. Finney (1792-1875) to the understanding of the term which had prevailed in the Church up to his time.

Indeed, Finney launched a radical and sustained attack on the whole theological structure of Reformed Protestantism in general, on the doctrines of sin, regeneration, and sanctification in particular, and on the ministers who held such views.[1] He proposed and adopted a series of 'new measures' in the conduct of evangelistic campaigns (which he referred to as 'revivals'), and began the modern phenomenon of mass evangelism.

Finney's own exposition of his ideas and practices on revival are found in his *Revivals of Religion*.[2]

Finney claimed that his new methods, based upon his new understanding, worked in producing revivals, together with thousands of converts. However, Finney's greatest successes occurred during periods when revival was already widespread; his methods did not produce revival; rather, he enjoyed the benefits of revival when it was in progress. He may be said to have been very successful in harvesting the results of revival, although some would say that his methods produced numbers of false converts. Other preachers, such as Asahel Nettleton, and a host of ministers, such as William Sprague and those who contributed accounts of revivals to his *Lectures on Revivals*, published in 1832, enjoyed the blessings of the revival which was in progress then without subscribing to Finney's theology or using his methods. On more than one occasion, revival broke out before Finney arrived in a town, or took place in other parts of the same town where he was ministering. In such cases he was anxious to reap the fruits of a revival which had already begun through the sovereign operation of God.

In 1845, Finney published a series of articles in the *Oberlin Evangelist*,[3] in which he expressed concern about the decline in the depth of the revivals which had occurred in the previous ten years, together with reservations concerning the number of converts from his work who fell away. He comments in his second letter:

> I have observed...that for the last ten years [that is, since he published his original *Lectures*] revivals of religion have been gradually becoming more and more superficial...There is very less much deep conviction of sin and deep breaking up of the heart; much less depth of humility and much less strength in all the graces exhibited by converts in late revivals, than all the converts from the revivals which occurred about 1830 and 1831, and for some time previous (Finney 1979:14).

1830-1831 was the time of his most successful mission in Rochester, New York, during a period of general awakening, especially in New York State. At this point, Finney is admitting that his 'new measures' which he and many others continued to use in the years following 1831 were not sufficient of themselves to produce deep and lasting conversions.

He puts much of the blame on the evangelists who had been spawned by his own methods, and also on ministers who are not preaching repentance as they should; but as Hardman points out, Finney was really changing his concept of the nature of revival and the means of producing it (Hardman 1987:384).

In addition, his admission regarding the falling-away of great numbers of his converts, which he blamed on the churches' failure to integrate them into their fellowships properly, could also be seen as indicating that his 'new measures' actually produced great numbers of temporary converts.

There is no doubt that Finney produced a 'sea-change' in the popular evangelical understanding of revival. However, it seems that the 'sea-change' is also a sea-mist, and even a fog, which obscures the real nature of revival.[4] In North America 'revivals' are held in churches, which are either evangelistic campaigns or meetings for Christian rededication. Books which talk about revival often quote Finney, and may incorporate some of his ideas; however, Finney's basic philosophy and practice were basically contrary to the classical, and, in the view of the present author, the biblical, understanding. His methods of producing converts, when used by other evangelists in his own day and subsequently, have continued to produce great numbers of temporary converts. This is not to indict all mass evangelists either in the past or the present; it means, however, that Finney's views of the nature of fallen humanity produce a method of evangelistic persuasion which is basically calculated to convince people *against their will* to accept Christ, which can only result in a later reversion to previous belief.

To reject Finney's ideas on producing revivals does not mean that we do nothing. As we have seen, revivals have come when the people of God have persistently prayed for revival. As Matthew Henry put it: 'When God intends to bless His people, the first thing He does is to start them a-praying.' There is no guarantee as to *when* he will bless, there is an absolute guarantee that He *will*.[5]

IS IT POSSIBLE TO ABORT A REVIVAL?

While we may disagree with Charles Finney on the possibility of beginning a revival by the right use of appropriate means, experience seems to suggest that there is more possibility of aborting, or bringing a revival to a premature end, than of producing one. The history of awakenings shows that by excesses, by lack of continued prayer, by needless divisions and criticism, it is tragically possible to abort revival.[6]

The Great Awakening in New England was brought to a premature end by the fanaticism of James Davenport. The revival impulse continued in isolated places, the Separate Baptists also experienced awakening, but the Awakening on a large scale in New England was definitely brought to a premature end by Davenport's excesses and the reaction they provoked.

Divisions among the revival leaders in Britain during the eighteenth century, most notably between the Wesley brothers and George Whitefield over the subjects of Predestination and Perfectionism, probably put brakes on the revival and may have prevented its full flowering.

In the American colonies prayer and interest in awakening declined and fell away as the movement for independence from Britain grew in the 1770s, as well as during the War of Independence. Construction of the new nation also occupied attention after the War. It seems that the Second Awakening at the close of the eighteenth century began five or six years earlier in Britain than the comparable movement in the United States. Similarly, the Second Awakening on both sides of the Atlantic came to a temporary halt during the Napoleonic Wars as attention was diverted to other things.

Finally the criticism of Evan Roberts by Rev Peter Price and his subsequent withdrawal from leadership in the Welsh Revival of 1904 may possibly have brought it to a premature end.

A number of these examples may admit of other explanations, but there is still evidence to support this possibility, and it should be a warning to us, if ever God gives us the privilege of being involved in genuine awakening, that we should be very careful not to do anything which could possibly hinder or bring such blessing to a premature end.[7]

Notes

[1] Of course he was not the first to mount such an attack. In the seventeenth century the Quakers George Fox and Robert Barclay had done so, and in the eighteenth century John Wesley and his colleague John Fletcher had done the same. However, Finney's distinctiveness lies in the fact that he combined such an attack with a radically new understanding of the nature of revival and the means of promoting it.

[2] First published in 1835, issued in a revised edition in 1868, and available in an accurate modern edition edited with an introduction by William McLoughlin (1960). Other modern editions are all heavily 'edited for today's reader'. The lectures have been immensely popular and influential, having been translated into other languages, and published, in whole or in part, numerous times since their first appearance. However, they are very uneven in quality and value, contain many virulent attacks on opponents (see especially Lecture XV), and are extremely unsatisfactory in key elements, such as the definition of religion, revival, etc (Lecture I). They are most valuable in their strong emphasis on prayer (Lectures IV, V, VI and VIII) and on the need for all Christians to be filled with the Holy Spirit (Lecture VII, although Finney's understanding of how this comes about and what are its results will not command the agreement of all Christians).

Finney's *Lectures on Systematic Theology*, published in 1846 and 1847 are also reprinted (in an abridged edition), as are his *Skeletons of a Course of Theological Lectures*, first published in 1840. The theological lectures make very heavy reading, are very philosophical in their basis and presentation (being based on the prevailing 'Common Sense' philosophy of the mid-nineteenth century), and make minimal use of Scripture. The method of presentation relies heavily on the sort of legal argument with which Finney was acquainted from his legal training, and which he made great use of in his evangelistic preaching.

[3] Republished in 1979 under the title *Reflections on Revival*. It is surprising that when in 1864 he was asked to edit a revised and enlarged edition of his *Lectures on Revivals* he re-issued the first edition virtually unchanged (except for rewriting the last two lectures, without changing any of the views expressed there), and did not include any of the new material which incorporated his 'second thoughts' (Finney ed McLoughlin 1960:lii). It is a

great pity that these second thoughts are not so well known and widely used as the original *Lectures*.

⁴ Some readers may feel that the writer has been far too severe in his criticisms of Charles Finney. He does not, however, intend to say anything derogatory about Finney as a servant of God, nor of the way in which God used him to bring great numbers to faith in Christ, nor of his many laudable social activities in the areas of human rights, etc. For more information on Finney, see Hardman's biography (Hardman 1987) and the modern edition of Finney's *Memoirs* (ed Rosell & Dupuis 1989). More positive assessments than that given here will be found in Dayton 1988:15-24 and Rosell in Sweet ed 1986.

⁵ A number of recent writers have suggested that Solomon Stoddard, Jonathan Edwards' grandfather, was the real initiator of the newer understanding of promoting revivals (see Schafer 1963:328-361; Hardman 1983:27-45; Stout 1986:99-101). It is true that Stoddard attacked his fellow ministers for failing to preach the right truths in the right way (see his *The Defects of Preachers Reproved* [1723], reprinted in Bushman 1989:11-16). However, he clearly held to the classical understanding of revival as evidenced by his statement in a sermon preached in 1712 on the doctrine 'There are some special seasons wherein God doth in a remarkable manner revive religion among His people', in which he says, 'God is very arbitrary in this Matter. The People of God are praying, and waiting for this Mercy. Psalm 85:6...*But God will take his own time for this Mercy* [Italics in the original]' (cited in *Christian History* vol VIII no 3:10).

⁶ Charles Finney, in Lecture XV of his *Lectures on Revivals* mentions a total of twenty-four 'hindrances to revivals', most of which are factors which in his view cause a revival to come to a premature end. We have taken up some of his points here (see Finney ed Harding 1913:314-348).

⁷ Another question which might be considered is whether it is possible by any sin which grieves the Holy Spirit or by any other action, *to abort the beginning of a revival*, ie to prevent a revival, which is imminent, from starting.

CHAPTER 16

THE IMPLICATIONS AND OUTWORKINGS OF REVIVAL

REVIVAL AND HOLINESS

THERE IS AN OBSERVABLE CONNECTION in the history of awakenings between revival and holiness. We have already seen that an overwhelming sense of the holiness of God frequently characterises revivals, bringing with it a crushing sense of personal, and often corporate, sin and guilt. The repentance which is produced in revival is a deep, radical, complete abhorrence of sin and turning away from it, with a heartfelt desire to have done with it completely. This then becomes a consuming passion in the lives of the new converts in revival. Sin is seen for what it really is, as God sees it, and it continues to be hateful to the young convert. Contrariwise, holiness is seen as beautiful and infinitely desirable. The new Christian longs after holiness, seeing it as a characteristic of his God, for whom he pants and desires (Psalm 42:1; Tippit 1987:65-74; Roberts 1988:71-98; Edwards 1990:59-67, 112-123).

In addition, we may say that the instruments God uses in revival are holy men and women whom he has been preparing by prayer and often by suffering and other means. The consuming desire for holiness has, therefore, already been showing itself before the revival actually breaks out. We can see this in men like Jonathan Edwards, David Brainerd, George Whitefield, John and Charles Wesley, Charles Finney, Evan

251

Roberts, Joe Church and his African friend Simeoni Nsibambi, Liviu Olah in Romania, and many, many others whom God has used.

Any movement which claims for itself to be revival, or even part of the divine preparation for revival, must be able to stand up to this test.

REVIVAL AND EVANGELISM

The definition and description of revival with which we began this book (Chapter I) emphasised the connection between revival and evangelism. When a group of God's people are revived, there is an inevitable effect on those in the immediate neighbourhood. They see that something has happened, make enquiries, and are then told by those who have been revived. This is what happened on the Day of Pentecost (Acts 2), and is what has often happened in subsequent times of revival.

In addition, those who have been revived feel bound to tell others what has happened to them, with a view to them sharing for themselves in the new experience. Such 'telling' often begins with nominal Christians in the same Christian communities, but soon spreads to outsiders, as the love which the revived feel for God and their neighbours includes those who are complete strangers to God's love for themselves. The witness of 'ordinary Christians' also is strong in revival, as they joyfully share with relatives, friends and neighbours what God has done for them.

When those who are revived are already ministers or preachers, their preaching takes on a completely new tone and content, and the evangelistic note becomes prominent. Many new preachers are often raised up as the result of revival, and these also swell the numbers of evangelists. So evangelism follows inevitably from revival (Edwards 1990:147-158).

Sometimes it may be said that travelling evangelists, who have already participated in the revival of a group of Christians, seem to carry the revival with them as they move from place to place. This has often happened, and may be seen from multitudes of examples. It happened with George Whitefield, with Evan Roberts and the teams of evangelists and young people in the 1904 Welsh Revival, with Jonathan Goforth in Manchuria, with the Bethel Teams in China, with James Stewart in the Baltic States and Hungary before the Second World War, with Edwin Orr in so many of his travels between the two World Wars and after the Second War, and with scores of others. Once again it needs to be emphasised that this is different from the idea that a revival can be 'promoted' by the use of the proper means, which has led to the misuse of the word to describe evangelistic campaigns or holiness meetings for Christians, where often nothing significant happens at all!

REVIVAL AND MISSION

Pioneer missionary work and the expansion of mission work already in existence have often been a result of revival. This was abundantly clear from our historical survey. A few examples may be repeated here to further underline the point.

One of the first examples of Protestant missionary work was that of John Eliot, the Mayhews and others to the North American Indians in the seventeeth century. If we are right in assessing the Puritan movement of the seventeenth century as an example of revival, then this may be seen as one of its fruits.

At the beginning of the eighteenth century, the first Protestant missionaries to India were Bartholomew Ziegenbalg and Henry Plutschau, who were products of Halle Pietism, itself the result of revival. The Moravian missionary movement, which began in 1732, and, which in a short time had sent missionaries to scores of countries, was the fruit of revival. In North America, the Great Awakening produced a new movement of mission to the Indians; the name of David Brainerd is the most prominent among the missionaries who took the gospel to the native inhabitants, but there were many more.[1]

By general consent, the Second Great Awakening at the end of the eighteenth and the beginning of the nineteenth centuries launched the modern Protestant worldwide missionary movement, with the formation of scores of missionary societies. The 'Resurgence' of 1830, the Prayer Revival in mid-century, and the Resurgence of 1882ff, provided hundreds, if not thousands, of new missionaries, together with significant movements into new areas and countries.[2]

The history of the modern Protestant missionary movement is, to a large extent, the history of revivals. As with evangelism, when the Church is revived and filled with new, divine life, there is an irresistible urge to communicate the message of new life to others, and a willingness to sacrifice all out of gratitude for the amazing grace of God experienced by those who consider themselves to be completely unworthy.

REVIVAL AND SOCIAL ACTION

As with missionary work, so social action has often followed from revival. The vast benevolent activity at Halle under August Herman Francke was the outcome of the revival under Pietism.

The results of the Evangelical Revival in the rescue of thousands from debased and debauched lives contributed indirectly to the alleviation of many of the social problems of England in the eighteenth century. John Wesley in particular was strong in the rules he gave for the lives of members of the Methodist societies, although there was no direct political action adopted by the leaders to cure social ills.

Wesley was influenced by the attitude of the Quakers concerning the abolition of slavery,[3] and produced tracts, articles and sermons arguing against slave-trading and slave-holding. One of his most powerful sermons against the slave trade was preached in Bristol, the home port of many of the slave traders (and the home town of the present writer!)

The Evangelical Revival in Britain also produced a new impetus in education, including schools for the under-privileged, the beginnings of what later became the Sunday School movement, and the formation of boarding schools such as the one that John Wesley founded for the sons of his preachers (Wood 1968:1-5).

In the Second Evangelical Revival, at the end of the eighteenth century, the mainly upper-class Anglican members of the 'Clapham Sect' fought for the abolition of the slave trade, using parliamentary influence to secure its legal abolition, while thousands of Methodists and Dissenters signed petitions and worked in other ways at the grass roots to undermine support for the slave trade (Howse 1953; Cairns 1986:276-285). Both groups were the products of revival.

The various social reforms undertaken in nineteenth-century England by Evangelicals, such as the Ragged School movement, the work of men such as George Muller in setting up orphanages (Muller, a German by birth, consciously copied the work at Halle), the alleviation of the lot of children and teenagers in various ways, the Temperance movement, the reclamation of prostitutes, prison reform, the care of the blind, the deaf, the mentally ill, the sick, the aged, soldiers and sailors, and other groups of working people—these were all the direct or indirect fruits of the revivals of the period (Heasman 1962).

In the American colonies, as we have noted, many colleges which later grew into universities, began as a direct result of the Great Awakening. Also in America at the beginning of the eighteenth century Cotton Mather, influenced in part by the work of Halle in its various benevolent enterprises, as well as the Pietist concept of the *collegia pietatis* for the deepening of the spiritual life of the church (he kept up a correspondence with Francke and other Pietists), and also by the 'reforming societies' which developed in England in the 1690s, helped to propagate the use of voluntary religious societies for the spread of piety and the suppression of moral disorders. Mather and the members of 'the several societies for the Suppression of Disorders' met to fast and pray for 'revival and reformation at home and abroad'. Mather's practical concern for widows, orphans, Indians, Negroes, and other needy groups, meant that 'Cotton Mather was without question the most public spirited colonial before Benjamin Franklin, who drew much of his inspiration from the Boston minister' (Bridenbaugh, 252, cited in Lovelace *ibid* 228; see the whole

section in Lovelace, 214-236). While Mather did not partici-
pate in revival, he may be described as a 'revival Christian', as
this was that for which he prayed and fasted through a large
part of his life. He failed to see the corporate basis of the
problems which he sought to solve by individual acts of
charity, but he was extremely socially aware.

The same may be said of Jonathan Edwards and other
leaders in the Great Awakening, in their strong advocacy of
charity and care for the downtrodden.[4] Moreover, their views
and activities did much to pave the way for the 'Benevolent
Empire' which grew out of the second Great Awakening,
with its network of voluntary societies, thousands in number,
organised to attack social problems.[5] 'Slavery, temperance,
vice, world peace, women's rights, Sabbath observance,
prison reform, profanity, education—all these and more had
specific societies devoted to their betterment' (Christian History 1990 VIII 3:31). They, and the good they accomplished,
were the direct results of revival. 'To a remarkable degree the
Benevolent Empire achieved its goals in the first half of the
nineteenth century, making lasting contributions to national
life, eliminating much evil, and bringing Christian values into
the mainstream of American life' (*ibid*).

Charles Finney included social reform in his programme
for awakening, and was very strong in the temperance crusade
and the anti-slavery movement. Among the twenty-four
'Hindrances to Revivals' which he deals with in Lecture XV
of his *Revivals of Religion*, the eighteenth and nineteenth
hindrances are

> 18. *Resistance to the Temperance reformation* will put a
> stop to revivals in a Church...
> 19. Revivals are hindered when ministers and *Churches
> take wrong ground in regard to any question involving
> human rights*. Take the subject of SLAVERY for
> instance... (Harding ed 1913:324-325).

Some historians have not shown with sufficient clarity the

dependence of the anti-slavery movement on the revival of 1830ff, but, according to one writer, Gilbert H. Barnes[6]

> The conjunction of so many elements of the Great Revival [1831] in the antislavery agitation was more than coincidence....In leadership, in method, and in objective, the Great Revival and the American Antislavery Society now were one. It is not too much to say that for the moment the antislavery agitation as a whole was what it had long been in larger part, *an aspect of the Great Revival in benevolent reform.*

As we noted in our historical survey, the YMCA was formed as a direct result of the Resurgence of 1830ff, thus continuing the social impact of the revival at the turn of the century.

These major examples could be reinforced by many more, but they serve to show that so often genuine revival, which begins with men and women coming into a new relationship with God, very soon has radical effects in efforts for the good of their fellow men, not just to 'save their souls', but also to improve their lives here in this world.

REVIVAL AND THE LAITY

In the history of the Church, revivals have often given lay people greater prominence in the life of the Church than they have enjoyed in other periods when institutionalisation has meant that the ordained clergy are in control and the laity are reduced to a fairly passive role. In such times of institutionalisation the quality of spiritual life of the clergy—or lack of it in times of deadness—has determined the general standard of life and vigour of the Church in general.

However, in times of revival and awakening the whole community of God's people has been affected, and the laity have come to far greater prominence. Sometimes the revival impulse has come initially to a group of lay people; sometimes it has included both ordained and lay; sometimes it has spread from the ordained ministers to lay people.

In the first case, there is the danger that the ordained leadership will see the new lay interest and activity as a threat to their own position, and so reject the revival movement for themselves. Even in the second or third scenarios, the new activity of lay people, often exuberant and not always free from excess, may still pose a threat to the established leadership and the way they think the life of the church should be run. Of course, the best possibility is when an enlightened leadership and a zealous laity work together.

In most cases when awakening has brought lay people to a new position of prominence in the life and activity of the church, the change has been irrevocable. The new degree of lay involvement in church, and especially para-church, activities has been permanent. The history of revival has seen a large number of para-church movements, such as the anti-slavery movements in Britain and the USA, the other activities of the 'Benevolent Empire', the Student Volunteer Movement, the YMCA and YWCA, and the 'Faith mission' movement, all developing from primarily lay initiative and being staffed primarily by lay people.

Also, in a number of cases, revival has brought lay leadership to the fore in national life, and has broken the exclusive clerical control of social life. The Great Awakening in North America had this effect. In the words of one historian:

> Ultimately they [the Revivalists such as Edwards, Whitefield and Gilbert Tennent] replaced the traditionally elite figures of authority, the clergy and traditional lay magistrates, with a new figure, a new man— any man who had been reborn in the Spirit and was living out the converted life. Thus the layman emerged as the central figure in the Christian community...[and ultimately in the secular community also] (Brauer 1976:26; see also Stout 1986:211 and Hatch 1989).

Other examples where revival movements have involved initial lay activity or where the laity have subsequently come to a new permanent place of prominence would include the Medieval protest movements and monastic movements which were usually lay-inspired; the Anabaptist movement of the sixteenth century which was almost entirely a lay movement; the renewed Moravian Church which was similarly a lay-inspired and lay-led activity; the Methodist societies, lay preachers etc (Wesley was an ordained clergyman of the Church of England, but he involved lay people in the leadership of his societies and in the whole spread of the movement); the leadership in the mid-century Prayer Revival and the resulting movements; many of the modern para-church movements such as Campus Crusade for Christ which grew out of local revivals (see Orr 1971:187-189).

Awakening and revival have often led to the emancipation of the laity from the dominance and control of the clergy, and have introduced 'every member ministry' and true 'body life' into the activity of the Church.

Notes

[1] The names of such men as Ebenezer Pemberton, John Sergeant, Gideon Hawley and John Brainerd are virtually unknown today for their missionary work among the Indians at the time of the Great Awakening.

[2] Pentecostalism, which began as part of the worldwide revival at the beginning of the twentieth century, has been one of the main forces behind the remarkable growth of the Church in Latin America, and to a lesser extent in Africa. Consequently, an integral connection may again be seen between revival, mission and evangelism.

[3] Before the Quakers argued against it, Richard Baxter, in his *Christian Directory*, condemned the slave trade as 'One of the worst kinds of Thievery in the World', although he did not object to Christians owning slaves if they took pains to bring the gospel to them (Lovelace 1979b:234).

[4] The Great Awakening is also seen as a preparation for the movement for independence for the American colonies from Britain (see eg Heimert

1966). One's assessment of the goodness or otherwise of this will depend on one's own nationality!

[5] According to Sydney Ahlstrom,

> In the long run the influence of Jonathan Edwards...is the most enduring result of the New England Awakening...A new and irrepressible expectancy entered the life of the churches. A national sense of intensified religious and moral resolution was born. Millennial hopes were rekindled...Edwards' powerful witness and his development of a distinct school of theology would help to nurture these results (Christian History *ibid* 19).

[6] In his book, *The Antislavery Impulse 1830-1844* (cited in *Christian History* 1989 VIII 3:31). See also Cole 1954; Dayton 1988.

CHAPTER 17

REVIVALS AND YOUNG PEOPLE

A SUBJECT WHICH HAS BEEN largely neglected in the study of revivals is that of the place of children and young people. A brief survey of some of the revivals of the past and present where children and young people have been involved, often in the beginning of an awakening, will show that we have here an important principle of divine operation at such times.

In Silesia in the eighteenth century the movement known as 'the children's uprising' began with children's prayer meetings. In the revival at Northampton in Jonathan Edwards' church, the movement was preceded with special meetings for the youth of the town and in the revival the young people were particularly affected. Indeed, it was begun through the conversion of a young woman 'who had been one of the greatest company-keepers in the whole town' (Edwards ed Goen 1972:149). One of the clearest instances of conversion in the revival described by Edwards was a four-year-old, Phebe Bartlet (Edwards *ibid* 199-205). In *Some Thoughts...* Edwards takes time to defend 'the religious meetings of children, to read and pray together, and perform religious exercises by themselves' and speaks of the several examples of children being converted at such meetings (*ibid* 407-408).

The revivals in 1742 at Cambuslang and Kilsyth in Scotland were preceded two years before by a prayer meeting consisting of sixteen children between the ages of ten and sixteen being held in a barn. In the revival that followed, many children, some only eight years old, were converted. The same was true in the revival in Aberystwyth in 1805 under the preaching of Thomas Charles, and in Dundee in 1839 under William Chalmers Burns and Robert Murray M'Cheyne.

George Muller records an instance of revival among the orphans in one of his homes in Bristol (Muller 1906:613-614). Two boys asked one of their masters if they might hold a prayer meeting. They were granted permission and 150 boys attended, around 100 continuing to meet on a regular basis. There was a marked change in their behaviour. All the boys of fourteen years and over were gathered together for a meeting. Of the 55 present, between 35 and 40 professed faith in Christ.

In the 1904 Welsh Revival, it was the simple testimony of a girl, Florrie Evans, which began the movement of spiritual blessing, and young people were active in its spread. In Denmark and Finland the revival of the same period affected young people in particular.

The student movements in the nineteenth and twentieth centuries, together with the awakenings in schools and colleges, particularly in North America, in the eighteenth, nineteenth and twentieth centuries, all witness to the same fact that revivals have often begun with young people and even children.[1]

Young men, still in their teens or in their early twenties have often been used in revivals. George Whitefield, James McQuilken, William Chalmers Burns, Andrew Gih and his teams of young Chinese evangelists, and James Stewart may be cited as examples.

Cynics may suggest that this is a further example of the fact that 'religious excitement' occurs most frequently among the immature. Believers will point to the fact that God is always pleased to use the simple to confound those who are wise in their own eyes (cf Matt 21:15-16; I Cor 1:26-29). They may also be provoked to ask the question as to whether children and young people are less closed to divine influences than those of supposedly maturer years.

Notes

[1] For further examples see Edwards 1990:163-172.

CHAPTER 18

REVIVAL, HISTORY AND THE PAROUSIA

I N THIS FINAL CHAPTER it is appropriate for us to step back and view the whole history of revival in the light of the historical outworking of the purposes of God in general, and also to look forward and see what relation, if any, exists between revivals and the Return of Jesus Christ, the Parousia.

REVIVALS AND HISTORY

Having surveyed the whole history of revivals, both those recorded in Scripture and those which have occurred over the Christian centuries, we are in a position to ask the question: Is Jonathan Edwards' dictum regarding outpourings of the Spirit and history which we cited in Chapter II above supported by the evidence? In his *History of Redemption* Edwards states that:

> From the fall of man to this day wherein we live the Work of Redemption in its effect has mainly been carried on by remarkable pourings out of the Spirit of God. Though there be a more constant influence of God's Spirit always in some degree attending his ordinances, yet the way in which the greatest things have been done towards carrying on this work always has been by remarkable pourings out of the Spirit at special seasons of mercy (Edwards, ed Wilson 1989:143).

The strange thing is that in his own historical survey in the same work he mentions very few examples of such outpourings! In the Old Testament period he only draws attention to five, at least one of these having a dubious exegetical basis, as we saw. In the New Testament he refers to more, but in the subsequent history of the Church, he mentions none before the Protestant Reformation in the sixteenth century. He draws attention to Halle Pietism and the awakening in the Connecticut Valley of 1734-1735, and then concentrates more on what he feels Scripture says about awakenings in the future. His view of the equation of the Medieval papacy with the Antichrist has prevented him from finding any movements of the Spirit during that time, but the evidence which he collects in support of his own statement is surprisingly sparse.

In the light of the actual history of the people of God in both Testaments and in the Christian centuries, it seems that his statement is an over-simplification. While revivals have contributed substantially to the development, vigour, life, growth and spread of the Church, many other factors are also involved.

It is certainly true that *since* Edwards' time, revivals *have* played a major part in the life, vitality, growth and spread of the Church, and the present worldwide Church, especially in its Protestant manifestation, is a phenomenon due in large part to the succession of revivals which have occurred since Edwards' day. Events since his time seem to justify his statement more than those before he wrote!

REVIVAL AND THE PAROUSIA

A final question we need to ask is: What connection, if any, exists between the phenomenon of revival and the Return of Jesus Christ? Revivals have happened periodically in history, as we have seen, and continue to occur, at least on a local level, up to the present time. What expectation may we have that they will continue to occur, and perhaps even increase, as the End approaches?

The idea that the future age of the Church here on earth

would be especially the Age of the Spirit may be found in different forms in the beliefs of the Montanists in the third century and that of Joachim of Fiore in the twelfth. Some of the Protestant Reformers and a considerable number of the Puritans believed in 'the hope of better times' to come, as the papacy lost its power and as Reformed Christianity increasingly triumphed in the world. This 'positive amillennialism', as it has been described, developed into fully-fledged postmillennialism in seventeenth-century writers like Thomas Brightman and Daniel Whitby. Jonathan Edwards integrated his theology of revivals and his postmillennialism into a scheme in which revivals would increasingly lead to the millennium. He actually hoped that 'the great and general awakening' which came to New England and the Middle Colonies in the 1740s was

> the dawning, or at least a prelude, of that glorious work of God, so often foretold in Scripture, which, in the progress and issue of it, shall renew the world of mankind (Goen ed. 1972: 353).[1]

These words were penned in 1742, when the effects of the Great Awakening were still evident. In 1747, when the revival was faltering, and, in many places, had been dissipated through excesses, opposition, and divisions, he still hopes that:

> a far more pure extensive and glorious revival of religion is not far off, which will more properly be the beginning of that work which in its issue shall overthrow the Kingdom of Antichrist, and of Satan through the world (Stein ed 1977: 427).

This revival, whenever and wherever[2] it eventually begins, will result in multitudes turning from vice and wickedness. 'Vital religion' will flourish, and conversions will take place on a scale hitherto unknown. Through the preaching of the gospel 'vast multitudes [shall be brought] savingly home to Christ'.

> Some shall be converted, and be the means of others' conversion ... And doubtless one nation shall be enlightened and converted after another, one false religion and false way of worship exploded after another (Wilson ed 1989:459).

'Violent and mighty opposition' will occur, as the combined forces of Antichrist, Mahometanism and heathenism will resist the spread of the gospel. This is foretold in Revelation 16 and 19, under the imagery of a mighty battle. In addition to opposition by external force, there will also be 'great opposition of subtile disputers, and carnal reasoning', great persecution in many places, 'great opposition by virulent reproaches' and 'great opposition by craft and subtilty' (ibid 464).

The victory of Christ and his Church, which is also represented as a total rout of the forces of evil (Rev 19:11ff.), will take place 'by his word and Spirit' as

> The devil is utterly baffled and confounded, and knows not what else to do; he now sees his Antichristian and Mohamedan and heathenish kingdoms through the world all tumbling about his ears. He and his most powerful instruments are now taken captives (ibid 465).

When this has been accomplished, 'the church will have an easy work of it', as the word of God is proclaimed throughout the world by a whole army of preachers. Heresies, infidelity and superstition will be abolished. Satan's twin kingdoms of 'Popery' and Islam will be overthrown. The nation of Israel will be converted, and the heathen nations of the world shall be 'wonderfully enlightened with the glorious gospel' as 'many shall go forth and carry the gospel unto them' (ibid 466-470).

'Then the millennium shall begin' (Stein ed. 1977: 196, 197), which 'is most properly the time of *the kingdom of heaven upon earth*', a time of 'great light and knowledge...a time of great holiness...a time wherein religion shall in every respect be uppermost in the world...times of great peace and love...a time of excellent order in the church of Christ...[when] the church of God shall..be beautiful and glorious on these accounts...a time of great temporal prosperity...a time of great rejoicing...[the time of] the church's glorious wedding-day...with Christ' (Wilson ed 1989:480-485). It will be 'of long continuance', being represented by the idea of a thousand years (Rev 20:4), and described as 'a joy of many generations' (Is 60:15 *ibid*).

The whole series of events leading up to the millennium, would begin with the 'extensive and glorious revival of religion' which Edwards longed for and at times dared to hope was commencing in his day, but which, as he eventually realised, did not, even though he never failed to eagerly study the religious and secular events of his day for hopeful signs.

He speaks of a 'wonderful swiftness' with which the gospel would spread, once the process began (Wilson ed 1989:460, 461). However, he also speaks of the work taking place 'gradually' (*ibid* 458) as did the return of the Jews from exile, and the overthrow of the pagan Roman Empire, which took about 300 years. 'Very swiftly, yet gradually' the eschatological events will unfold. In the *Humble Attempt*, written in 1747, he speculates that even if the initial revival began immediately, an amazing and unparalleled progress would be necessary for the whole process to be completed by the year 2000 (Stein ed 1977: 410, 411). The battles foretold are not to be thought of as single events, but as series of events happening in different places and apparently unrelated, possibly with various stages (in the 'Apocalyptic Series' Notebook No.77, in Stein ed *ibid* 173-184). Quite clearly, the generation which witnessed the beginning of the series of events would not be alive to see the conclusion, although Edwards did speculate on the knowledge that the saints in heaven have of events taking place here on earth (eg in the Miscellanies, see No.529 in Hickman ed 1834: II.621, 622).

One of the merits of Edwards' postmillennial scheme is that revival and missions occupy a key place in God's overall plan for the redemption of mankind according to him. Indeed, in his scheme the greatest period of spiritual awakening and missionary activity is yet to take place. This does not mean that the church is to wait for the great revival to begin before it engages in missionary work. Rather, prayerful anticipation of the commencement of that great event is to be accompanied by vigorous mission activity here and now. The certainty that the event will be accomplished in God's appointed time is a spur and an encouragement, especially when the actual results are small. Edwards' revivalist postmillennialism was a major motivation for mission in the great missionary movement of the nineteenth century.

Cotton Mather (1663-1728), Jonathan Edwards' older contemporary in New England, may be taken as an example of a different eschatological scheme, but one which also integrates revivals into a full eschatological programme. He may be described as a positive, revivalist premillennialist (Lovelace 1979: 71, 245). Mather developed the views of 'the great Mede' (Joseph Mede [1586-1638]), in a number of ways. Most importantly, he felt that the millennium would be inaugurated by the visible appearing of Christ himself. He would come as a thief in the night, to a world morally asleep, although a world which had already been warned by earthquakes and other signs of the end, which Mather believed were happening with increasing frequency in his own day. Christ would come with clouds of fire and smoke, accompanied by legions of angels singing his praises. He would destroy the Antichrist and his armies with fire, and then chain Satan for a thousand years. The saints living on earth at the time would be caught up to Christ, raised above the terrible conflagration which would be destroying God's enemies and refining the earth, and, together with saints who had already died, be given new, transformed bodies. Once the burning was ended, the City of

God in the New Heavens would rule over the saved nations of the New Earth, the nucleus of which will be made up of those caught up to meet Christ at his return, but who will soon multiply and reproduce, build houses and plant vineyards. The saints who had already died before the return of Christ and who have also received new bodies will reign with Christ over the saints on the New Earth; in fact, will serve them as the angels at present serve the saints. So there will be sweet communion between the two groups, even though one really belongs on earth, and the other in heaven. Indeed, Christ himself will occasionally walk among men on the New Earth openly and visibly.

The end of the millennial period will come with the appearance of Gog and Magog, rising from Hell, and led by the Devil in a last, vain bid. All will end in fire and destruction, and be followed by the Last Judgment. Sinners will be dispatched to Hell for ever, and the saints will enjoy eternal communion with Christ in the Third Heaven.

Mather expected to see the End in his own lifetime, perhaps in 1716, although subsequent recalculation meant that 1736 might be the date, or even 1775 or 1780, but 1735 or 1736 remained the most likely (Lovelace *ibid* 65-68).

More importantly for our study, Mather also believed that the outpouring of the Holy Spirit foretold in Joel 2: 28-32 would take place before the Parousia, and would inaugurate a 'New Reformation' (*ibid* 65,66).

The importance of the prophecy in Joel indicates a very key element in Mather's scheme. According to Mather, 'the Church was enlarged and Governed' by the gifts of the Spirit for 200 years following the ascension of Christ. But 'the Carnal Spirit of this World' entered the Church and 'the Grieved Paraclete withdrew'. After the time of Antichrist is ended, 'the Dove' ie the Holy Spirit will return in fulfillment of Joel 2, and the 'Extraordinary Gifts of the Holy Spirit' will be restored to the Church. Indeed, 'That Effusion of the Spirit, by which the Primitive Church flourished, might be but as Drops, which will be followed with Mighty Showers, for the Accomplishment of this Prophecy to be expected in the Latter Days' (Mather 1721:71-72). When this happened, the Church would be reformed, the gospel would be preached with great success throughout the world, and the Jews would be converted to Christ (*ibid* 47-48).

The idea that the prophecy of Joel 2:28-32 still awaits its greatest and final fulfilment in a future period of worldwide revival is found in a number of writers in the twentieth century, as for example Arthur Wallis (1956:35-42). Wallis is important as the 'founding father' of the modern 'Restoration Movement', a branch of the Charismatic Movement, in Britain. The Restoration Movement basically embraces Dispensationalist teaching on the Second Coming and related subjects. However, although J. N. Darby's pessimism regarding historic Christendom is still held, there is a strong injection of optimism in the hope for a great revival yet to take place, which will have worldwide repercussions.

As we have noted already, the Charismatic Renewal is seen by many Charismatics, not as revival itself, but as a preparatory movement for the coming great revival. This hope rests to a large extent on visions and prophecies which a number of the leaders in the movement claim to have received. David Wilkerson's well-known 'Vision' is predominently pessimistic regarding the Churches, although he does speak of a revival of Spirit-filled Christians who will be persecuted by the unrenewed part of the Church. Bryn Jones, a very prominent leader in the British Renewal Movement, records a vision of the coming great revival which he had when he was a Bible College student (see 'Suddenly all heaven broke loose!' in Matthew ed 1990:113-122). According to him, 'God was saying an astonishing thing: *The coming spiritual visitation will not be so much a torrential downpour as a steady and continuous visitation of the Holy Spirit* [italics his]' (*ibid* 117). The Holy City of Revelation refers to the Church, according to Jones, into which the nations of the world will enter from all parts of the globe (*ibid* 121). It seems that this is very close to the postmillennialism of Jonathan Edwards, although the basic Dispensationalist Pre-millennialism is still held to by Jones and others in the movement.[3]

Among mainstream Evangelicals, there are also those, like Billy Graham (see his address at the Lausanne Congress in Douglas ed 1974) who see the possibility of both declension in the world and revival in the Church taking place concurrently.

It seems, therefore, that expectation of and prayer for revival are linked, in the minds of many, with the hope of the Parousia and all that it brings. Whatever the precise nature of our eschatological scheme, and whether or not it rests upon new 'revelations', we should work and pray both for revival and the return of Jesus Christ.

We can pray in the words of James Montgomery's great revival hymn:

> O Spirit of the living God,
> In all Thy plenitude of grace,
> Where'er the foot of man hath trod,
> Descend on our apostate race.
>
> Give tongues of fire and hearts of love
> To preach the reconciling word;
> Give power and unction from above,
> Whene'er the joyful sound is heard.
>
> Be darkness at Thy coming light;
> Confusion, order in Thy path;
> Souls without strength inspire with might;
> Bid mercy triumph over wrath.
>
> O Spirit of the Lord, *prepare*
> *All the round earth her God to meet;*
> Breathe Thou abroad like morning air,
> Till hearts of stone begin to beat.

Baptize the nations; far and nigh
The triumphs of the cross record;
The Name of Jesus glorify
Till every kindred call Him Lord.

Notes

[1] It was these words, together with other supposed comments by Edwards, which Charles Chauncy and other opponents of the Awakening interpreted as claiming that the Millennium had begun in Northampton in 1734! (Chauncy 1743, repr 1975: 371-373).

[2] It may begin in many places at the same time, according to Edwards (Wilson ed 1989:460).

[3] Others in the movement seem to have abandoned it (see Wright 1991: 7).

REFERENCES CITED

(This is not intended to be a complete bibliography on the subject of Revival, but is limited to those works referred to in the text. A work by Richard Owen Roberts, *A Preliminary Bibliography of Published Books and Pamphlets on Revival With Annotations and Historical Notices*, Wheaton, 1982, provides details of around 2,000 volumes on the subject. The work by Earl E. Cairns mentioned below gives between 400 and 500 volumes.)

Allen, William E. (1951) *The History of Revivals of Religion*, Lisburn, Ulster

Ambler, R. W. (1989) *Ranters, Revivalists and Reformers: Primitive Methodism and Rural Society South Lincolnshire 1817-1875*, Hull

Appasamy, A. J. (1964) *Write the Vision*, London

Armstrong, Maurice (1948) *The Great Awakening in Nova Scotia, 1776-1809*, Hartford, Conn.

Autrey, C. E. (1960) *Revivals of the Old Testament*, Grand Rapids

Baker, Ernest (1906) *The Revivals of the Bible*, London (Repr 1988)

Barnes, Gilbert Hobbs (1933) *The Anti-Slavery Impulse, 1830-1844*, New York

Beale, Peter (1986) 'Jonathan Edwards and the Phenomena of Revival' Unpublished paper

Beardsley, Frank G. (1904) *A History of American Revivals*, New York

Beaver, R. Pierce (1957-8) 'The Concerts of Prayer for Mission', in *The Ecumenical Review* X (1957-8) pp 420-427

Bebbingdon, D. W. (1989) *Evangelicalism in Modern Britain: A History from the 1730s to the 1980s*, London

Bede, The Venerable (1962) *Ecclesiastical History of the English Nation*, ET Pelican Classics, Harmondsworth

Benham, D. (1895) *The Memorial Days of the Renewed Church of the Brethren*, London

Bennett, Richard (1987) *Howell Harris and the dawn of Revival* (first published in Welsh 1909), Bryntirion

Bibliotheca Sacra (1871) 'What Can Be Done For Augmenting The Number Of Christian Ministers?', in *Bibliotheca Sacra* XXVII no 9 pp 84-97

Blair, William Newton (1957) *Gold in Korea*, Topeka, Kansas

Bloch-Hoell, N. (1964) *The Pentecostal Movement*, Oslo

Boles, John B. (1972) *The Great Revival, 1787-1805: The Origins of the Southern Evangelical Mind*, Lexington, Kentucky

Bonar, Andrew A. (1893) *The Diary of Andrew A. Bonar*, Edinburgh

Bonomi, Patricia U. & Eisenstadt, Peter R. (1982) 'Church Adherence in the Eighteenth-Century British American Colonies', *William and Mary Quarterly* 3rd Series, XXXIX (1982) pp 245-286.

Bonomi, Patricia U. (1986) *Under the Cope of Heaven: Religion, Society and Politics in Colonial America* New York & London

Bourdeaux, Lorna & Bourdeaux, Michael (1987) *Ten Growing Soviet Churches*, Eastbourne

Bradley, James E. (n.d.) 'Some Theological and Ethical Aspects of Miracles in the Early Church'. Unpublished paper.

Braithwaite, W. C. (1912) *The Beginnings of Quakerism*, London, Revised edition 1955.

Brauer, Jerald C. (1986) 'Puritanism, Revivalism, and the Revolution', in *Religion and the American Revolution* ed Jerald C. Brauer

Brewer, Peter D. (1990) 'Revivalists and Refugees: An Interpretation of Baptist Work in the Caribbean', in *Bulletin of the Scottish Institute for Missionary Studies* (1990) pp 16-30

Broadbent, Ernest H. (1930) *The Pilgrim Church*, London

Brock, Peter (1957) *The Political and Social Doctrines of the Unity of Brethren in the 15th and Early 16th Centuries*, The Hague

Bruce, F. F. (1959) *The Spreading Flame: The Rise and Progress of Christianity*, London

Bryant, David (1985) *With Concerts of Prayer*, Glendale

Buchanan, James (1843) *The Office and Work of the Holy Spirit*, Edinburgh (Repr 1966)

Burgess, Stanley M. & McGee, Gary B. ed (1988) *Dictionary of Pentecostal and Charismatic Movements*, Grand Rapids

Burns, James (1909) *Revivals: Their Laws and Leaders*, London

Bushman, Richard L. ed (1969) *The Great Awakening: Documents on the Revival of Religion, 1740-1745*, Chapel Hill & London

Cadbury, Henry J. (1948) *George Fox's Book of Miracles*, New York

Cairns, Earle E. (1986) *An Endless Line of Splendor: Revivals and Their Leaders from the Great Awakening to the Present*, Wheaton

Campbell, Duncan (1954) *The Lewis Awakening, 1949-1953*, Edinburgh

Candler, Warren Akin (1904) *Great Revivals and the Great Republic*, Nashville

Cartledge, Mark J. (1991) 'Charismatic prophecy and New Testament prophecy', in *Themelios* 17.1 (1991) pp 17-19

Cartwright, Peter (1956) *Autobiography of Peter Cartwright*, New York

Carwardine, Richard A. (1978) 'The Welsh Evangelical Community and "Finney's Revival" ', in *Journal of Ecclesiastical History* 26.4 (October 1978) pp 463-480

Carwardine, Richard A. (1978) *Trans-Atlantic Revivalism: Popular Evangelicalism in Britain and America, 1790-1865*, Greenwood, Connecticut

Chauncy, Charles (1743) *Seasonable Thoughts on the State of Religion in New-England*, Boston (Repr edn 1975)

Christian History (1985) *Christian History: Jonathan Edwards and the Great Awakening* Vol IV no 4 (1985)

Christian History (1986) *Christian History: Pietism. A Much Maligned Movement Re-examined* Vol V no 2 (1986)

Christian History (1989) *Christian History; The Waldensians*, Vol VIII no 2 (1989)

Christian History (1989) *Christian History: Spiritual Awakenings in North America* Vol VIII no 3 (1989)

Church of Scotland (1840) *The Revival of Religion: Addresses by Scottish Evangelical Leaders delivered in Glasgow in 1840*, Edinburgh (Repr edn 1984)

Church, J. E. (1981) *Quest for the Highest: An autobiographical account of the East African Revival*, Exeter

CLC (1954) *This Is That*, London

Coalter, Milton J. Jr (1980) 'The Radical Pietism of Count Nicholas Zinzendorf as a Conservative Influence on the Awakener, Gilbert Tennent' in *Church History* (1980) pp 35-46

Coalter Milton J. Jr (1986) *Gilbert Tennent, Son of Thunder: A Case Study of Continental Pietism's Impact on the First Great Awakening in the Middle Colonies*, Westport

Cole, Charles C. (1954) *The Social Ideas of the Northern Evangelists, 1826-1860*, New York

Colton, Calvin (1832) *The History and Character of American Revivals, 1733-1832*, London

Cooley, Frank L. (1973) 'The Revival in Timor', in *South-East Asia Journal of Theology* 14.2 (1973) pp 78-93

Crawford, Don (1972) *Miracles in Indonesia: God's Power Builds His Church*, Wheaton

Crawford, Michael J. (1991) *Seasons of Grace: Colonial New England's Revival Tradition in its British Context*, New York & Oxford

Cross, Whitney R. (1950) *The Burned-over District: The Social and Intellectual History of Enthusiastic Religion in Western New York, 1800-1850*, Ithaca, NY

Dallimore, Arnold A. (1970 & 1980) *George Whitefield: The Life and Times of the Great Evangelist of the Eighteenth-Century Revival*, London

Dallimore, Arnold A. (1988) *A heart set free: The life of Charles Wesley*, Welwyn

Davenport, F. M. (1917) *Primitive Traits in Religious Revivals: A Study in Mental and Social Evolution*, New York

Davies, R. E. (1990) 'Second Baptist Church, Oradea, Romania', in *Church Growth Digest*, Year 11 Issue 2 (Winter 1989/90) pp 3-5

Davies, R. E. (1990) 'Baptists in Poland—Past and Present', in *Religion in Communist Lands* 18.1 (Spring 1990) pp 52-63

Dayton, Donald (1976) *Discovering an Evangelical Heritage*, Peabody, Mass

Dolan, Jay P. (1978) *Catholic Revivalism: The American Experience, 1830-1900*, South Bend

Douglas, J. D. (1964) *Light in the North*, Exeter

Douglas, J. D. ed (1974) *Let The Earth Hear His Voice*, Wheaton

Douglas, J. D. ed (1978) *The New International Dictionary of the Christian Church*, Grand Rapids

Douglass, Philipp D. (1991) 'Yonggi Cho and the Korean Pentecostal Movement: Some Theological Reflections', in *Presbyterion* 17/1 (1991) pp 16-34

Durnbaugh, Donald F. (1985) *The Believers' Church*, Scottdale

Edwards, Brian H. (1990) *Revival! A people saturated with God*, Darlington

Edwards, Jonathan ed Hickman, Edward (1834) *The Works of Jonathan Edwards, A. M.* 2 vols, London (repr 1974)

Edwards, Jonathan ed Edwards, Tryon, DD (1852) *Charity and its Fruits*, New York (repr 1969)

Edwards, Jonathan ed Faust, Clarence H. & Johnson, Thomas H. (1935) *Jonathan Edwards: Representative Selections, with Introduction, Bibliography, and Notes*, New York, etc.

Edwards, Jonathan ed Helm, Paul (1971) *Treatise on Grace and other posthumously published writings*, Cambridge & London

Edwards, Jonathan ed Townsend, Harvey G. (1972) *The Philosophy of Jonathan Edwards From His Private Notebooks*, Westport

Edwards, Jonathan ed Smith, John E. (1959) *The Works of Jonathan Edwards: Volume 2 Religious Affections*, New Haven

Edwards, Jonathan ed Goen, C. C. (1971) *The Works of Jonathan Edwards: Volume 4 The Great Awakening*, New Haven & London

Edwards, Jonathan ed Stein, Stephen J. (1977) *The Works of Jonathan Edwards: Volume 5 Apocalyptic Writings*, New Haven & London

Edwards, Jonathan ed Pettit, Norman (1985) *The Works of Jonathan Edwards: Volume 7 The Life of David Brainerd*, New Haven & London

Edwards, Jonathan ed Ramsey, Paul (1989) *The Works of Jonathan Edwards: Volume 8 Ethical Writings*, New Haven & London

Edwards, Jonathan ed Wilson, John F. (1989) *The Works of Jonathan Edwards: Volume 9 A History of the Work of Redemption*, New Haven & London

Elwell, Walter ed (1984) *Dictionary of Evangelical Theology*, Grand Rapids

Erskine, John (1742) *The Signs of the Times Consider'd: or, the high Probability, that the Present Appearances in New-England, and the West of Scotland, are a Prelude of the Glorious Things promised to the Church in the latter Ages*, Edinburgh

Evans, Eifion (1959) *When He Is Come: An Account of the 1858-1860 Revival in Wales*, Bala

Evans, Eifion (1974) *The Welsh Revival of 1904*, Bryntirion

Fawcett, Arthur (1971) *The Cambuslang Revival*, 1971

Finney, Charles Grandison (1913) *Revivals of Religion: Lectures by Charles Grandison Finney, With the Author's Final Additions and Corrections, Newly revised and Edited with Introduction and Original Notes by William Henry Harding*, London

Finney, Charles G. (1960) *Lectures on Revivals of Religion*, Ed William G. McLoughlin, Cambridge, Mass.

Finney, Charles G. (1976) *Finney's Systematic Theology*, Minneapolis (Originally published as *Finney's Lectures on Systematic Theology*, edited by J H Fairchild 1851 [Abridged edition in one volume from *Lectures on Systematic Theology*, 2 vols, 1846-1847])

Finney, Charles G. (1976) *The Heart of Truth*, Minneapolis (Originally published as *Skeletons of a Course of Theological Lectures*, 1840)

Finney, Charles G. ed Dayton, Donald (1979) *Reflections on Revival*, Compiled by Donald Dayton, Minneapolis

Finney, Charles G. ed Rosell, Garth M. & Dupuis, Richard A. G. (1989) *The Memoirs of Charles G Finney: The Complete Restored Text*, Grand Rapids

Foster, Charles I. (1960) *An Errand of Mercy: The Evangelical United Front, 1790-1837*, Chapel Hill NC

Foster, John (1948) 'The Centenary of Jonathan Edwards's "Humble Attempt" ', in *International Review of Missions* XXXVII pp 375-381

Fountain, David (1988) *Lord Radstock and the Russian Awakening*, Southampton

Fox, George ed Penney, N. (1911) *Journals*, London

Fox, George ed Nickalls, J. L. (1952) *Journals*, London

Garret, Clarke (1987) *Spirit Possession and Popular Religion. From the Camisards to the Shakers*, Baltimore

Gaustad, Edwin Scott (1957) *The Great Awakening in New England*, New York

Gehman, Richard (1986) 'The East African Revival', in *East African Journal of Evangelical Theology*, 5.1 (1986) pp 36-56

Gewehr, Wesley M. (1930) *The Great Awakening in Virginia, 1740-1790*, Durham, N.C.

Gilley, Sheridan (1990) 'Catholic Revival in the Eighteenth Century', in *Protestant Evangelicalism: Britain, Ireland, Germany and America c.1750-c.1950: Essays in Honour of W. R. Ward* ed Keith Robbins, Oxford pp 99-108

Gillie, John (1845) *Historical Collections Relating to Remarkable Periods of the Success of the Gospel* Reprinted with a Preface and Continuation to 1845 by Horatius Bonar, Kelso (Repr 1981)

Gillies, John (1772) *Memoirs of the Life of the Reverend George Whitefield, M.A.*, London

Goen, C. C. (1962) *Revivalism and Separatism in New England 1740-1800*, Hamden, Connecticut

Goff James R. Jr (1988) *Fields White Unto Harvest: Charles F Parham and the Missionary Origins of Pentecostalism*, Fayetteville & London

Goforth, Jonathan (nd) *'By My Spirit'*, London & Edinburgh

Green, Michael (1960) *Evangelism in the Early Church*, London

Greenfield, John (1929) *Power From On High, or The Two Hundredth Anniversary of the Great Moravian Revival 1727-1927*, London

Griffin, Clifford S. (1960) *Their Brothers' Keepers: Moral Stewardship in the United States, 1800-1865*, New Brunswick

Guelzo, Allen C. (1988) 'The Making of a Revivalist: Finney and the heritage of Edwards', in *Christian History* Vol VII no 4 pp 28-30

Hall, David D. (1972) *The Faithful Shepherd: A History of the New England Ministry in the Seventeenth Century*, Chapel Hill NC

Hamilton, John T. & Kenneth G. (1967) *A History of the Moravian Church: The Renewed Unitas Fratrum, 1722-1957*, Bethlehem, Pennsylvania

Hamilton, Victor P. (1990) *The New International Commentary on the Old Testament: Genesis*, Grand Rapids

Hannah, John D. (1977) 'The Layman's Prayer Revival of 1858', in *Bibliotheca Sacra* 134 (Jan-March 1977)

Hardman, Keith J. (1983) *The Spiritual Awakeners: American Revivalists from Solomon Stoddard to Dwight L. Moody*, Chicago

Hardman, Keith J. (1987) *Charles Grandison Finney, 1792-1875*, Syracuse NY & Darlington

Harnack, A. von (1962) see von Harnack

Hatch, Nathan O. (1989) *The Democratization of American Christianity*, New Haven & London

Heasman, Kathleen (1962) *Evangelicals in Action: An Appraisal of their Social Work in the Victorian Era*, London

Heier, Edmund (1970) *Religious Schism in the Russian Aristocracy, 1860-1900—Radstockism and Pashkovism*, The Hague

Heimert, Alan (1966) *Religion and the American Mind from the Great Awakening to the Revolution*, Cambridge, Mass

Heimert, Alan & Miller, Perry ed (1967) *The Great Awakening: Documents Illustrating the Crisis and Its Consequences*, Indianapolis & New York

Heitzenrater, Richard Paul (1972) *John Wesley and the Oxford Methodists, 1725-1735*, Doctoral dissertation. Duke University (cited in Snyder 1980)

Heymann, Frederick G. (1955) *John Zizka and the Hussite Revolution*, Princeton

Hinson, E. Glenn (1981) *The Evangelization of the Roman Empire: Identity and Adaptability*, Macon, Ga.

Hoffman, F. W. (1956) *Revival Times in America*, Boston

Hollenweger, Walter J. (1972) *The Pentecostals: The Charismatic Movement in the Churches*, Minneapolis

Hopkins, Hugh E. (1977) *Charles Simeon of Cambridge*, Grand Rapids

Houghton, Frank (1954) *Amy Carmichael of Dohnavur*, London

Howe, John (1846) *The Outpouring of the Holy Spirit; or, The Prosperous State of the Christian Interest before the End of Time, by a Plentiful Effusion of the Holy Spirit: Considered in Fifteen Chapters on Ezekiel XXXIX: The Doctrinal Puritans 29*, London

Howse, Ernest Marshall (1953) *Saints in Politics: The 'Clapham Sect' and the Growth of Freedom*, London

Hughes, Selwyn (1990) *Revival: Times of Refreshing*, Sunbury-on-Thames

Hulse, Erroll (1991) *Give him no rest: A call to prayer for revival*, Darlington

Humphrey, Heman (1859) *Revival Sketches and Manual*. New York

Irenaeus (1979) 'Against Heresies' in *The Ante-Nicene Fathers*, ed Roberts, Alexander & Donaldson, James, Grand Rapids

Isaac, Rhys (1988) *The Transformation of Virginia*

Jenkins, T. Omri (1989) *Five Minutes to Midnight: James Stewart and mission to Europe*, Darlington

Jensen, Paul (1986) *Evangelical Awakenings and Revivals on Seventh-Day Adventist Campuses in North America 1967-1972*, Unpublished paper Fuller Theological Seminary, Pasadena

Johnson, Charles A. (1955) *The Frontier Camp Meeting*, Dallas

Johnson, Paul (1976) *A History of Christianity*, New York

Jones, R. Tudur (1985) *The Great Reformation*, Leicester

Jones, J. W. (1887) *Christ in the Camp, or Religion in Lee's Army*, Richmond, Va.

Kaiser, Walter (1986) *Quest for Renewal: Personal Revival in the Old Testament*, Grand Rapids

Keim, Paul (1983) 'Profile of a Polish Pastor', in *Keston News Service*, (Feb 24, 1983) Keston, Kent

Keller, Charles Roy (1942) *The Second Great Awakening in Connecticut*, New Haven

Kent, John (1978) *Holding the Fort: Studies in Victorian Revivalism*, London

Kidner, F. D. (1987) *The Message of Jeremiah*, Leicester

Kim, Myung Hyuk (1990) 'Lessons from the Prayer Habits of the Church in Korea', in *Teach Us To Pray*, ed Donald M. Carson, Grand Rapids pp 231-246

Knox, Ronald (1950) *Enthusiasm: A Chapter in the History of Religion, with special reference to the XVII and XVIII Centuries*, Oxford

Koch, Kurt (1972) *The Revival in Indonesia*, Grand Rapids

Koch, Kurt E. (1973) *Revival Fires in Canada*, Grand Rapids

Kydd, Ronald A. N. (1984) *Charismatic Gifts in the Early Church*, Peabody, Mass

Lamb, David (1991) *The Radical Shrub: A Movement of Intervarsity on the West Coast, 1978-91*, Unpublished paper, Fuller Theological Seminary

Lambert, Frank (1990) ' "Pedlar in Divinity": George Whitefield and the Great Awakening, 1737-1745', in *The Journal of American History* 77 (1990) pp 812-837

Lambert, Frank (1991) 'The Great Awakening as Artefact: George Whitefield and the Construction of Intercolonial Revival, 1739-1745', in *Church History* 60.2 (1991) pp 223-246

Lambert, Tony (1991) *The Resurrection of the Chinese Church*, London

Latimer, Robert Sloan (1907) *Dr. Baedeker and his Apostolic Work in Russia*, London

Latourette, Kenneth Scott (1937) *A History of the Expansion of Christianity. Volume I, The First Five Centuries*, New York

Latourette, Kenneth Scott (1939) *A History of the Expansion of Christianity. Volume IV, The Great Century*, New York

Latourette, Kenneth Scott (1953) *A History of Christianity*, London

Lees, Bill & Lees, Shirley (1987) *Is It Sacrifice?*, Leicester, Singapore & Bromley

Lees, Shirley (1979) *Drunk Before Dawn*, London

Lescellius, R. H. (1990) 'Revival and the History of the Church', in *Reformation Today*, (1990) Leeds pp 3-10

Lewis, A. J. (1962) *Zinzendorf the Ecumenical Pioneer*, London

Littell, Franklin H. (1964) *The Origins of Sectarian Protestantism*, Boston

Lloyd-Jones, D. Martyn (1960) 'Revival: An Historical and Theological Survey', in *How Shall they Hear?*, London

Lloyd-Jones, D. Martyn (1986) *Revival: can we make it happen?*, Basingstoke

Lloyd-Jones D. M. (1989) 'Jonathan Edwards and the Crucial Importance of Revival', in *The Puritans: Their Origins and Successors*, Edinburgh, pp 348-371

Longenecker, Richard N. (1981) 'The Acts of the Apostles' in *The Expositor's Commentary* ed Gaebelin, Frank C, Grand Rapids

Lovegrove, Deryck (1988) *Established Church, Sectarian People: Itinerancy and the transformation of English Dissent, 1780-1830*, Cambridge

Lovelace, Richard F. (1979a) *Dynamics of Spiritual Life: An Evangelical Theology of Renewal*, Exeter

Lovelace, Richard F. (1979b) *The American Pietism of Cotton Mather: Origins of American Evangelicalism*, Grand Rapids

Luther, Martin ed Tappert, Theodore G. (1955) *Luther: Letters of Spiritual Counsel*, Philadelphia

Lutzer, Erwin (1976) *Flames of Freedom*, Chicago

Lyall, Leslie (1954) *Flame for God: John Sung*, London

Lyall, Leslie (1985) *God Reigns in China*, London

M'Cheyne, Robert Murray ed Bonar, Andrew A. (1844) *The Memoir and Remains of Robert Murray M'Cheyne*, Enlarged Edition 1892. Edinburgh (Repr edn 1966)

MacFarlan, D. (1847) *The Revivals of the Eighteenth Century particularly at Cambuslang London & Edinburgh* Repr edn 1980.

MacInnes, John (1951) *The Evangelical Movement in the Highlands of Scotland 1688-1800*, Aberdeen

MacMullen, Ramsey (1984) *Christianizing the Roman Empire (A.D. 100-400)* New Haven and London

Manton, John D. (1969) 'German Pietism and the Evangelical Revival', in *By Schisms Rent Asunder*, London pp 6-17

Maria, Giuseppe (1852) *The Life of Blessed Leonard of Port-Maurice*, London (cited in Gilley 1990)

Mather, Cotton (1957) *Diary of Cotton Mather* ed Worthington Chauncy Ford 2 vols, New York

Mather, Cotton (1702) *Magnalia Christi Americana*, London (Repr edn New York 1972)

Matthew, David ed (1990) *Revive Us Again!; Realistic Thinking on Revival*, Bradford

Maxson, Charles Hartshorn (1920) *The Great Awakening in the Middle Colonies*, Chicago

McLoughlin, William G. Jr (1959) *Modern Revivalism from Charles G. Finney to Billy Graham*, New York

McLoughlin, William G. (1967) *Isaac Backus and the American Pietistic Tradition*, Boston

McLoughlin, William G. (1978) *Revivals, Awakening and Reform*, Chicago

McNemar, Richard (1968) *The Kentucky Revival*, New York

Meredith, Ian (1989/90) 'Emotional Manifestations and Revivals', in *Church Growth Digest* Year 11 Issue 2 (Winter 1989/90) pp 10-11

Miller, Perry (1952) 'Jonathan Edwards and the Great Awakening', repr in *Errand into the Wilderness*, Cambridge, Mass, 1956

Miller, Perry (1949) *Jonathan Edwards*, New York

Monsen, Marie (1961) *The Awakening*, London

Moody, William R. (nd) *The Life of D L Moody*, London

Morrell, David James (1987) *Some Aspects of Revivalist and Charismatic Movements in England, 1800-1862*, M.Phil. thesis, University of Manchester

Muller, George (1906) *Autobiography of George Muller, or, A Million and a Half in Answer to Prayer*, London & Bristol

Mumper, Sharon (1991) 'Gypsies sing new song as revival spreads throughout the world', in *Pulse* (September 27, 1991) p 4

Murray, Iain H. (1971) *The Puritan Hope: A Study in Revival and the Interpretation of Prophecy*, London

Murray Iain H. (1982) *David Martyn Lloyd-Jones: The First Forty Years 1899-1939*, Edinburgh

Murray, Iain H. (1987) *Jonathan Edwards: A New Biography*, Edinburgh

Murray, John J. (1990) *Revivals in Lewis*. Lectures given at Carey Conference 1990 (Tape cassette)

Nagler, Arthur Wilford (1918) *Pietism and Methodism, or The Significance of German Pietism in the Origin and Early Development of Methodism*, Nashville

Neill, Stephen (1986) *A History of Christian Missions*, Harmondsworth. Revised by Owen Chadwick

Noel, C. C. (1985) 'Missionary preachers in Spain: teaching social virtues in the eighteenth century', in *American Historical Review* 90 (cited in Gilley 1990)

Olford, Stephen F. (1962) *Heart-Cry for Revival: Expository Sermons on Revival*, Westwood, NY.

Open Doors (1990) *Open Doors: Cuba Special* Open Doors with Brother Andrew, (May 1990)

Open Doors (1991) *Open Doors*, Open Doors with Brother Andrew, (July 1991)

Open Doors (1991) *Open Doors*, Open Doors with Brother Andrew (Nov 1991)

Orr, J. Edwin (1949) *The Second Evangelical Awakening in Britain*, London

Orr, J. Edwin (1952) *The Second Evangelical Awakening in America*, London

Orr, J. Edwin (1971) *Campus Aflame: Dynamic of Student Religious Revolution*, Glendale

Orr, J. Edwin (1973) *The Flaming Tongue: The Impact of 20th Century Revivals*, Chicago

Orr, J. Edwin (1974) *The Fervent Prayer: The Worldwide Impact of the Great Awakening of 1858*, Chicago

Orr, J. Edwin (1975) *The Eager Feet: Evangelical Awakenings 1790-1830*, Chicago

Orr, J. Edwin (1981) *The Re-Study of Revival and Revivalism*, Pasadena

Orr, J. Edwin (1984) *The Outpouring of the Spirit in Revival and Awakening and Its Issue in Church Growth*, Pasadena

Osborn, H. H. (1991) *Fire in the Hills*, Crowborough, East Sussex

Overton, John Henry (1885) *Life in the English Church (1660-1714)*, London

Owen, John ed Goold, William H. (1854) *The Works of John Owen D.D.*, Edinburgh

Packer, J. I. (1961) 'Jonathan Edwards and the Theology of Revival', in *Increasing in the Knowledge of God*, London

Packer, J. I. (1971) 'Revival', in *Christian Graduate* (1971) pp 97-100

Packer, J. I. (1980) 'Puritanism as a Movement of Revival', in *Evangelical Quarterly*, (1980) pp 2-16

Packer, J. I. (1984) *Keep in Step With the Spirit*, Leicester

Packer, J. I. (1988) 'Revival', in *New Dictionary of Theology*, ed Sinclair Ferguson & David Wright, Leicester

Payne, Ernest A. (1941) *The Prayer Call of 1784*, London

Payne, Ernest A. (1943) 'The Evangelical Revival and the Beginnings of the Modern Missionary Movement', in *The Congregational Quarterly* XXI pp 223-236

Pelikan, Jaroslav (1971) *The Christian Tradition: A History of the Development of Doctrine*, Vol I, Chicago

Peters, George W. (1973) *Indonesia Revival: Focus on Timor*, Grand Rapids

Pibworth, Nigel R. (1987) *The Gospel Pedlar: The Story of John Berridge and the Eighteenth Century Revival*, Welwyn

Plowman, Edward E. (1971) *The Jesus Movement in America*, New York

Prime, Samuel Irenaeus (1859) *The Power of Prayer Illustrated in the Wonderful Displays of Divine Grace at the Fulton Street and Other Meetings in New York and Elsewhere*, New York (cited in Finney ed Rosell & Dupuis)

Prince, Thomas (1745) *The Christian History Containing Accounts of the Revival and Propagation of Religion in Great Britain and America for the Years 1743,1744*, Boston (cited in Tracy 1842, Gaustad 1957 etc)

Prozesky, Martin H. (1977) 'The Emergence of Dutch Pietism', in *Journal of Ecclesiastical History* 28.1 (January 1977) pp 29-37

Ravenhill, Leonard (1959) *Why Revival Tarries*, Minneapolis

Reid, William ed (1968) *Authentic Records of Revival*, London

Richardson, Alan & Bowden, John (1989) *New Dictionary of Christian Theology*, 2nd edn, London

Richie, J. (nd) *Floods Upon the Dry Ground*, London

Riss, Richard M. (1988) *A Survey of 20th-Century Revival Movements in North America*, Peabody, Mass

Roberts, Richard Owen (1988) *Revival*, Wheaton

Robe, James (1840) *The Revival of Religion at Kilsyth, Cambuslang and Other Places in 1742*, Glasgow

Rosell, Garth M. (1986) 'Asahel Nettleton and the Emergence of the Finney Revivals', in *American Christianity: A Case Study Approach*, ed White, Ronald C., Weeks, Louis B., & Rosell, Garth M., Grand Rapids

Sairsingh, Krister (1986) *Jonathan Edwards and the Idea of Divine Glory: His Foundational Trinitarianism and Its Ecclesial Import*. Harvard. Unpublished Ph.D. dissertation.

Sawatsky, Walter (1981) *Soviet Evangelicals Since World War II*, Scottdale, Pennsylvania

Schafer, Thomas G. (1963) 'Solomon Stoddard and the Theology of the Revival', in *A Miscellany of American Christianity* ed Stuart C. Henry, Durham NC pp 328-361

Schaff-Herzog (1909) 'French Prophets', in *The New Schaff-Herzog Encyclopaedia of Religious Knowledge*, New York

Scott, C. Anderson (1910) 'Camisards', in *Encyclopaedia of Religion and Ethics*, ed James Hastings, Edinburgh

Shearer, R. E. (1966) *Wildfire: Church Growth in Korea*, Grand Rapids

Simon, John S. (1921) *John Wesley and the Religious Societies*, London

Smeaton, George (1889) *The Doctrine of the Holy Spirit*, Edinburgh

(Smith, A. C. Stanley) (1938) *The Ruanda Revival, By a Missionary*, London

Smith, A. C. Stanley (1946) *Road to Revival: The Story of the Ruanda Mission*, London

Smith, A. C. Stanley (1951) *Supplement to Road to Revival: The Story of the Ruanda Mission continued from 1946 to 1951*, Croydon, Surrey

Smith, H. Shelton, Handy, Robert T., Loetscher, Lefferts A. (1960) *American Christianity: An Historical Interpretation with Representative Documents, Volume I 1607-1820*, New York

Smith, Timothy L. (1957) *Revival and Social Reform:American Protestantism on the Eve of the Civil War*, New York

Smith, Wilbur M. (1937) *The Glorious Revival under Hezekiah*, Grand Rapids

Snyder, Howard A. (1980) *The Radical Wesley & Patterns for Church Renewal*, Downers Grove, Illinois

Snyder, Howard A. (1989) *Signs of the Spirit: How God Reshapes the Church*, Grand Rapids

Spinka, Matthew (1968) *John Hus: A Biography*, Westport, Conecticut

Sprague, William B. (1832) *Lectures on Revivals of Religion*, Albany. NY (Repr edn 1958)

Spurgeon, Charles H. (1860) *New Park Street Pulpit*, London

Spurgeon, Charles H. (1875) *Metropolitan Tabernacle Pulpit*, London

Spurgeon, Charles H. (1959) *Revival Year Sermons*, London

Stanley, Brian (1978) 'The East African Revival: African Initiative Within a European Tradition', in *The Churchman*, 92.1 (1978) pp 6-22

Stewart, Ruth (?) *James Stewart, Missionary* (cited in Jenkins 1989)

Stoeffler, F. Ernest (1965) *The Rise of Evangelical Pietism*, Leiden

Stoeffler, F. Ernest (1973) *German Pietism During the Eighteenth Century*, Leiden

Stoeffler, F. Ernest ed (1976) *Continental Pietism and Early American Christianity*, Grand Rapids

Stott, J. R. W. (1990) *The Message of Acts*, Leicester

Stout, Harry S. (1986) *The New England Soul: Preaching and Religious Culture in Colonial New England*, New York & Oxford

Stout, Harry S. (1991) *The Divine Dramatist: George Whitefield and the Rise of Modern Evangelism*, Grand Rapids

Stratton, Gary D. (1991) *The Lost Secret of Spiritual Awakening: A Case Study in Youth Revival* Unpublished paper, Fuller Theological Seminary

Strickland, A. B. (1934) *The Great American Revival: a case study in historical evangelism, with implications for today*, Cincinnati, Ohio

Strong, Augustus Hopkins (1899) *Christ in Creation and Ethical Monism*, Philadelphia

Sweet, Leonard I. (1976) 'The View of Man Inherent in New Measures Revival', in *Church History* 45 (June 1976) pp 206-211

Sweet, Leonard I. ed (1986) *The Evangelical Tradition in America*, Grand Rapids

Sweet, William Warren (1973) *The Story of Religion in America*, Grand Rapids

Synan, Vinson, ed (1975) *Aspects of Pentecostal-Charismatic Origins*, Plainfield, NJ.

Tanis, James R. (1967) *Dutch Calvinistic Pietism in the Middle Colonies: A Study in the Life and Theology of Theodorus Jacobus Frelinghuysen*, The Hague

Tari, Mel (1971) *Like a Mighty Wind*, Eastbourne

Taylor, Howard and Taylor, Mary (1911) *Hudson Taylor in Early Years*, London

Taylor, Howard and Taylor, Mary (1918) *Hudson Taylor and the China Inland Mission*, London

Taylor, J. V. (1958) *The Process of Growth in an African Church*, London

Thompson, J. A. (1980) *The New International Commentary on the Old Testament: The Book of Jeremiah*, Grand Rapids

Thornbury, John F. (1977) *God Sent Revival: The Story of Asahel Nettleton and the Second Great Awakening*, Welwyn

Tippit, Sammy (1987) *Fire in Your Heart*, Amersham-on-the-Hill, Bucks

Today (1990) 'Rumours of Glory', *Today*, (December 1990) pp 4-5,46

Torrey, R. A. (1924) *The Power of Prayer and the Prayer of Power*, New York

Tracy, Joseph (1842) *The Great Awakening: A History of the Revival of Religion in the Time of Edwards and Whitefield*, Boston & New York

Tracy, Patricia (1979) *Jonathan Edwards, Pastor: Religion and Society in Eighteenth Century Northampton*, New York

Trotter, Mrs Edward (nd) *Lord Radstock: An Interpretation and a Record*, London

Tyler, Bennet (1844) *Nettleton and His Labours: The Memoir of Dr Asahel Nettleton, Remodelled in some parts by Andrew A Bonar*, Edinburgh (Repr edn 1975)

Tyler, Bennet (1846) *New England Revivals, As They Existed at the Close of the Eighteenth, and the Beginning of the Nineteenth Centuries*, Boston (Repr edn 1980)

Verduin, Leonard (1964) *The Reformers and Their Stepchildren*, Grand Rapids

von Campenhausen, Hans (1964) *Fathers of the Latin Church*, London

von Harnack, Adolf (1908) *The Mission and Expansion of Christianity in the First Three Centuries*, ET Moffatt, James, New York

Wagner, Doris (1991) 'Learning from the Argentine Revival', *Equipping the Saints*, Vineyard Fellowship, Anaheim CA (Winter 1991) pp 28-30

Wagner, Murray L. (1983) *Peter Chelcicky: A Radical Separatist in Hussite Bohemia*, Scottdale, Pennsylvania

Wagner, William L. (1978) *New Move Forward in Europe*, South Pasadena

Wallace, Anthony F. C. (1966) *Religion: An Anthropological View*, New York

Wallis, Arthur (1956) *In the Day of Thy Power: The Scriptural Principles of Revival*, London

Wang, David (1990) 'Lessons form the Prayer Habits of the Church in China', in *Teach Us To Pray*, ed Donald M Carson, Grand Rapids pp 247-254

Ward, W. R. (1979) 'The Relations of Enlightenment and Religious Revival in Central Europe and in the English-Speaking World', in *Reform and Reformation: England and the Continent c1500-c1750*, ed Derek Baker, Oxford pp 281-298

Ward, W. R. (1981) 'Power and Piety: The Origins of Religious Revival in the Early Eighteenth Century', in *Bulletin of the John Rylands Library of Manchester*, lxiii (Spring 1981) pp 231-252

Ward, W. R. (1982) 'Orthodoxy, Enlightenment and Religious Revival', in *Studies in Church History*, xvii (1982) pp 275-296

Ward, W. R. (1988) 'The Renewed Unity of the Brethren: Ancient Church, New Sect or Interconfessional Movement?', in *The Bulletin of the John Rylands Library of Manchester*, lxxi (1988) pp 77-92

Ward, W. R. (1989) ' "An Awakened Christianity". The Austrian Protestants and Their Neighbours in the Eighteenth Century', in *Journal of Ecclesiastical History*, 40.1 (January 1989) pp 53-73

Warren, Max (1954) *Revival: An Enquiry*, London

Watt, Eva Stuart (1939) *Floods on Dry Ground: Revival in the Congo*, London

Weinlick, John R. (1956) *Count Zinzendorf*, New York & Nashville

Weisberger, Bernard A. (1958) *They Gathered at the River: The Story of the Great Revivalists and Their Impact upon Religion in America*, Boston

Wenham, Gordon J. (1987) *The Word Biblical Commentary: Genesis 1-15*, Waco, Texas

Wesley, John (nd) *The Journal of the Rev. John Wesley A.M. in 4 Volumes*, Everyman's Library. London

Wesley, John ed Curnock, Nehemiah (1938) *The Journal of the Rev. John Wesley A.M.*, Standard edition. London

Westerkamp, Marilyn J. (1988) *Triumph of the Laity: Scots-Irish Piety and the Great Awakening, 1625-1760*, New York & Oxford

Westermann, Claus (1974) *Genesis*, I, Philadelphia

Westgarth, J. W. (1946) *The Holy Spirit and the Primitive Mind: A Remarkable Account of a Spiritual Awakening in Darkest Africa*, London

White, John (1986) *Excellence in Leadership: the Pattern of Nehemiah*, Leicester

White, John (1988) *When the Spirit Comes with Power: Signs and Wonders Among God's People*, London

White, Ronald C. Jr, Weeks, Louis B., & Rosell, Garth M. (1986) *American Christianity: A Case Study Approach*, Grand Rapids

White, Ronald C. Jr (1991) *The Beauty of Holiness: The life of Phoebe Palmer*, New York

Whitefield, George (1960) *George Whitefield's Journals*, London

Whittaker, Colin (1990) 'God Gives the Increase', *Today* (September 1990) 17-19,45

Willard, W. W. (1950) *Fire on the Prairie*, Wheaton

Williams, George H. (1962) *The Radical Reformation*, Philadelphia

Williamson, H. G. M. (1982) *The New Century Bible: I & II Chronicles*, London

Wood, A. Skevington (1960) *The Inextinguishable Blaze: Spiritual Renewal and Advance in the Eighteenth Century*, London

Wood, A. Skevington (1967) *The Burning Heart. John Wesley: Evangelist*, Exeter

Wood, Arthur Skevington (1968) 'The Contribution of the Evangelical Revival to Education', in *The Christian Graduate* XXI no 3 (Sept 1968) pp 1-6

World Evangelization Information Service (1991) 'Religious Revival Sweeps Some Post-Marxist Countries' in *World Evangelization Information Service* (9/9/91) p 1

Worsley, Peter (1968) *The Trumpet Shall Sound*, New York

Wright, David F. (1976) 'Why were the Montanists condemned?', in *Themelios*, 2.1 (Sept 1976) pp 15-22

Wright, Nigel T. (1991) 'Restorationism and the 'House church' movement', in *Themelios* 16.2 (1991) pp 4-9

Wright, Nigel T. (1991b) 'Kansas City Prophets: an assessment' in *Themelios* 17.1 (1991) pp 20-21

Zinzendorf, Nicholas ed Forell, George (1973) *Zinzendorf: Nine Public Lectures on Important Subjects in Religion*, Iowa City

INDEX

287